ESSAYS IN
DIVINITY

BY

JOHN DONNE

ESSAYS IN DIVINITY

BY

JOHN DONNE

Edited by
EVELYN M. SIMPSON

OXFORD
AT THE CLARENDON PRESS
1952

Oxford University Press, Amen House, London E.C. 4

GLASGOW NEW YORK TORONTO MELBOURNE WELLINGTON
BOMBAY CALCUTTA MADRAS CAPE TOWN

Geoffrey Cumberlege, Publisher to the University

PRINTED IN GREAT BRITAIN

PREFACE

IT is just three hundred years since this little book was
first issued, and ninety-six years have passed since
the only other edition, an annotated one by the late
Augustus Jessopp, was published in 1855. My first tribute
must be one of gratitude to my old friend for the help
which I have received from his scholarly notes. When as
a young graduate I began to work at Donne's prose, I was
encouraged by the letters which he, then an old man of
almost ninety, used to send me. He was delighted that one
of the younger generation should be preparing to carry on
the work which he had begun to do in editing Donne's
prose, but which he had been obliged to abandon for lack
of support.

My thanks are due to Colonel C. H. Wilkinson, Librarian
of Worcester College, Oxford, for permission to collate the
dedication to Sir Henry Vane which is complete in the
Worcester College copy, though it has been cancelled in
most known copies; also to Mr. W. G. Hiscock, Sub-
Librarian of Christ Church, Oxford, for permission to
collate the Christ Church copy. I am obliged to the
Delegates of the Clarendon Press for permission to reprint
in my Introduction some pages of Chapter IX of the
second edition (1948) of my *Study of the Prose Works of
John Donne*. I must also thank the Principal and Fellows
of Newnham College, Cambridge, for their grant of a
Research Fellowship for three years, which enabled me to
continue my work on this book and on Donne's Sermons.

My friend Miss Helen Gardner, Fellow of St. Hilda's
College, has given me some valuable suggestions for the
notes. Finally, my thanks are due to my husband, Percy
Simpson, for his continued advice and encouragement.

E. M. S.

OXFORD
October, 1951

CONTENTS

INTRODUCTION

THE *Essays in Divinity* have less literary value than the *Devotions* or the *Sermons*, but they are of great importance for those who wish to study the development of Donne's thought. They are linked with *Biathanatos*, *Ignatius his Conclave*, and the verse *Anniversaries*, which preceded them, and with the *Sermons* which followed them. They are vital for the understanding of Donne's position during the difficult years which preceded his entry into Holy Orders, when he was hesitating on the threshold. The exact date of their composition is uncertain, but from the address 'To the Reader' prefixed by Donne's son to the edition of 1651 it has generally been deduced that they were written at the end of 1614 or the beginning of 1615.[1] The address runs thus:

'It is thought fit to let thee know, that these *Essayes* were printed from an exact Copy, under the Authors own hand: and, that they were the voluntary sacrifices of severall hours, when he had many debates betwixt God and himself, whether he were worthy, and competently learned to enter into Holy Orders. They are now publish'd, both to testifie his modest Valuation of himself, and to shew his great abilities; and, they may serve to inform thee in many Holy Curiosities. *Fare-well.*'

This, however, is less conclusive than Gosse imagined. Donne had had 'many debates . . . whether he were worthy, and competently learned to enter into Holy Orders' for a number of years before he actually took the final step. Several dates between 1611 and January 1615 might fit this statement, but the general tone of the *Essays*

---

[1] Gosse, *Life and Letters of Donne*, ii. 321: 'This narrows the date of their composition to December 1614 and January 1615.' Ramsay, *Les Doctrines médiévales chez Donne*, p. 118: 'Son ordination eut lieu en janvier 1615. C'est pendant les mois qui la précédèrent qu'il se donna pour tâche d'écrire les *Essais de Théologie.*' Gosse and Ramsay both ignore the statement in the dedication to Sir Harry Vane by the younger Donne that the *Essays* were written when his father was 'obliged in Civill business, and had no ingagement in that of the Church'. See p. 3 *infra*, and the note on p. 109.

makes it clear that they were written later than *Ignatius his Conclave*, and that Donne's interests were beginning to be predominantly theological. His concern with the 'new philosophy' is still there, but it is much less urgent than in the two *Anniversaries* and *Ignatius his Conclave*. He shows himself interested in the Jewish Cabalists, in Hermes Trismegistus, Zoroaster, and the Koran, but Augustine and Aquinas are beginning to assert their authority over these extremely unorthodox thinkers. He is beginning to think of himself as a preacher, and can write 'Though these lack thus much of Sermons, that they have no Auditory, yet as Saint *Bernard* did almost glory, that Okes and Beeches were his Masters, I shall be content that Okes and Beeches be my schollers, and witnesses of my solitary Meditations.'[1]

The *Essays in Divinity* have never been as popular with readers as the *Devotions*. This is partly due to their fragmentary character, and also to the fact that their style is much less polished. They are essentially private meditations, whereas the *Devotions* were carefully prepared for the press. Coffin has emphasized their importance in the history of Donne's thought, but other writers on Donne have been much less sympathetic.[2] Many have neglected any discussion of the book. Gosse called it 'a dull little book', and his suggestion that it was written to be laid before Arch-

---

[1] See p. 41.

[2] Coffin, *John Donne and the New Philosophy*, p. 249. 'Whether or not we accept the younger Donne's statement that they ⟨the *Essays*⟩ were written for his father's own satisfaction on the threshold of his going into the ministry, we must believe that they were "private" rather than public discourses, in which he wished to clear up in his mind certain fundamental religious problems. In this respect they are more fitting as a companion piece to the *Anniversaries* than as a prelude to his assumption of holy orders. Donne has been confronted, through a study of the new philosophy rendering the old conception of a unified world scheme entirely hopeless, with the necessity of discovering other means whereby the natural world may be significantly related to a new universal order. . . . Donne looks to pagan and Christian alike, occultist and orthodox Christian, for means to help him; hence, the generous attitude toward Catholic and Protestant, cabalist and occult mystic, and Greek philosopher.'

bishop Abbot before Donne's ordination as a proof of his orthodoxy,[1] is a most infelicitous one. Abbot was a narrow-minded man, bitterly hostile to the Church of Rome,[2] and his suspicions of Donne, if he had any, would have been increased rather than allayed by a treatise in which the author wrote: 'So Synagogue and Church is the same thing, and of the Church, *Roman* and *Reformed*, and all other distinctions of place, Discipline, or Person, but one Church, journying to one *Hierusalem*, and directed by one guide, Christ Jesus.'[3] Misled by his own unwarranted assumption that Donne needed to clear himself in Abbot's eyes of complicity in the Somerset divorce, Gosse was prepared to judge the *Essays* harshly. He remarked: 'When we examine the *Essays in Divinity*, however, for evidence of Donne's state of soul at this juncture, we meet with considerable disappointment. There is no revelation here of the writer's personal experience; nothing is for edification. These short homilies are more like the notes of a theological professor who is lecturing on Genesis and the early chapters of Exodus, than the out-pourings of a man who is trembling on the threshold of the Holy of Holies. There is a total absence of unction, even of spiritual enthusiasm; the essays are scholastic exercises and no more.'[4]

[1] Gosse, ii. 63. On the previous page Gosse states: 'It is more than probable that Abbot, who was very well informed, was aware, as Donne feared that he might be, of Donne's activity for Somerset in the business of the nullity. Very possibly the documents which Donne drew up for the favourite, and which still exist, had passed under the eyes of Abbot.' As we know, these documents were written by Sir Daniel Dunne and not by Donne, and the mere composition of an epithalamium for a marriage which had been graced by the King's presence could hardly have been a valid reason for refusing ordination to Donne. Incidentally we may notice that Abbot had nothing to do with Donne's ordination. The right of conferring Orders is vested in the diocesan bishop, and Donne was duly ordained by John King, Bishop of London, the diocese in which he was to serve.

[2] Abbot had the temerity to write a protest in 1622 to King James against the latter's proposed decree of toleration for Catholics, in which he inveighed against 'that most *Damnable* and *Heretical Doctrine* of the *Church* of *Rome*, the Whore of *Babylon*'.

[3] See the whole passage on pp. 51-2.   [4] Gosse, ii. 63.

The book itself, if studied attentively, refutes this last charge. It is the kindest, the happiest, the least controversial of Donne's prose works. The melancholy which pervaded his mind during the writing of the *Anniversaries* has vanished. His subject during the first half of the book is the creation of the world, and he looks upon the world with admiring eyes. He speaks of the Book of Creatures, in which man may see God the Creator. 'Certainly, every Creature shewes God, as a glass, but glimeringly and transitorily, by the frailty both of the receiver, and beholder: Our selves have his Image, as Medals, permanently and preciously delivered.'

There is a gentleness which is very pleasant in such a passage as this:

'Let no smalnesse retard thee: if thou beest not a Cedar to help towards a palace . . . yet thou art a shrub to shelter a lambe, or to feed a bird; or thou art a plantane, to ease a childs smart; or a grasse to cure a sick dog.'[1]

Death is hardly mentioned,[2] and there is no morbid discussion of disease or corruption. Gosse himself excepted the prayers contained in the volume from his general censure of its supposed dullness. He considered one of them so fine an expression of Donne's feelings that he wished to detach it from the rest of the book, and ascribed it to a period three years later, when he believed that Donne, in his agony of grief over his wife's death, passed through the crisis of conversion.[3] He failed, however, to

[1] See p. 66. This should be compared with Donne's remark that 'the Indian priests expressed an excellent charity, by building Hospitalls and providing chirurgery for birds and beasts lamed by mischance, or age, or labour' (*Letters*, 1651, p. 47). He was certainly an animal-lover in an age when cruelty to animals was fashionable.

[2] On p. 76 Donne says 'the slumber of death shall overtake us'.

[3] Gosse, ii. 102–3. Gosse quoted in particular the sentence, 'And as, though thy self hadst no beginning, thou gavest a beginning to all things in which thou wouldst be served and glorified; so, though this soul of mine, by which I partake thee, begin not now, yet let this minute, O God, this happy minute of thy visitation, be the beginning of her conversion, and shaking away confusion, darknesse, and barrennesse; and let her now produce Creatures, thoughts, words, and deeds agreeable to thee.'

see that this prayer and its companions are intimately connected with the whole argument of the book. The first prayer sums up Donne's meditations on the Name of God, and on the creation of heaven and earth out of nothing. The second and third apply his meditations on Exodus to his own experience, and have an intensely personal note. Here is a passage from the prayer on p. 75 which shows how a piece of intimate self-revelation can flower out of the dry wood of a discussion of the first verse of the Book of Exodus.

'Thou hast delivered me, O God, from the Egypt of confidence and presumption, by interrupting my fortunes, and intercepting my hopes; And from the Egypt of despair by contemplation of thine abundant treasures, and my portion therein; from the Egypt of lust, by confining my affections; and from the monstrous and un-naturall Egypt of painfull and wearisome idleness, by the necessities of domestick and familiar cares and duties. Yet as an Eagle, though she enjoy her wing and beak, is wholly prisoner, if she be held by but one talon; so are we, though we could be delivered of all habit of sin, in bondage still, if Vanity hold us but by a silken thred. But, O God, as mine inward corruptions have made me mine own *Pharaoh*, and mine own *Egypt*; so thou, by the inhabitation of thy Spirit, and application of thy merit, hast made me mine own Christ; and contenting thy self with being my Medicine, allowest me to be my Physician.'

The central position occupied by the *Essays* is shown by their intimate connexion with the verse *Anniversaries* and certain of the *Divine Poems* on the one hand, and with the early *Sermons* on the other.

The verbal links with the two *Anniversaries* are worth enumeration. In *The first Anniversary* Donne had written:

Vouchsafe to call to minde that God did make
A last, and lasting'st peece, a song. He spake
To *Moses* to deliver unto all,
That song, because hee knew they would let fall
The Law, the Prophets, and the History,
But keepe the song still in their memory.[1]

[1] Grierson, *Poems of Donne*, i. 245.

In the *Essays in Divinity* he writes:

'And God himself in that last peice of his, which he commanded
Moses to record, that Heavenly Song which onely himself compos'd
. . . this which himself cals a Song, was made immediately by himself, and *Moses* was commanded to deliver it to the Children; God
choosing this way and conveyance of a Song . . . because he knew
that they would ever be repeating this Song, . . .'[1]

In *The second Anniversary*, 425–8, we find:

> But as the Heathen made them severall gods,
> Of all Gods Benefits, and all his Rods,
> (For as the Wine, and Corne, and Onions are
> Gods unto them, so Agues bee, and Warre).[2]

This is expanded in the *Essays* thus:

'Have they furthered, or eased thee any more, who not able to
consider, whole and infinit God, have made a particular God, not
only of every power of God, but of every benefit? . . . Out of this
proceeded *Dea febris*, and *Dea fraus*, and *Tenebræ*, and *Onions*, and
Garlike. For the *Egyptians*, most abundant in Idolatry, were from
thence said to have Gods grow in their gardens.'[3]

The same thought is expressed in the *Sermons*:

'The Gentiles were not able to consider God so; not so entirely,
not altogether; but broke God in pieces, and changed God into
single money, and made a fragmentarie God of every Power, and
Attribute in God, of every blessing from God, nay of every male-
diction and judgment of God. . . . *Feare* came to be a God, and a
Fever came to be a God.'[4]

More important than these parallels[5] is the likeness in
theme between the *Anniversaries* and some passages of the
Essays. In the poems Donne takes a view of the universe,
through which the soul ascends to heaven. 'This slow-pac'd
soule, which late did cleave To a body, and went but

---

[1] See p. 92.   [2] Grierson, i. 263.   [3] See p. 22.
[4] *LXXX Sermons*, 50. 502.
[5] A smaller example may be found in *The second Anniversary*, 281–2
(Grierson, i. 259): 'Wee see in Authors, too stiffe to recant, A hundred
controversies of an Ant'; and *Essays*, p. 14: '. . . there are marked an
hundred differences in mens Writings concerning an *Ant*.'

by the bodies leave' stays not in the air, and knows not
whether she has passed through the element of fire.

> She baits not at the Moone, nor cares to trie
> Whether in that new world, men live, and die. . . .
> But ere she can consider how she went,
> At once is at, and through the Firmament.
> And as these starres were but so many beads
> Strung on one string, speed undistinguish'd leads
> Her through those Spheares, as through the beads, a string,
> Whose quick succession makes it still one thing:
> As doth the pith, which, lest our bodies slacke,
> Strings fast the little bones of necke, and backe;
> So by the Soule doth death string Heaven and Earth. . . .'[1]

The whole passage with its mention of the planets Venus,
Mercury, Mars, Jupiter, and Saturn, and finally of the
firmament and the fixed stars, gives a wonderful impression
of the immensities of outer stellar space. Again and again
in these two poems, and in the *Funerall Elegie*, attached to
The first Anniversary, Donne makes mention of the 'new
Starres' which Kepler and Galileo had revealed to the
world.

> But, as when heaven lookes on us with new eyes,
> Those new starres every Artist exercise,
> What place they should assign to them they doubt,
> Argue, and agree not till those starres goe out.[2]

By the time that Donne wrote *Essays in Divinity* the
excitement produced in him by the discoveries of the new
astronomy had largely disappeared. He no longer appended marginal notes, referring to the works of Kepler
and Galileo, as he had done in *Biathanatos* and *Ignatius
his Conclave*. But the wide cosmic view still persists in
the first book of the *Essays*—that which is devoted to the
creation of the world. In one of the most eloquent passages
in the book he returns to the contemplation of the universe,
the fixed stars, the planets, and finally the earth itself:

'So that this *Heaven* and *Earth*,[3] being themselves and all be-

---

[1] Grierson, i. 256–7.   [2] Ibid. 247 (*A Funerall Elegie*, 67–70).
[3] A reference to the text on which Donne is meditating, Genesis
I. I: 'In the beginning God created Heaven and Earth.'

tween them, is this World; the common house and City of Gods and
men, in *Cicero*'s words;[1] and the corporeal and visible image and
son of the invisible God, in the description of the *Academicks*:
which being but one, (for *Universum est omnia versa in unum*) hath
been the subject of Gods labor, and providence, and delight,
perchance almost six thousand years; whose uppermost first moving
Orbe is too swift for our thoughts to overtake, if it dispatch in every
hour three thousand times the compass of the Earth ⟨marginal
reference "Gilbert. de Magn." l. 6. c. 3.⟩, and this exceeds fifteen
thousand miles.[2] In whose firmament are scattered more *Eyes*
(for our use, not their owne) then any Cyphers can esteeme or
expresse. For, how weake a stomack to digest knowledge, or how
strong and misgovern'd faith against common sense hath he, that
is content to rest in their number of 1022 Stars?[3] whose nearer
regions are illustrated with the Planets, which work so effectually
upon man, that they have often stop'd his further search, and been
themselves by him deified.... Of the glory of which (i.e. the world),
and the inhabitants of it, we shall best end in the words of *Sirach*'s
Son,[4] *When we have spoken much, we cannot attain unto them; but the
sum of all is, that God is all.*'[5]

Donne goes on to claim that the true possessor of the
earth is not the King of Spain, though it is said that 'the
Sun cannot hide himself from his Eye, nor shine out of
his Dominions', nor the Sultan of Turkey, nor any other
potentate, however wide his sway, but it is the wise man,
who uses the world without setting his heart upon it, and
sees himself as the tenant who holds it in trust from God,
the true owner.

[1] Cicero, *De Natura Deorum*, lib. ii, c. 6.

[2] Coffin, op. cit., p. 84, n. 54, comments on this passage. He argues
that Donne's 'compass of the Earth', which exceeds fifteen thousand
miles, refers to its diameter, but in the seventeenth century (see *O.E.D.*)
compass meant circumference or circle, not diameter. Burton writes in
The Anatomy of Melancholy, ii. ii. 3: 'If the earth be 21,500 miles
in compasse, its Diameter is 7,000.' In any case Donne's figures are wide
of the mark.

[3] Dr. Jessopp was the first to point out that here also Donne is following Gilbert. The Ptolemaic catalogue of stars gave 1,022 as the total
number. This passage should be compared with Donne's attack in
Biathanatos, p. 146, on '*Aristotles* Schollers' who go on maintaining that
the heavens are inalterable, in spite of the discovery of new stars.

[4] Ecclesiasticus xliii. 27. [5] See pp. 33–34.

'What are these ⟨i.e. kings and princes⟩ our fellow-ants, our fellow-durt, our fellow-nothings, compared to that God whom they make but their pattern? And how little have any of these, compared to the whole Earth? whose hills, though they erect their heads beyond the Country of Meteors, and set their foot, in one land, and cast their shadow into another, are but as warts upon our ⟨read, her⟩ face: And her vaults, and caverns, the bed of the winds, and the secret streets and passages of al rivers, and Hel it self, though they ⟨marg. ref. Munster l. 1. c. 16⟩ afford it three thousand great miles, are but as so many wrinkles, and pock-holes.'[1]

This passage is closely linked with a great passage in *The first Anniversary*, 286–301, in which we have the same reflection that in comparison with the whole extent of the earth, the highest hills and the deepest caverns are but 'warts' and 'pock-holes':

But keepes the earth her round proportion still?
Doth not a Tenarif, or higher Hill
Rise so high like a Rocke, that one might thinke
The floating Moone would shipwracke there, and sinke? . . .
If under all, a Vault infernall bee,
(Which sure is spacious, except that we
Invent another torment, that there must
Millions into a straight hot roome be thrust)
Then solidnesse, and roundnesse have no place.
Are these but warts, and pock-holes in the face
Of th' earth?[2]

In the body of the *Essays in Divinity*, as distinct from the prayers, there is very little affinity with *La Corona* and the *Holy Sonnets*. The *Essays* are for the most part impersonal, while the *Divine Poems* are intensely personal, the record of Donne's inner strife. There is, however, one link which may be mentioned. The *Holy Sonnets* draw on the apocalyptic imagery of the Book of Revelation for their background of 'the round earth's imagin'd corners',[3]

[1] See pp. 35–36. See also *LXXX Sermons*, 73. 747, where there is a reference to the same passage in Sebastian Münster's *Cosmographia* which inspired the conjectures about hell in *The first Anniversary*.

[2] Grierson, i. 240.

[3] *Holy Sonnets*, vii. 1, see Rev. vii. 1: 'I saw four Angels standing on the four corners of the Earth.'

the angels' trumpets,[1] the rising of the dead from earth
and sea,[2] the dyeing of souls in Christ's blood which makes
them white,[3] the description of Christ as 'the Lamb slain
from the foundation of the world'.[4] Similarly the *Essays
in Divinity* open with a reference to Rev. iii. 7, and continue with references on page 17 to Rev. i. 8, on page 30
to 'the last great fire' (Rev. xx. 9, 10, 14, 15), on page 31,
'some have prayed to have *Hils fall upon them*' (Rev. vi. 16),
on page 52 to the '*Multitude in white before the Lamb,
which none could number*', and the '*number of them which
were sealed 144,000*' (Rev. vii. 4, 9), and on page 76 to the
Last Judgement (Rev. xx. 11–13). Donne had a special
affection for the Book of Revelation, and preached a
number of sermons on texts taken from it (e.g. *LXXX
Sermons*, nos. 19 and 44; *Fifty Sermons*, nos. 4 and 32).

In the prayers found in the *Essays*, on the other hand,
there is a kinship of spirit with the *Holy Sonnets*. Here, in
prosaic language, is that plea to God for an overpowering
access of grace which shall overcome the stubbornness of
Donne's will—a plea which reaches its finest expression in
the intensity of *Holy Sonnet* XIV: 'Batter my heart, three-
person'd God.'

The *Essays* are also linked with *Catalogus Librorum*, one
of Donne's minor prose works which cannot be dated
exactly. It was probably composed about 1604 or 1605,
and about 1611 Donne intended to revise it, for in a letter[5]
to Goodyer he asked his friend to return a number of
papers, among them 'Catalogus librorum satyricus', so that
he might give them a final revision. Among the authors
who are mentioned in *Catalogus* and also in *Essays in
Divinity* are Raymond of Sebund (or Sebundus, as Donne
calls him), Pico della Mirandola, and the German humanist Reuchlin, as well as two minor writers, Petrus Galatinus
and F. Zorgi, whom Donne calls 'Francis George'. All

---

[1] *Holy Sonnets*, vii. 1, 2, and Rev. viii. 2, 6–12.
[2] Ibid. 2–7, and Rev. xx. 13, 14.
[3] Ibid. iv. 13, 14, and Rev. vii. 14.
[4] Ibid. xvi. 5, 6, and Rev. xiii. 8.
[5] Printed in the 1633 edition of Donne's *Poems*, p. 352.

these are mentioned with a touch of satire[1] in *Catalogus*,
while in the *Essays* Donne shows himself frankly interested in their work. The change seems to show that in the
interval he had studied more deeply, and had been more
favourably impressed by the mystical and cabalistic speculations of Pico, Reuchlin, and Zorgi. Certainly in the
Essays he writes admiringly of 'Francis George, that
transcending Wit', and approves his calculation 'that in
the Decalogue there are just so many letters, as there are
precepts in the whole law', while in *Catalogus* (Item 6) he
had made great fun of this author, and had ascribed to him
a mythical treatise on the numbering of the hairs of the
tail of Tobit's dog. Also in *Catalogus* Donne had made a
good-natured joke about the 'super-seraphical John Picus',
who in his 'Judaeo-Christian Pythagoras' was able to prove
'the numbers 99 and 66 to be identical if you hold the
leaf upside down'. In the *Essays* Donne treats Pico much
more seriously, though he criticizes him as 'a man of an
incontinent wit, and subject to the concupiscence of inaccessible knowledges and transcendencies'. He praises
Pico and Zorgi because 'they have many delicacyes of
honest and serviceable curiosity, and harmless recreation
and entertainment', and continues: '. . . there be some
Cankers, (as *Judaisme*) which cannot be cured without
the *Cabal*; which is (especially for those diseases) the
Paracelsian Phisick of the understanding, and is not unworthily (if it be onely applyed where it is so medicinable)
call'd *præambulum Evangelii*.'

While the book has many links with Donne's previous
works, it marks at the same time a new departure. It is the
first of the definitely theological works, the precursor of the
Sermons and the *Devotions*. It lays down, though somewhat tentatively, the lines of Donne's later thought. The
universe is to be seen in relation to God, otherwise the
perspective will be distorted. The world is God's world,
and is therefore no longer 'this rotten world', as Donne had
called it in *The first Anniversary*, but 'this glorious world',
as he now terms it. We hear nothing in the *Essays* of the

---

[1] The satire on Sebundus and Galatinus is very slight.

decay and disillusionment which occupy so much of the
Anniversaries. Donne is absorbed in studying the eternal
purpose of God in the world, and in contemplating the
mercy, power, and justice of God. As yet we have no discussion of those distinctively Christian doctrines of the
Incarnation and the Atonement, which were to occupy so
large a place in the Sermons. These are implicit in much
of the argument, but for the moment Donne is concerned
with God as the Creator of the Universe.

There are a number of close verbal parallels between the
Essays and some undated sermons, which probably belong
to the early years of Donne's ministry. Thus the discussion
of God's revelation of Himself by name, which occupies
pages 23–24 of the *Essays*, is reproduced fairly closely in
a sermon on one of the penitential Psalms:

'So that it is truly said, there is no name given by man to God,
Ejus essentiam adaequatè representans. And *Hermes* says humbly and
reverently, *Non spero*, I cannot hope, that the maker of all Majesty,
can be call'd by any one name, though compounded of many. I
have therefore sometimes suspected, that there was some degree of
pride, and overboldness, in the first naming of God; the rather,
because I marke, that the first which ever pronounced the name,
God, was the Divell; and presently the woman; who in the next
chapter proceeded further, and first durst pronounce that sacred
and mystick name of foure letters. For when an Angell did but
Ministerially represent God wrastling with *Jacob*, he reproves
Jacob, for asking his name; *Cur quaeris nomen meum?* And so also
to *Manoah, Why askest thou my Name, quod est mirabile?* And God,
to dignify that Angell which he promises to lead his people, says
Fear him, provoke him not, etc. *For my Name is in him*; but he tels
them not what it is. But since, necessity hath enforced, and Gods
will hath revealed some names. For in truth, we could not say this,
God cannot be named, except God could be named.'

'God is come nearer to us then to others, when we know his
Name. For though it be truly said in the Schoole, that no name can
be given to God, *Ejus essentiam adaequatè repraesentans*, No one
name can reach to the expressing of all that God is; And though
Trismegistus doe humbly, and modestly, and reverently say, *Non
spero*, it never fell into my thought, nor into my hope, that the
maker and founder of all Majesty, could be circumscribed, or im-

prisoned by any one name, though a name compounded and complicated of many names, as the Rabbins have made one name of God, of all his names in the Scriptures; Though *Iacob* seeme to have been rebuked *for asking Gods name*, when he wrastled with him; And so also the Angel which was to do a miraculous worke . . . would not permit *Manoah* to enquire after his name, *Because*, as he sayes there, *that name was secret and wonderfull*; And though God himselfe, to dignifie and authorize that *Angel*, which he made his Commissioner, and the Tutelar and Nationall Guide of his people, sayes of that *Angel*, to that people, *Feare him, provoke him not, for my Name is in him*, and yet did not tell them, what that name was; Yet certainly, we could not so much as say, God cannot be named, except we could name God by some name; we could not say, God hath no name, except God had a name; for that very word, *God*, is his name.'[1]

In the same sermon there is another passage in which the argument of the *Essays* is reproduced in almost identical words. It is too long to quote in full, but it begins in the *Essays* with the words, 'This is the Name, which the *Jews* stubbornly deny ever to have been attributed to the *Messias* in the Scriptures',[2] and in the sermon, 'This is that name which the Jews falsly, but peremptorily . . . deny ever to have been attributed to the *Messias*, in the Scriptures.'[3]

An undated sermon preached at Lincoln's Inn, and therefore belonging to the earlier part of Donne's ministry, contains a passage in which a verse of Canticles is applied, as it had been in the *Essays*, to the divisions of the Christian Church, and Donne's longing for unity.[4] The earliest of Donne's sermons which we possess, that preached at Greenwich on 30 April 1615, has a passage which is closely parallel to a passage in the *Essays in Divinity*. In the *Essays* we read:

'In the first constitution of the *Roman* Empire . . . they easily foresaw, that men would soon decline and stray into a chargeable and

---

[1] *LXXX Sermons*, 50. 501. The marginal references are to Gen. 32. 29, Judges 13. 18, and Exodus 23. 20, references which are also found in the margin of the parallel passage of the *Essays*.

[2] Pp. 24–25. [3] *LXXX Sermons*, 50. 502.

[4] P. 52, and *Fifty Sermons*, 21. 183.

sumptuous worship of their Gods; And therefore they resisted it with this law, *Deos frugi colunto*. This moderated their sacrifices. . . .'[1]

In the *XXVI Sermons* we read:

'And whereas the Heathens needed laws to restrain them, from an expensive, and wastful worship of their Gods, every man was so apt to exceed in sacrifices and such other religious duties, til that law, *Deus* (read, *Deos*) *frugi Colunto* Let men be thrifty and moderate in religious expenses, was enacted. . . .'[2]

These are merely samples of the continuity of thought and expression between the *Essays* and the *Sermons*, and they could be multiplied almost indefinitely.

The form of the book is sufficiently described by its title, *Essays in Divinity*. It differs from Donne's other theological works in that it has no regular structure. The sermons are divided into several parts carefully planned and leading up to a definite conclusion. The work which is most like the *Essays* is the *Devotions upon Emergent Occasions*, but this conforms to a rigid plan; it has twenty-three chapters, each of which marks a stage in Donne's illness or his recovery, and each is divided into a meditation, an expostulation, and a prayer. This gives unity to the book; and we feel a certain personal interest in watching the development of Donne's sickness, which at last reaches its crisis, and then there is a gradual relaxation of tension, as recovery becomes established. The earlier book of *Essays* has no such central interest. Donne's plan was to take the first verse of the first two books of the Bible, and to compose a series of short dissertations and meditations on each. The two main divisions are both followed by a prayer or prayers, and one or two short prayers are inserted into the body of the book. The meditations, like those in the *Devotions*, are not 'meditations' in the technical sense. They are, as Donne described them, short essays, in which the headings, 'Of the Bible', 'Of Genesis', 'Of God', 'Diversity in Names', and the like, express very inadequately what Donne was trying to convey. He was to find a ministry of sixteen years too short to give a full

---

[1] P. 65.　　　　　　　　　　　[2] *XXVI Sermons*, 11. 160.

exposition of his views on the nature of God, and of His
self-revelation in the Scriptures. Here he merely 'essayed'
to put down a few scattered thoughts, of which some were
drawn from his miscellaneous reading, some from the
commentaries of established theologians, some from his
own experience. He is least interesting when he is repro-
ducing the commentaries. It is when he speaks from the
depths of his own experience of life that he challenges our
attention. This book is like the 'treasure trove' which a
child brings back from a day on the sea-shore. Some of it
is worthless, some ugly, some trivial, but here and there
we find an exquisitely fashioned sea-shell, some brightly
coloured sea-weed, or even a piece of precious amber or
cornelian.

The prayers are generally finer than the meditations.
To one reader at least they seem to be more spontaneous
than those in the *Devotions*, and to spring more evidently
from the depths of the heart. 'Thou hast set up many
candlesticks, and kindled many lamps in mee; but I have
either blown them out, or carried them to guide me in by
and forbidden ways . . . Yet, O God, have mercy upon
me, for thine own sake have mercy upon me. Let not sin
and me be able to exceed thee, nor to defraud thee, nor
to frustrate thy purposes: But let me, in despite of Me, be
of so much use to thy glory, that by thy mercy to my sin,
other sinners may see how much sin thou canst pardon.'

Without a careful study of these prayers it is easy for
a reader to miss the real significance of the book. Donne's
work is not simple; it is full of undertones and overtones.
From the prayer at the end of Book I we discover that in
pondering on the Genesis story of Creation he has seen
in it a symbol of that continuous act of creation by which
God dispels the 'confusion, darknesse, and barrennesse' in
the soul of John Donne, and makes it 'produce Creatures,
thoughts, words and deeds agreeable to' Himself. The
relation of Heaven and Earth to one another is seen as a
symbol of the relation between soul and body. In making
Heaven God did not neglect Earth, but made them
'answerable and agreeable to one another'. So Donne prays

that his 'Soul's Creatures' may have such a temper and harmony that he may not by a misdevout consideration of the next life become 'stupidly and trecherously negligent of the offices and duties which thou enjoynest amongst us in this life; nor so anxious in these, that the other (which is our better business, though this also must be attended) be the less endeavoured'.

Similarly at the close of Book II the first prayer expounds the spiritual significance of the essays on the Exodus. In the body of the book Donne has already warned his readers to be on the watch for a deeper meaning. 'If this be in the bark, what is in the tree? If in the superficiall grass, the letter; what treasure is there in the hearty and inward Mine, the Mistick, and retired sense? Dig a little deeper, O my poor lazy soul, and thou shalt see that thou, and all mankind, are delivered from an Egypt, and more miraculously then these.' This inward and mystic sense is not mere allegorizing, against which he utters a caution.[1] It springs from a recognition that God the Creator, who has manifested Himself in history, is also the eternal Spirit who brings light and life into the darkness of men's minds. This doctrine, which is fundamental in the Sermons, links these crude *Essays* firmly with Donne's later and greater work.

The style of the book is not that of Donne at his best. In the evolution of his prose, as in that of his thought, the *Essays* mark a period of transition. In *Biathanatos*, *Pseudo-Martyr*, and *Ignatius his Conclave*, Donne had forged a prose style admirably suited for controversy. Now, however, Donne was beginning to prepare himself for a new career in which preaching was to be one of his principal tasks. He needed to evolve a different style in which he could exhort, meditate aloud, and pray for and with his hearers. Hitherto, if we may judge from the *Divine Poems*, he had found it easier to meditate in verse than in prose,

---

[1] See p. 40: '. . . the curious refinings of the Allegoricall Fathers, which have made the Scriptures, which are stronge toyles, to catch and destroy the bore and bear which devast our Lords vineyard, fine cobwebs to catch flies.'

but he knew that from the time of his ordination prose would have to be the chief instrument of his thought. Here in the *Essays* he labours at this new task, but at first his style is clumsy and involved. The first twenty-five pages contain numerous sentences in which there are so many subordinate and co-ordinate clauses that the reader loses the thread of the thought. There are far too many parentheses enclosed in brackets, and there is a certain amount of padding, as in the last paragraph of the introductory section 'Of Genesis': 'And thus much necessarily, or conveniently, or pardonably, may have been said, before my Entrance, without disproportioning the whole work.'

We must also remember that we possess the *Essays* in their rough state, without the final polish which Donne was wont to give to his work before publication. He had prepared *Pseudo-Martyr* and *Ignatius his Conclave* for the press, and later he was to do the same for the *Devotions* and a number of the sermons. The difference between the earlier form of *A Sermon of Valediction*, as found in five manuscripts and in *Sapientia Clamitans*, and the revised version in *XXVI Sermons* shows how much revision, even as late as 1619, Donne's prose might need before it was fit for publication.

Yet in spite of its faults of style the book is lightened by many flashes of memorable thought expressed in fitting words. When Donne gets away from the tedious discussions of the first few sections, and lets his imagination wander over the wide prospect from the creation of the universe to its final dissolution, he anticipates some of the harmonies of Sir Thomas Browne's meditations in *Urn Burial*:

'Truly, the *Creation* and the *last Judgement*, are the *Diluculum* and *Crepusculum*, the *Morning* and the *Evening* twi-lights of the long day of this world. Which times, though they be not utterly dark, yet they are but of uncertain, doubtfull, and conjecturall light. Yet not equally; for the break of the day, because it hath a succession of more and more light, is clearer then the shutting in, which is overtaken with more and more darknesse; so is the birth of the world more discernable then the death, because upon this

God hath cast more clouds: yet since the world in her first infancy did not speak to us at all (by any Authors;) and when she began to speak by *Moses*, she spake not plain, but diversly to divers understandings; we must return again to our strong hold, *faith*, and end with this, *That this Beginning was, and before it, Nothing.* It is elder then darknesse, which is elder then light; And was before Confusion, which is elder then Order, by how much the universall Chaos preceded forms and distinctions. A beginning so near *Eternity*, that there was no *Then*, nor a minite of *Time* between them. Of which, Eternity could never say, *To morrow*, nor speak as of a future thing, because this *Beginning* was the first point of time, before which, whatsoever God did, he did it uncessantly and unintermittingly; which was but the *generation of the Son*, and *procession of the Spirit*, and *enjoying one another*; Things, which if ever they had ended, had begun; And those be terms incompatible with Eternity. And therefore Saint Augustin says religiously and exemplarily, *If one ask me what God did before this beginning, I will not answer, as another did merrily, He made Hell for such busie inquirers: But I will sooner say, I know not, when I know not, then answer that, by which he shall be deluded which asked too high a Mystery, and he be praysed, which answered a lie.*'[1]

Again, Donne's meditations on the transitory nature of human fame have some kinship with a famous chapter of *Urn Burial*:

'Amongst men, all Depositaries of our Memories, all means which we have trusted with the preserving of our Names, putrifie and perish. . . . The very places of the *Obeliscs*, and *Pyramides* are forgotten, and the purpose why they were erected. Books themselves are subject to the mercy of the Magistrate: and as though the ignorant had not been enemie enough for them, the Learned unnaturally and treacherously contribute to their destruction, by rasure and mis-interpretation. . . . But Names honour'd with a place in this book, cannot perish, because the Book cannot. Next to the glory of having his name entred into the *Book of Life*, this is the second, to have been matriculated in this Register, for an example or instrument of good. *Lazarus* his name is enrolled, but the wicked rich mans omitted.'[2]

There is nothing here of the sustained eloquence, the purple and gold of the Sermons, but here and there we

---

[1] Pp. 19–20.   [2] Pp. 43–44.

find a happy phrase such as 'the building of this great
patriarchal Catholick Church, of which every one of us is
a little chappel'. Probably the noblest passage in the book
is that in which Donne sets forth his conviction that Rome,
Canterbury, and Geneva are all branches of the one 'universal, Christian, Catholick Church'. He expresses his desire
for a measure of outward reunion, 'That then the Church,
discharged of disputations, and misapprehensions, and this
defensive warr, might contemplate Christ clearly and uniformely. For now he appears to her, as in Cant. 2. 9.
*He standeth behind a wall, looking forth of the window,
shewing himself through the grate.* But then, when all had
one appetite, and one food, one nostrill and one perfume,
the Church had obtained that which she then asked, *Arise
ô North, and come ô South, and blow on my garden, that the
spices thereof may flow out.* For then, that *savour of life
unto life* might allure and draw those to us, whom our
dissentions, more then their own stubbornness withhold
from us.'[1]

[1] Pp. 48–52.

BIBLIOGRAPHICAL NOTE

THE *Essays in Divinity* form a duodecimo volume
with the collation A⁸, B–K¹², L⁴. Signature A1 is
blank, and remains intact in the Bodleian copy.
A2 is occupied by the title, which is here reproduced in
facsimile.

Signatures A3–A7 originally contained the dedication,
'To the Great Example of Honour and Devotion, Sir H.
Vane, Junior'. The address, 'To the Reader', follows
on A8.

In this form the book was published early in 1651/2, for
Thomason bought his copy on 11 January. John Donne
the younger evidently thought it politic to cancel the dedication to Vane and reissue the book later in 1652 in company with the *Paradoxes, Problemes*, which he dedicated to
Francis Lord Newport. In this issue the leaves containing
the original dedication are omitted, and the 'Address to
the Reader' follows the title-page, being pasted on the
edge of a cancelled leaf. The text begins with pagination
on B1, and occupies 213 pages. It is followed by four
prayers, which occupy eleven pages.

The juxtaposition of the *Essays* and the *Paradoxes* is sufficiently startling, and in reality they are separate publica-
tions, the *Essays* having been issued by Richard Marriott,
and printed by T. M. (almost certainly Thomas Maxey),
while the *Paradoxes* were published by Humphrey Mose-
ley, and printed by T. N. (Thomas Newcomb). Apparently
only a few copies of the *Essays* appeared separately, and it
is plain from the younger Donne's dedication to Lord
Newport that in 1652 he had decided to make the two
books into one volume. There, as was first pointed out by
Dr. Geoffrey Keynes, he laboured the point that the
volume contained 'the *Essays* of *two Ages*, where you may
see the *quicknesse* of the first, and the *firmness* of the
latter . . . Here then you have the *entertainment* of the
Authors *Youth*; and the *Assumption* of his *Wit* when it
was employed in more *Heavenly* things.'

This dedication to Lord Newport is dated '*From my house in Cov. Gard. March 2. 1652*', which evidently means 1652/3, for *Ignatius his Conclave*, which is included in the volume, and is mentioned on the title-page of the *Paradoxes*, has its own title-page with the date 1653.

The original dedication of the *Essays* to Sir Harry Vane is here reproduced from one of the two perfect copies known, that in the Library of Worcester College, Oxford. The other is in the possession of Dr. Keynes. Two copies containing part of the dedication are known—the Thomason copy in the British Museum (shelf-mark E 1362), and the copy in Christ Church Library, Oxford. Both of these lack A3 and A6. I have collated the Worcester College copy with those leaves which remain in the Christ Church copy, and have found that the latter has an earlier uncorrected state of sheet A with the reading on A4 verso 'the Author was obliged in a civil business', which is corrected to 'the Author was obliged in Civill business' in the Worcester copy. On A8 verso, lines 4–6, the Christ Church copy has 'publish'd . . . himself . . . ', where the Worcester copy and my own (which has the cancel of A3–7) supply commas after both words. Also in the body of the work on H2 recto, the two last lines, Christ Church has 'tribute ju-|ly'. In the Bodleian, Worcester, and my own copies 'ju-|ly' has been corrected to 'just-|ly', and in order to make room for the 'st' of 'just-', the printer has curtailed 'tribute' to 'tribut'.

The book was not reprinted during the seventeenth and eighteenth centuries, and it was not included in Alford's *Works of Donne* (1839). In 1855 Dr. Augustus Jessopp produced an edition with introduction and notes. This was published in London by John Tupling, and is now extremely rare. Jessopp modernized the spelling and punctuation, and introduced a number of additional headings and subdivisions, as well as some emendations, but his text is reasonably accurate, except towards the end of the volume. The value of the edition lies chiefly in its excellent notes, some of which have been reproduced here followed by the initial (J.).

NOTE

CONTRACTIONS in the text have been expanded. Since square brackets are frequently used in the original edition to denote quotations, as in Donne's *Biathanatos*, these have been retained for this purpose, and editorial insertions of letters or numbers in the body of the text have been marked by angular brackets.

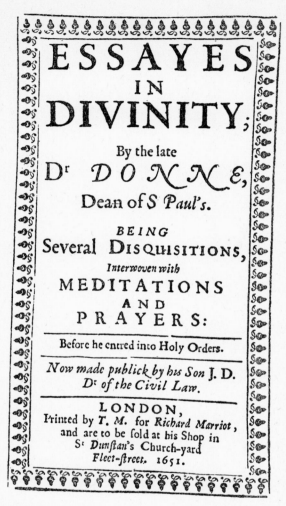

ESSAYES
IN
DIVINITY,

By the late
Dr DONNE,
Dean of S Paul's.

BEING
Several DISQUISITIONS,
Interwoven with
MEDITATIONS
AND
PRAYERS:

Before he entred into Holy Orders.

Now made publick by his Son J. D.
Dr of the Civil Law.

LONDON,
Printed by T. M. for Richard Marriot,
and are to be sold at his Shop in
St Dunstan's Church-yard
Fleet-street. 1651.

This facsimile was taken from the editor's own copy. Certain copies, such as the Worcester College copy, show a trace of a small broken t after the S of 'S Paul's'.

To the *Great Example* of Honour and Devotion,[1]
Sr H. *VANE Junior.*

Sir,

    Since it is acknowledg'd that if the Patrons of Scholers had
5 *not contributed more to the Commonwealth of Learning, then*
the Writers themselves, by giving both incouragement and
protection to their Labours, Achilles *had been but an Embrion*
of Homer's *brain, and* Æneas *proved a false conception of*
Virgil's *wit, (which are now two of the fairest products in the*
10 *world;) I cannot doubt, Sir, but that in owning these less, yet*
more lawfull issues of this modern Author, you will prove a
greater Mecænas *then those former Writers ever had, in*
giving a livelihood to these Ofsprings, that had no provision
left them by their Father.
15   *And to beg this favour, they come (Sir) with the greater*
confidence, because being writ when the Author was obliged
in Civill[2] *business, and had no ingagement in that of the*
Church, the manner of their birth may seem to have some
analogie with the course you now seem to steer; who being so
20 *highly interested in the publick Affairs of the State, can yet*
allow so much time to the exercise of your private Devotions;
which, with the help of your active wisdom, hath so setled us,
as the tempestuous North-windes are not like to blast in the
Spring before it come to a full growth, nor the South to over-
25 *ripen, till it arrive at such a perfection as may equall the*
birth of PALLAS; which could be produced from nothing but
the very brains of JUPITER; who although shee came
arm'd from thence, yet it had not been sufficient to have had
a God for her Father, if she had not had METIS to her
30 *Mother. Which shews us, that the Union is so inseparable*
between Counsell and Strength, that our Armies abroad
depend more upon your advice, then upon their own force; and
that they would prove but a Body without a Soul, if they were

---

[1] To the Great Example, etc.] Printed from the copy in Worcester
College Library, Oxford. The copy in Christ Church Library, Oxford,
has A4, 5, 7 (A3, 6 missing).
[2] *in Civill* Worc.: *in a civil* Ch. Ch.

not animated as well as recruted by your Direction. And
although it bee objected, that the Sword be no good Key to
open the Gates of Heaven, yet it was thought fit to protect
and defend Paradise, *and keep out even ADAM himself, who*
was the first and lawfull Heir, and who had for ever enjoyed 5
his Prerogative, if he had not exceeded his Commission, in
devouring that which hee was forbidden to taste. Sir, I have
no Application but of this Book to your protection, and of my
self to your Commands.

Your most   10
humble Servant,
JOHN DONNE.

To the Reader

It is thought fit to let thee know, that these *Essayes* were
printed from an exact Copy, under the Authors own 15
hand: and, that they were the voluntary sacrifices of
severall hours, when he had many debates betwixt God
and himself, whether he were worthy, and competently
learned to enter into Holy Orders. They are now publish'd,
both[1] to testifie his modest Valuation of himself, and[2] to 20
shew his great abilities; and, they[3] may serve to inform
thee in many Holy Curiosities.

Fare-well.

[1] publish'd, both *1651 corr.*: publish'd both *1651 originally.*
[2] himself, and *1651 corr.*: himself and *1651 originally.*
[3] and, they *1651 corr.*: and they *1651 originally.*

ESSAYES IN DIVINITY

⟨BOOK I⟩

In the Beginning God created Heaven and Earth. Gen. 1. 1.

I do not therefore sit at the door, and meditate upon
5 the threshold, because I may not enter further; For he
which is *holy and true, and hath the key of David, and open-* Apoc. 3. 7.
eth and no man shutteth, and shutteth and no man openeth;
hath said to all the humble in one person, *I have set before*
thee an open door, and no man can shut it, for thou hast a little
10 *strength.* And the holy Scriptures, signified in that place, Lyra.
as they have these properties of a well provided Castle,
that they are easily defensible, and safely defend others.
So they have also this, that to strangers they open but a
litle wicket, and he that will enter, must stoop and humble
15 himselfe. To reverend Divines, who by an ordinary calling
are Officers and Commissioners from God, the great Doors
are open. Let me with *Lazarus* lie at the threshold, and
beg their crums. *Discite à me,* sayes our blessed Saviour, Mat. 11.
Learn of me, as Saint *Augustine* enlarges it well, not to do ⟨29.⟩
20 Miracles, nor works exceeding humanity; but, *quia mitis*
sum; learn to be humble. His humility, to be like us, was
a Dejection; but ours, to be like him, is our chiefest exalta-
tion; and yet none other is required at our hands. Where Prov. 11.
this Humility is, *ibi Sapientia.* Therfore it is not such a ⟨2.⟩
25 groveling, frozen, and stupid Humility, as should quench
the activity of our understanding, or make us neglect the
Search of those Secrets of God, which are accessible. For, Tho.
Humility, and Studiousnesse, (as it is opposed to curiosity, ⟨Aquinas⟩
and transgresses not her bounds) are so near of kin, that 2ª, 2æ.
30 they are both agreed to be limbes and members of one 161.&166.
vertue, *Temperance.*

These bounds *Daniel* exceeded not; and yet he was *Vir*
Desideriorum, and in satisfaction of so high Desires, to him Dan. 10.
alone were those visions discovered. And to such desires 11.
35 and endeavours the Apostle encourageth the *Corinths,*[1] 1 Cor. 12.
31.

[1] *Corinths*] Corinthians 7.

*Æmulamini Charismata meliora, Desire you better gifts, and
I wil yet shew you a better way.* It is then humility to study
God, and a strange miraculous one; for it is an ascending
humility, which the Divel, which emulates even Gods
excellency in his goodnesse, and labours to be as ill, as he   5
is good, hath corrupted in us by a pride, as much against
reason; for he hath fill'd us with a descending pride, to
forsake God, for the study and love of things worse then
our selves. This averts us from the Contemplation of God,
and his Book. In whose inwards, and *Sanctum Sanctorum*,   10
what treasure of saving mysteries do his Priests see, when
we on the threshold see enough to instruct and secure us?
for he hath said of his lawes, *Scribes ea in limine*; and both
the people, and Prince himselfe, were to worship at the
threshold.   15

Before we consider each stone of this threshold, which
are 1. The *time, In the begin⟨n⟩ing*: 2. The *person, God*:
3. The *Action, He created*: And 4. the *Work, Heaven and
Earth*; we will speak of two or three other things, so many
words. Of the *Whole Book*; Of the *Author* of those first   20
5 Books; And of this *first book*. For earthly princes look for
so many pauses and reverences, in our accesses to their
table, though they be not there.

Of the Bible

God hath two Books of life; that in the *Revelation*, and   25
else where, which is an eternall Register of his Elect; and
this *Bible*. For of this, it is therefore said, *Search the Scriptures, because in them ye hope to have eternall life.* And more
plainly, when in the 24. of *Ecclesiasticus* Wisdome hath
said in the first verse, *Wisdome shall praise her self,*[1] saying, 30
He created me from the beginning, and I shall never fail,
v. 12. *I give eternall things to all my Children, and in me
is all grace of life and truth,* v. 21. *They that eat me shall
have the more hunger, and they that drink me shall thirst the
more,* v. 24. At last, in v. 26. *All these things are the book of*   35
life, and the Covenant[2] *of the most high God, and the law of*

Deut. 6. 9.
Ezek. 46.

Apoc. 3. 5.
Joh. 5. 39.

---

[1] Wisdome shall praise her self *1651.*
[2] *Covenant* Ed. following Geneva Bible: *Covenants* 1651.

Moses. And as our orderly love to the understanding this Book of life, testifies to us that our names are in the other; so is there another book subordinate to this, which is *liber creaturarum.* Of the first book, we may use the words of
5 *Esay, It is a book that is sealed up, and if it be delivered to* Isa. 29. 11. *one (Scienti literas) that can read, he shall say, I cannot, for it is sealed.* So far removed from the search of learning, are those eternall Decrees and Rolls of God, which are never certainly and infallibly produced and exemplified *in*[1]
10 *foro exteriori,* but onely insinuated and whisper'd to our hearts, *Ad informandum conscientiam Judicis,* which is the Conscience it selfe. Of the Second book, which is the *Bible,* we may use the next verse; *The book shall be given* (As interpreters agree, *open*) *Nescienti Literas, to one which*
15 *cannot read: and he shall be bid read, and shall say, I cannot read.* By which we learn, that as all mankind is naturally one flock feeding upon one Common, and yet for society and peace, Propriety, Magistracy, and distinct Functions are reasonably induc'd; so, though all our soules have
20 interest in this their common pasture, the book of life, (for even the ignorant are bid to read;) yet the Church has wisely hedged us in so farr, that all men may know, and cultivate, and manure their own part, and not adventure upon great reserv'd mysteries, nor trespass upon this
25 book, without inward humility, and outward interpretations. For it is not enough to have *objects,* and *eyes* to see, but you must have *light* too. The first book is then impossible; the second difficult; But of the third book, the[2] book of *Creatures,* we will say the 18th verse, *The deaf shall heare*
30 *the word of this book, and the eyes of the blinde shall see out of obscurity.* And so much is this book available to the other, that *Sebund,* when he had digested this book into Ray. Seb. a written book, durst pronounce, that it was an Art, which *in prolo.* teaches al things, presupposes no other, is soon learned,
35 cannot be forgotten, requires no books, needs no[3] witnesses, and in this, is safer then the Bible it self, that it cannot be falsified by Hereticks. And ventures further Tit. 166. after, to say, That because his book is made according to

---

[1] *in*] in *1651.*   [2] the] the the *1651.*   [3] no *J*: on *1651.*

the Order of Creatures, which express fully the will of
God, whosoever doth according to his booke, fulfils the
will of God. Howsoever, he may be too abundant in affirming, that *in libro creaturarum* there is enough to teach us all
particularities of Christian Religion, (for *Trismegistus* going 5

De im-
manifesto
Deo mani-
festissimo.
Rom. 2.
farr, extends not his proofs to particulars;) yet St *Paul* clears
it thus far, that there is enough to make us inexcusable, if
we search not further. And that further step is the knowledg of this Bible, which only, after Philosophy hath
evicted and taught us an Unity in the Godhead, shews 10
also a Trinity. As then this life compared to blessed

Greg.
Hom.
35. in
Evang.
eternity, is but a death, so the books of Philosophers,
which only instruct this life, have but such a proportion
to this book: Which hath in it *Certainty*, for no man
assigns to it other beginning then we do, though all allow 15
not ours: *Dignity*, for what Author proceeds so *sine teste*?
(and he that requires a witnesse, believes not the thing,
but the witnesse;) and a *non Notis*; (for he which requires
reason believes himselfe, and his own approbation and
allowance of the reason.) And it hath *Sufficiency*; for it 20
either rejecteth or judgeth all Traditions. It exceeds all
others in the *object*, for it considers the *next life*; In the
way, for it is written by *revelation*; yea the first piece of
it which ever was written, which is the Decalogue, by
Gods own finger. And as *Lyra* notes, being perchance too 25
Allegoricall and Typick in this, it hath this common with
all other books, that the *words* signifie *things*; but hath this
particular, that all the *things* signifie *other things*.

There are but two other books, (within our knowledge)
by which great Nations or Troops are govern'd in matter 30
of Religion; The *Alcoran*, and *Talmud*; of which, the first
is esteemed, only where ours is not read. And besides the
common infirmity of all weak, and suspicious, and crasie
religions, that it affords salvation to all good men, in any

Epist. Pii
secundi ad
Morbis.
Turcar.[1]
Religion, yea, to Divels also, with our singular *Origen*, is 35
so obnoxious and self-accusing, that, to confute it, all
Christian Churches have ever thought it the readiest and
presentest way to divulge it. And therefore *Luther*, after

[1] *Morbis. Turcar.*] *Morisb. Tunam* 1651.

it had received *Cribrationem*, a sifting by *Cusanus*, per- *Præfat. ad*
swades an Edition of the very Text, because he thinks the *lect. ad lib.*
Roman Church can no way be shak'd more, then thus to *de moribus*
Turcarum.
let the world see, how Sister-like those two Churches are.
5 But that man of infinite undertaking, and industry, and
zeal, and blessings from the Highest, had not seen the
Alcoran when he writ this, though he mention it: Nor
Cusanus his book certainly; for else he could not have said,
that the Cardinall had only excerpted and exhibited to the
10 world the infamous and ridiculous parts of it, and slipt
the substantiall; for he hath deduc'd an harmony, and
conformity of Christianity out of that book. *Melancthon* *Præmonit.*
also counsels this Edition, *Ut sciamus quale Poema sit*. And *ad Edit.*
Bibliander observes, that it is not only too late to sup- *Alcor.*
15 presse it now, but that the Church never thought it fit to
sup⟨p⟩resse it; because (saith he) there is nothing impious *Apolog.*
in it, but is formerly reprehensively registred in the *pro Edit.*
Alcor.
Fathers. As *Cusanus* hath done from the *Alcoran*, *Galatinus*
hath from the *Talmud* deduced all Christianity, and more. *De arcanis*
20 For he hath proved all *Roman* traditions from thence. We *Cathol.*
grudge them not those victories: but this flexibility and *veritatis.*
appliablenesse to a contrary religion, shews perfectly, how
leaden a rule those lawes are. Without doubt, their books
would have been received with much more hunger then
25 they are, if the Emperour *Maximilian*, by *Reuchlyns*[1]
counsell, had not allowed them free and open passage. If
there were not some compassion belong'd to them who
are seduced by them; I should professe, that I never read
merrier books then those two. Ours therefore, begun, not
30 only in the first stone, but in the intire foundation, by
Gods own finger, and pursued by his Spirit, is the only
legible book of life; and is without doubt devolv'd from
those to our times. For God, who first writ his Law in the
Tables of our hearts; and when our corruption had defaced
35 them, writ it again in *Stone-tables*; and when *Moses* zealous *Exod. 31.*
anger had broken them, writ them again in *other tables,* *18.*
leaves not us worse provided, whom he loves more, both *Exod.*
because he ever in his providence fore-saw the *Jews* defec- *34. 1.*

---

[1] *Reuchlyns*] *Reuchlyus* 1651: Reuchlin's *J*.

tion, and because in a naturall fatherly affection, he is delighted with his Sons purchases. For that interruption which the course of this book is imagin'd by great Authours *Irenæus.* to have had, by the perishing in the Captivity, cannot *Tertul.* possibly be allowed, if either Gods promise, or that history 5 *Clem. Al.* be considered; nor, if that were possible, is it the lesse the *Euseb.* *Hiero. &c.* work of God, if *Esdras* refresh'd and recompiled it by the same spirit which was in the first Authour; Nor is it the lesse ancient, no more then a man is the lesse old, for having slept, then walked out a day. Our age therefore 10 hath it; and our Church in our language; for since the *Def. Conc.* *Jesuit Sacroboscus,* and more late interpreters of the *Trent* *Trid. c. 1.* Councell, have abandoned their old station, and defence of the letter of the Canon, pronouncing the vulgate Edition to be authentick, (which they heretofore assumed for 15 the controverted point) and now say, that that Canon doth only preferre it before all Latine Translations; and that not *Absolutè*, (so to avoid *barbarismes*) but *In ordine ad fidem et mores*; and have given us limits and rules of allowable infirmities in a Translation, as corruptions not 20 offensive to faith, observing the meaning, though not the words, If the Hebrew text may bear that reading, and more such: We might, if we had not better assurances, rely upon their words, that we have the Scripture, and nearer perfection, then they. 25

Of Moses

The Author of these first five books is *Moses.* In which number, compos'd of the first even, and first odd, because Cabalistick learning seems to most *Occupatissima vanitas,* I will forbear the observations, both of *Picus* in his *Hep-* 30 *taplus,*[1] and in the Harmony of *Francis George,* that tran-*In Gen.* scending Wit, whom therefore *Pererius* charges to have *l. 1. c. 8. audax nimis, et ad devia et abruta opinionum præceps ingenium,* though they have many delicacyes of honest and serviceable curiosity, and harmless recreation and 35 entertainment. For as Catechisers give us the milk of Religion, and positive Divines solid nutriment, so when our

[1] *Heptaplus* J: *Hepsaplus* 1651.

conscience is sick of scruples, or that the Church is wounded
by schismes, which make *solutionem continui*, (as Chirur-
gians speak) though there be proper use of controverted
Divinity for Medicine, yet there be some Cankers, (as
5 *Judaisme*) which cannot be cur'd without the *Cabal*;
which is (especially for those diseases,) the *Paracelsian* *Arch-*
Phisick of the understanding, and is not unworthily (if it *angelus*
be onely applyed where it is so medicinable) call'd *præ-* *Apol.*
Cabal.
ambulum Evangelii. [*They of the Synagogue of Satan, which* *Apoc. 3.*
10 *call themselves Jews, and are not, but do lie*] as though they *9.*[1]
were still in the desert, and under the incommodities of
a continuall straying and ignorance of their way, (and so
they are, and worse; for then they onely murmured against
their guide, for not performing Gods promises, now, they
15 have no promise) are not content with their *Pillar of fire*,
this *Moses*, but have condens'd to themselves a *Pillar of*
Cloud, *Rabbi Moses*, call'd the *Egyptian*, but a *Spaniard*. *Drus. in*
[*A Mose ad Mosem non surrexit qualis Moses*] they say. *Not. ad*
nomen
This man quarelling with many imperfections, and some *Tetra.*
20 contradictions in our *Moses* works, and yet concurring
with the Jews in their opinion of his perfectness, if he
were understood, accomplish'd and perfected their *legem*
Oralem; which they account to be delivered by God to
our *Moses* in his forty dayes conversation with him, and
25 after delivered to *Esdras*, and so descended to these Ages.
His lateness and singularity, makes him not worth thus
many words: We will therefore leave *this Moses*, and
hasten to the dispatch of the *other*. Who, because he was
principal Secretary to the Holy Ghost, (I dispute not
30 other dignities, but onely priority in time) is very credible,
though he be his owne Historiographer. Therefore, though
his owne books best shew who, and what he was, let us
endeavour otherwise to bring those men to some reverence
of his Antiquity, who bring no taste to his Philosophy, nor
35 faith to his Story. *Pererius* seems peremptory that no Author *In Gen.*
is elder. I thinke it moved him, that *Henoch's* booke, men- *c. 1.*
tioned in the Epistle of *Jude*, is perish'd: So is the booke *Epist.Jud.*
of the Battails of the Lord (for any thing we know,) and

---

[1] Apoc. 3. 9] Apoc. 5. 9. *1651*.

Num. 21.
14.
that is not spoken of till *Num.* **21.** 14. and then as of a
future thing. He makes it reasonable evident, that *Linus,*
Orpheus, and all *Greeke* learning came after, and from him.
But if we shall escape this, that *Abraham's* booke *De* 5
formationibus is yet alive, by suspecting and pronouncing
Apol. it supposititious, (yet *Archangelus* saies, he hath it, and
Cabal. hath commented it, and *Francis George* often vouches it;)
Problem. how shall we deliver our selves from *Zoroasters* Oracles?
Fra. whom *Epiphanius* places in *Nembrots* time, and *Eusebius*
Patricius. in[1] *Abraham's;* since his language is *Chaldaick,* his works 10
Heurnius miraculously great, (for his Oracles are twenty hundred
de Philoso. thousand verses)[2] and his phrase more express, and clear,
Barbaric. and liquid, in the Doctrine of the Trinity, then *Moses?*
l. 2. For where sayes this, as the other, [*Toto mundo lucet Trias,*
cujus Monas est princeps?] From whence shall we say that 15
Hermes Trismegistus sucked his not only Divinity, but
Christianity? in which no Evangelist, no Father, no Coun-
cell is more literall and certain. Of the fall of Angels,
Renovation of the world by fire, eternity of punishments,
his *Asclepius* is plaine. Of Regeneration who sayes more 20
Asclep. then [*Nemo servari potest ante regenerationem, et regenera-*
Dial. *tionis generator est Dei filius, homo unus?*] Of imputed
De regen- Justice, with what Autor would he change this sentence,
erat. et [*Justificati sumus in Justitia absente?*] Of our corrupt will,
silentio.
De fato. and Gods providence he says, [*Anima nostra relicta à Deo,* 25
eligit corpoream naturam; at electio ejus est secundùm provi-
dentiam Dei.] To say with *Goropius,* that there was no such
man, because the publick pillars and statues in which were
engraved morall Institutions were called *Hermæ,* is im-
probable, to one who hath read *Patricius* his answers to 30
him. And if it be true which *Buntingus* in his Chronology
undisputably assumes, that he was the Patriarch *Joseph,*
as also that *Goropius* confounds *Zoroaster* and *Japhet,* then
Minerva *Moses* was not the first Author. But *Hermes* his naming of
mundi. *Italy,* and the 12. Constellations in the Zodiaque, are 35
Arguments and impressions of a later time. To unentangle
our selvs in this perplexity, is more labour then profit, or
perchance possibility.

     ¹ in] *in* 1651.   ² verses)] verses, *1651.*

Therefore, as in violent tempests, when a ship dares bear
no main sayl, and to lie stil at hull, obeying the uncertain
wind and tyde, puts them much out of their way, and
altogether out of their account, it is best to put forth such
5 a small ragg of sail, as may keep the barke upright, and
make her continue neer one place, though she proceed
not; So in this question, where we cannot go forward to
make *Moses* the first Author, for many strong oppositions,
and to ly hulling upon the face of the waters, and think
10 nothing, is a stupid and lazy inconsideration, which (as   Rom. 1.
Saint *Austin* says) is the worst of all affections, our best
firmament and arrest will be that reverent, and pious, and
reasonable credulity, that God was Author of the first
piece of these books, the *Decalogue*: and of such Authors
15 as God preordained to survive all Philosophers, and all
Tyrants, and all Hereticks, and be the Canons of faith and
manners to the worlds end, *Moses* had the primacy. So that
the Divine and learned book of *Job*, must be content to be
disposed to a later rank, (as indeed it hath somwhat a
20 Greek taste) or to accept *Moses* for Author. For to confess,
that it was found by *Moses* in *Madian*, were to derogate
from the other prerogative generally afforded to him.
Here therefore I will temperatly end this inquisition.
Hierom tells me true, [*Puerile est, et circulatorum ludo*   Epist. ad
25 *simile, docere quod ignores.*] And besides, when I remember   Paul. de
that it was God which hid *Moses*'s body, And the Divell   lib. Divin.
which laboured to reveal it, I use it thus, that there are   Deut. 34.
some things which the Author of light hides from us, and   Jud. 1.9.[1]
the prince of darkness strives to shew to us; but with
30 no other light, then his firebrands of Contention, and
curiosity.

Of Genesis

Picus Earl of *Mirandula* (happier in no one thing in this
life, then in the Author which writ it to us) being a man
35 of an incontinent wit, and subject to the concupiscence   S⟨r⟩ Tho.[2]
of inaccessible knowledges and transcendencies, pursuing   More.
the rules of *Cabal*, out of the word *Bresit*, which is the   In fine
title of this first Book, by vexing, and transposing, and   Heptap.[3]

[1] 9] 5 *1651.*   *Tho.*] *John* 1651.   [2] *Heptap.*] *Heptaph.* 1651.

anagrammatizing the letters, hath express'd and wrung
out this Sum of Christian Religion [*The Father, in and
through the Son, which is the beginning, end, and rest, created
in a perfect league, the head, fire and foundation* (which he
calls Heaven, Air and Earth) *of the great man*] (which he 5
calls the World). And he hath not onely delivered *Moses*
from any dissonance with other sound Philosophers, but
hath observed all other Philosophy in *Moses*'s words; and
more, hath found all *Moses*'s learning in every verse of
Moses. But since our merciful God hath afforded us the 10
whole and intire book, why should wee tear it into rags, or
rent the seamless garment? Since the intention of God,
Gen. 5. 1. through *Moses*, in this, was, that it might be to the Jews
a *Book of the generation of Adam*; since in it is purposely
propounded, That all this Universe, *Plants*, the chiefest 15
contemplation of Naturall Philosophie and Physick, and
1 Reg. 4. no small part of the Wisdom of *Solomon*, [*who spake of
33. plants, from Cedar to Hyssop*:] And *Beasts*, who have often
the honour to be our reproach, accited for examples of
vertue and wisdome in the scriptures, and some of them 20
seposed for the particular passive service of God in Sacrifices (which hee gave to no man but his Son, and withheld from *Isaac*:) And *Man*, who (like his own eye) sees
all but himself, in his opinion, but so dimly, that there are
marked an hundred differences in mens Writings concern- 25
ing an *Ant*: And *Spirits*, of whom we understand no more,
then a horse of us: and the receptacles and theaters of all
these, *Earth, Sea, Air, Heaven*, and all things were once
nothing: That Man chusing his own destruction, did what
he could to annihilate himself again, and yet received a 30
promise of a Redeemer: That Gods mercy may not be
distrusted, nor his Justice tempted, since the generall
Deluge, and *Joseph*'s preservation are here related, filling
an History of more then 2300 yeers, with such examples
as might mollifie the Jews in their wandering. I say, since 35
this was directly and onely purposed by *Moses*; to put him
in a wine-presse, and squeeze out Philosophy and particular Christianitie, is a degree of that injustice, which all
laws forbid, to torture a man, *sine indiciis aut sine proba-*

tionibus.[1] Of the time when *Moses* writ this booke, there
are two opinions which have good guides, and good followers. I, because to me it seems reasonable and clear, that
no Divine work preceded the Decalogue, have before
5 engaged my selfe to accompany *Chemnitius*, who is per- *Exam.*
swaded by *Theodoret*, *Bede*, and Reason (because here is *Conc.*
intimation of a Sabboth, and distinction of clean and *Trid.*
unclean in beasts,) that this book was written after the
Law; And leave *Pererius*, whom *Eusebius* hath won to
10 thinke this booke was written in *Madian*, induc'd only by
Moses forty years leisure there; and a likelihood, that this
Story might well conduce to his end, of reclining the Jews
from *Egypt*.

And thus much necessarily, or conveniently, or pardon-
15 ably, may have been said, before my Entrance, without[2]
disproportioning the whole work. For even in *Solomon's*
magnificent Temple, the Porch to the Temple had the
proportion of twenty Cubits to sixty. Our next step is
upon the *threshold* it self, *In the beginning*, &c.

20   PART I

'In the Beginning whereof, O onely Eternall God, of *In the Be-*
'whose being, beginning, or lasting, this beginning is no *ginning.*
'period, nor measure; which art no Circle, for thou hast
'no ends to close up; which art not within this *All*, for it
25 'cannot comprehend thee; nor without it, for thou fillest
'it; nor art it thy self, for thou madest it; which having
'decreed from all eternity, to do thy great work of Mercy,
'our Redemption in the fulnesse of time, didst now create
'*time* it selfe to conduce to it; and madest thy glory and
30 'thy mercy equal thus, that though thy glorious work of
'Creation were first, thy mercifull work of Redemption
'was greatest. Let me in thy beloved Servant *Augustine's* *Conf.*
'own words, when with an humble boldnesse he begg'd *li. ⟨xi⟩.*
'the understanding of this passage, say, *Moses writ this,* *c. 3.*
35 '*but is gon from me to thee; if he were here, I would hold*
'*him, and beseech him for thy sake, to tell me what he meant.*

---

[1] *sine probationibus* J: *semiprobationibus* 1651.
[2] without] with out *1651*.

'*If he spake Hebrew, he would frustrate my hope; but if*
'*Latine, I should comprehend him. But from whence should*
'*I know that he said true? Or when I knew it, came that*
'*knowledge from him? No, for within me, within me there is*
'*a truth, not Hebrew, nor Greek, nor Latin, nor barbarous;* 5
'*which without organs, without noyse of Syllables, tels me*
'*true, and would enable me to say confidently to Moses, Thou*
'*say'st true.*'

[1]Thus did he whom thou hadst filled with faith, desire
reason and understanding; as men blest with great for- 10
tunes desire numbers of servants, and other Complements

Aq.2.q.46. of honour. But another instrument and engine of thine,
A. 2. whom thou hadst so enabled, that nothing was too
minerall nor centrick for the search and reach of his wit,
hath remembred me; *That it is an Article of our Belief,* 15
that the world began. And therefore for this point, we are
not under the insinuations and mollifyings of perswasion,
and conveniency; nor under the reach and violence of
Argument, or Demonstration, or Necessity; but under the
Spirituall, and peaceable Tyranny, and easie yoke of sud- 20
den and present Faith. Nor doth he say this, that we
should discharge our selves upon his word, and slumber in
a lazy faith; for no man was ever more endeavourous then
he in such inquisitions; nor he in any, more then in this
point. But after he had given answers to all the Arguments 25
of reasonable and naturall men, for a beginning of this
world; to advance Faith duly above Reason, he assignes
this with other mysteries only to her comprehension. For
Reason is our Sword, Faith our Target. With that we prevail against others, with this we defend our selves: And 30
old, well disciplined Armies punished more severely the
loss of this, then that.

This word, *In the beginning,* is the beginning of this
book, which we finde first placed of all the holy books;
And also of the Gospel by Saint *John,* which we know to 35
be last written of all. But that *last* beginning was the *first;*
for *the Word was with God,* before God created Heaven
and Earth. And *Moses* his *In the Beginning,* hath ever been

[1] Thus . . . that.] *Quotation marks continued* 1651.

used powerfully, and prosperously, against Philosophers
and Hereticks relapsed into an opinion of the worlds
eternity. But Saint *John's In the Beginning*, hath ever had
strength against the Author of all errour, the Divel him-
5 self, if we may beleeve the relations of exorcists, who in
their dispossessings, mention strange obediences of the
Divell at the naked enunciation of that word. It is not then
all *one* Beginning; for here God *Did*, there he *Was*. That
confesses a *limitation of time*, this excludes it. The great *Caninius*
10 Philosopher, (whom I call so, rather for his Conversion, *Conc.*
then his Arguments) who was *Arius* his Advocate at the *To. 1.*
first *Nicene* Councell, assign'd a beginning between these *Nic.*
two beginnings; saying, that after *John's eternal Beginning*,
and before *Moses's timely beginning*, Christ had his begin-
15 ning, being then created by God for an instrument in his
generall Creation. But God forbid that anything should
need to be said against this, now. We therefore confessing
two Beginnings, say, that this first was *simul cum tempore*,
and that it is truly said of it, *Erat quando non erat*, and that
20 it instantly vanished; and that the last Beginning lasts yet,
and ever shall: And that our Mercifull God, as he made
no Creature so frail and corruptible as the *first* Beginning,
which being but the first point of time, dyed as soon as it
was made, flowing into the next point; so though he made
25 no creature like the *last* Beginning, (for if it had been as
it, eternall, it had been no creature;) yet it pleased him to
come so neer it, that our soul, though it began with that
first Beginning, shall continue and ever last with the *last*.
We may not dissemble, nor dare reprove, nor would avoid
30 another ordinary interpretation of this *Beginning*, because
it hath great and agreeing autority, and a consonance with
our faith: which is, that by the *beginning* here, is meant
the *Son* our Savior; for that is elsewhere said of him, *I am* *Rev. 1. 8.*
first and last, which is, and was, and is to come. And hereby
35 they would establish his coeternity, and consubstantial-
ness, because he can be no creature, who is present at
the first Creation. But because although to us, whom
the Spirit hath made faithfully credulous, and filled us
with an assurance of this truth, every conducing, and

convenient application governs and commands our assent, because it doth but remember us, not teach us. But to the *Jews*, who roundly deny this Exposition, and to the *Arians*, who accept it, and yet call Christ a creature, as fore-created for an Assistant in this Second Creation; these 5 detortions have small force, but as Sun-beams striking obliquely, or arrows diverted with a twig by the way, they lessen their strength, being turned upon another mark then they were destined to. And therefore by the Example of our late learned Reformers, I forbear this interpreta- 10 tion; the rather, because we are utterly dis-provided of any history of the Worlds Creation, except we defend and maintain this Book of *Moses* to be Historical, and therefore literally to be interpreted. Which I urge not with that peremptorinesse, as *Bellarmine* doth, who answers all the 15 Arguments of *Moses*'s silence in many points maintained *De Purg.* by that Church, with this only, *Est liber Historiarum, non* *l. 1. c. 15. Dogmatum.* For then it were unproperly argued by our John 5. Saviour, *If ye believed Moses, ye would believe me, for he writ of me.* There is then in *Moses*, both History and Pre- 20 cept, but evidently distinguishable without violence. That then this Beginning *was*, is matter of faith, and so, infallible. *When* it was, is matter of *reason*, and therefore various and perplex'd. In the Epistle of *Alexander the Great* to his Mother, remembred by *Cyprian* and *Augustin*, 25 there is mention of 8000. years. The *Caldeans* have delivered observations of 470000 years. And the *Egyptians* of 100000. The *Chineses* vex us at this day, with irreconciliable accounts. And to be sure, that none shall prevent them, some have call'd themselves *Aborigenes*. The poor 30 remedy of Lunary and other planetary years, the silly and contemptible escape that some Authors speak of running years, some of years expired and perfected; or that the account of dayes and monthes are neglected, cannot ease us, nor afford us line enough to fathom this bottom. The 35 last refuge uses to be, that prophane history cannot clear, but Scripture can. Which is the best, because it is halfe *Bib. Sanct.* true; But that the later part is true, or that God purposed *l. 5.* to reveal it in his Book, it seems doubtfull, because *Sextus*

Senensis reckons almost thirty severall supputations of the years between the Creation, and our blessed Saviours birth, all of accepted Authors, grounded upon the Scriptures; and *Pererius* confesses, he might have encreased the num-
5 ber by 20. And they who in a devout melancholy delight themselves with this Meditation, that they can assigne the beginning of all Arts which we use for Necessity or Orna-ment; and conclude, that men which cannot live without such, were not long before such inventions, forget both
10 that many Nations want those commodities yet, and that there are as great things perish'd and forgot⟨t⟩en, as are now remaining. Truly, the *Creation* and the *last Judge-ment*, are the *Diluculum* and *Crepusculum*, the *Morning* and the *Evening* twi-lights of the long day of this world. Which
15 times, though they be not utterly dark, yet they are but of uncertain, doubtfull, and conjecturall light. Yet not equally; for the break of the day, because it hath a succes-sion of more and more light, is clearer then the shutting in, which is overtaken with more and more darknesse; so
20 is the birth of the world more discernable then the death, because upon this God hath cast more clouds: yet since the world in her first infancy did not speak to us at all (by any Authors;) and when she began to speak by *Moses*, she spake not plain, but diversly to divers understandings; we
25 must return again to our strong hold, *faith*, and end with this, *That this Beginning was, and before it, Nothing.* It is elder then darknesse, which is elder then light; And was before Confusion, which is elder then Order, by how much the universall Chaos preceded forms and distinctions. A
30 beginning so near *Eternity*, that there was no *Then*, nor a minite of *Time* between them. Of which, Eternity could never say, *To morrow*, nor speak as of a future thing, because this *Beginning* was the first point of time, before which, whatsoever God did, he did it uncessantly and uninter-
35 mittingly; which was but the *generation of the Son*, and *procession of the Spirit*, and *enjoying one another*; Things, which if ever they had ended, had begun; And those be terms incompatible with Eternity. And therefore Saint *Conf. l.* 11. Augustin says religiously and exemplarily, *If one ask me cap.* 12.

what God did before this beginning, I will not answer, as
another did merrily, He made Hell for such busie inquirers:
But I will sooner say, I know not, when I know not, then
answer that, by which he shall be deluded which asked too
high a Mystery, and he be praysed, which answered a lie.'   5

PART 2

Now we have ended our Consideration of this beginning,
we will begin with that, which was before it, and was
Author of it, *God* himself; and bend our thoughts first
upon *himself*, then upon his *Name*, and then upon the   10
particular Name here used, *Elohim*.

Of God

Men which seek God by reason, and naturall strength,
(though we do not deny common notions and generall
impressions of a soveraign power) are like Mariners which   15
voyaged before the invention of the Compass, which were
but Costers, and unwillingly left the sight of the land.
Such are they which would arrive at God by this world,
and contemplate him onely in his Creatures, and seeming
Demonstration. Certainly, every Creature shewes God,   20
as a glass, but glimeringly and transitiorily, by the frailty
both of the receiver, and beholder: Our selves have his
Image, as Medals, permanently, and preciously delivered.
But by these meditations we get no further, then to know
what he *doth*, not what he *is*. But as by the use of the   25
Compass, men safely dispatch *Ulysses* dangerous ten years
travell in so many dayes, and have found out a new world
richer then the old; so doth Faith, as soon as our hearts
are touched with it, direct and inform us in that great
search of the discovery of Gods Essence, and the new   30
Hierusalem, which Reason durst not attempt. And though
the faithfullest heart is not ever directly, and constantly
upon God, but that it sometimes descends also to Reason;
yet it is ⟨not⟩ thereby so departed from him, but that it
still looks towards him, though not fully to him: as the   35
Compass is ever Northward, though it decline, and have
often variations towards East, and West. By this faith, as

by reason, I know, that God is all that which all men can
say of all Good; I beleeve he is somewhat which no man
can say nor know. For, *si scirem quid Deus esset, Deus essem.*
For all acquired knowledg is by degrees, and successive;
5 but God is impartible, and only faith which can receive it
all at once, can comprehend him.[1]

Canst thou then, O my soul, when faith hath extended
and enlarged thee, not as wind doth a bladder (which is
the nature of humane learning) but as God hath displaid
10 the Curtain of the firmament, and more spaciously; for
thou comprehendest that, and him which comprehends it:
Canst thou be satisfied with such a late knowledg of God,
as is gathered from *effects*; when even reason, which feeds
upon the crums and fragments of appearances and veri-
15 similitudes, requires *causes?* Canst thou rely and leane
upon so infirm a knowledg, as is delivered by negations?
And because a devout speculative man hath said, *Nega-*   Dyon.
tiones de Deo sunt veræ, affirmationes autem sunt incon-   2. ca.
venientes, will it serve thy turn to hear, that God is that   Cæl.
20 which cannot be named, cannot be comprehended, or   Hierar.
which is nothing else? When every negation implyes some
privation, which cannot be safely enough admitted in God;
and is, besides, so inconsiderable a kind of proofe, that
in civill and judic⟨i⟩all practice, no man is bound by it,
25 nor bound to prove it. Can it give thee any satisfaction,
to hear God called by concrete names, *Good, Just, Wise*;
since these words can never be without confessing *better,*
wiser, and *more just?* Or if he be called *Best,* etc. or in such
phrase, the highest degree respects some lower, and mean
30 one: and are those in God? Or is there any Creature, any
Degree of that *Best,* by which we should call God? Or
art thou got any neerer, by hearing him called Abstractly,
Goodness; since that, and such, are communicable, and
daily applied to Princes? Art thou delighted with Argu-
35 ments arising from Order, and Subordination of Creatures,
which must at last end in some one, which ends in none?
Or from the preservation of all this Universe, when men
which have not had faith, and have opposed reason to

---

[1] comprehend him.] *Paragraph continued* 1651.

reason, have escaped from all these, without confessing
such a God, as thou knowest; at least, without seeing
thereby, what he is? Have they furthered, or eased thee
any more, who not able to consider whole and infinit God,
have made a particular God, not only of every power of 5
God, but of every benefit? And so filled the world (which
our God alone doth better) with so many, that *Varro*
could account 30000 and of them 300 *Jupiters*. Out of
this proceeded *Dea febris*, and *Dea fraus*, and *Tenebræ*[1], and
Onions, and *Garlike*. For the *Egyptians*, most abundant in 10
Idolatry, were from thence said to have Gods grow in their
Apol. l. 5. gardens. And *Tertullian*, noting that Gods became mens
Creatures, said, *Homo incipit esse propitius Deo*, because
Gods were beholden to men for their being. And thus did
a great Greek Generall, when he pressed the Ilanders for 15
money, tell them, that he presented two Gods, *Vim et
Suasionem*; and conformably to this they answered, that
they opposed two Gods, *Paupertatem et Impossibilitatem*.
And this multiplicity of Gods may teach thee, that the
resultance of all these powers is *one* God, and that no place 20
nor action is hid from him: but it teacheth not, who, nor
what he is. And too particular and restrain'd are all those
descents of God in his word, when he speaks of a body,
and of passions, like ours. And such also is their reverend
silence, who have expressed God in Hieroglyphicks, ever 25
determining in some one power of God, without larger
extent. And lastly, can thy great capacity be fulfilled with
that knowledg, which the *Roman* Church affords of God?
which, as though the state of a Monarchy were too terrible,
and refulgent for our sight, hath changed the Kingdome 30
of heaven into an Olygarchy; or at least, given God leasure,
and deputed Masters of his Requests, and Counsellers in
his great Starr-chamber?

   Thou shalt not then, O my faithfull soul, despise any
of these erroneous pictures, thou shalt not destroy, nor 35
demolish their buildings; but thou shalt not make them thy
foundation. For thou beleevest more then they pretend
to teach, and art assured of more then thou canst utter.

[1] *Tenebræ*] *Tenebris* 1651.

For if thou couldest express all which thou seest of God,
there would be somthing presently beyond that. Not that
God growes, but faith doth. For, God himself is so unutter-
able, that he hath a name which we cannot pronounce.

5   *Of the Name of God*

Names are either to avoid confusion, and distinguish particulars, and so every day begetting new inventions, and the
names often overliving the things, curious and entangled
Wits have vexed themselves to know, whether in the world
10 there were more things or names;) But such a name, God
who is one needs not; Or else, names are to instruct us, and
express natures and essences. This *Adam* was able to do. And
an enormous pretending Wit of our nation and age under-
took to frame such a language, herein exceeding *Adam*,
15 that whereas he named every thing by the most eminent
and virtuall property, our man gave names, by the first
naked enuntiation whereof, any understanding should
comprehend the essence of the thing, better then by a
definition. And such a name, we who know not Gods
20 essence cannot give him. So that it is truly said, there is
no name given by man to God, *Ejus essentiam adæquatè*   Aq. 1.
representans. And *Hermes* says humbly and reverently, *Non*   q. 13.
spero, I cannot hope, that the maker of all Majesty, can be   Ar. 1.
call'd by any one name, though compounded of many. I   Asclep.
25 have therfore sometimes suspected, that there was some
degree of pride, and overboldness, in the first naming of
God; the rather, because I marke, that the first which   Gen. 3. 1.
ever pronounced the name, *God*, was the Divell; and presently after the woman; who in the next chapter pro-   Gen. 4. 1.
30 ceeded further, and first durst pronounce that sacred and
mystick name of foure letters. For when an Angell did but   Gen.32.29.
Ministerially represent God wrastling with *Jacob*, he reproves *Jacob*, for asking his name; *Cur quæris nomen meum?*
And so also to *Manoah*, *Why askest thou my Name, quod*   Jud.13.18.
35 *est mirabile?* And God, to dignify that Angell which he
promises to lead his people, says, *Fear him, provoke him*   Exod. 23.
not, &c. *For my Name is in him*; but he tels them not what   20.
it is. But since, necessity hath enforced, and Gods will

hath revealed some names. For in truth, we could not say this, God cannot be named, except God could be named. To handle the Mysteries of these names, is not for the straitness of these leaves, nor of my stock. But yet I will take from *Picus*, those words which his extream learning needed not, *Ex lege, spicula linquuntur pauperibus in messe*, the richest and learnedst must leave gleanings behind them. Omitting therefore Gods attributes, *Eternity, Wisdom*, and such; and his Names communicable with Princes, and such; there are two Names proper, and expressing his Essence: One imposed by us, *God*; The other taken by God, the Name of *four* letters; for the Name, *I am*, is derived from the same root. The Name imposed by us, comes so near the other, that most Nations express it in four letters; and the *Turk* almost as Mistically as the Hebrew, in *Abgd*, almost ineffably:[1] And hence perchance was derived the *Pythagorean* oath, by the number of four. And in this also, that though it be given from Gods Works, not from his Essence, (for that is impossible to us) yet the root signifies all this, *Curare, Ardere*, and *Considerare*; and is purposed and intended to signifie as much the Essence, as we can express; and is never afforded absolutely to any but God himself. And therefore *Aquinas*, after he had preferred the Name *I am*, above all, both because others were from *formes*, this from *Essence*; they signified some determined and limited property, this whole and entire God; and this best expressed, that nothing was past, nor future to God; he adds, yet the Name, *God*, is more proper then this, and the Name of four letters more then that. Of which Name one says, that as there is a secret property by which we are changed into God, (referring, I think, to that, *We are made partakers of the godly nature*) so God hath a certain name, to which he hath annexed certain conditions, which being observed, he hath bound himself to be present. This is the Name, which the *Jews* stubbornly deny ever to have been attributed to the *Messias* in the Scriptures. This is the name, which they say none could utter, but the priests, and the knowledg

Proem. in Heptap. 5

Aq. 1. 20
q. 13.
Ar. 8.

Ar. 11. 25

30
Tetragr.
Reuclin. de verbo Mirifico.
l. 2.[2] *c.* 6.
2 Pet. 1.4. 35

---

[1] ineffably] in effably *1651*.　　　[2] *l.* 2] *l.* 1. *1651*: Lib. ii. *J*.

of it perished with the Temple. And this is the name by
which they say our Blessed Saviour did all his miracles,
having learned the true use of it, by a Scedule which he
found of *Solomon's* and that any other, by that means,
5 might do them.

How this name should be sounded, is now upon the Jehovah.
anvile, and every body is beating and hammering upon it.
That it is not *Jehova*, this governs me, that the *Septuagint*
never called it so; Nor Christ; nor the Apostles, where
10 they vouch the old Testament; Nor *Origen*, nor *Hierome*,
curious in language. And though negatives have ever their
infirmities, and must not be built on, this may, that our
Fathers heard not the first sound of this word *Jehova*. For
(for any thing appearing,) *Galatinus*, in their Age, was the
15 first that offered it. For, that *Hierome* should name it in
the exposition of the eighth *Psalm*, it is peremptorily
averred by *Drusius*, and admitted by our learnedst Doctor, *De*
that in the old Editions it was not *Jehova*. But more then *Nomine*[1]
any other reason, this doth accomplish and perfect the *Tetrag.*
20 opinion against that word, that whereas that language *Rainolds*
hath no naturall vowels inserted, but points subjected of *de Idol.* 2,
the value and sound of our vowels, added by the *Masorits*, 2, 18.
the Hebrew Criticks, after *Esdras*; and therefore they
observe a necessity of such a naturall and infallible con-
25 currence of consonants, that when such and such consonants meet, such and such vowels must be imagined, and
sounded, by which they have an Art of reading it without *Genebr. de*
points; by those rules, those vowels cannot serve those *leg. Orient.*
Consonants, nor the name *Jehova* be built of those four *sine*
30 letters, and the vowels of *Adonay.* *punctis.*[2]

Elohim

Of the name used in this place, much needs not. But as old
age is justly charged with this sickness, that though it
abound, it ever covets, though it need less then youth did:
35 so hath also this decrepit age of the world such a sickness;
for though we have now a clearer understanding of the
Scriptures then former times, (for we inherit the talents

[1] *Nomine* J: *Nōie* 1651.   [2] *sine punctis*] *sinepunctis* 1651.

and travels[1] of al Expositors, and have overlived most of the
prophecies,) and though the gross thick clouds of *Arianism*
be dispersed, and so we have few enemies; yet we affect,
and strain at more Arguments for the *Trinity*, then those
times did, which needed them more. Hereupon hath an 5
opinion, that by this name of *God*, *Elohim*, because it is
plurally pronounced in this place, and with a *singular*
verbe, the Trinity is insinuated, first of any begun by
L. 1. Sent. Peter *Lumbard*, been since earnestly pursued by *Lyra*,
Dist. 2. *Galatin*, and very many. And because *Calvin*, in a brave 10
religious scorn of this extortion, and beggarly wresting of
Scriptures, denyes this place, with others usually offered
for that point, to concern it, and his defender *Paræus*
denyes any good Author to approve it, *Hunnius* opposes
Antipar. Luther, and some after, but none before, to be of that 15
fo. 9. opinion. But, lest any should think this a prevarication in
me, or a purpose to shew the nakedness of the Fathers of
our Church, by opening their disagreeing, though in no
fundamentall thing, I will also remember, that great pillars
of the Roman Church differ with as much bitterness, and 20
less reason in this point. For, when *Cajetan* had said true,
that this place was not so interpretable, but yet upon false
Eloah. grounds, That the word *Elohim* had no singular, which is
Job 2. and evidently false, *Catharinus* in his Animadversions upon
36. *Cajetan*, reprehends him bitterly for his truth, and spies 25
not his Errour: And though *Tostatus* long before said the
same, and *Lumbard* were the first that writ the contrary,
he denies any to have been of *Cajetan's* opinion. It satisfies
me, for the phrase, that I am taught by collation of many
places in the Scriptures, that it is a meer Idiotism. And 30
for the matter, that our Saviour never applyed this place
to that purpose: And that I mark, the first place which the
Fathers in the *Nicen* Councel objected against *Arius* his
Philosopher, was, *Faciamus hominem*, and this never men-
Isa. 65. tioned. Thus much of him, who hath said, *I have been* 35
found by them which have not sought me: And therefore
most assuredly in another place, *If thou seek me, thou shalt
finde me*. I have adventured in his Name, upon his Name.

[1] travels] travails *J*.

Our next consideration must be his most glorious worke
which he hath yet done in any time, the *Creation.*

PART 3

Mundum tradidit disputationi eorum, ut non inveniat homo Eccles.
5 *opus quod operatus est Deus ab initio usque ad finem.* So that 3. 11.[1]
God will be glorified both in our searching these Mys-
teries, because it testifies our liveliness towards him, and
in our not finding them. Lawyers, more then others, have
ever been Tyrants over words, and have made them accept
10 other significations, then their nature enclined to. Hereby
have Casuists drawn the word *Anathema,* which is *con-*
secrated or separated, and *separated* or seposed for Divine
use, to signify necessarily *accursed,* and cut off from the
communion of the Church. Hereby Criminists have com-
15 manded *Heresie,* which is but election, (and thereupon
Paul gloryed to be of the *strictest Heresie, a Pharisee;*[2] and Act. 26.[3] 5.
the Scepticks were despised, because they were of no Here-
sie) to undertake a capitall and infamous signification. Laert.
Hereby also the Civilists have dignified the word *Privi-* Acacius de
20 *ledge,* whose ancientest meaning was, a law to the dis- Privil. l. 1.
advantage of any private man (and so *Cicero* speaks of one cap. 1.
banished by priviledg, and lays the names, *cruel* and *capitall*
upon Priviledg) and appointed it to express only the
favours and graces of Princes. Schoolmen, which have
25 invented new things, and found out, or added Suburbs to
Hell, will not be exceeded in this boldness upon words.
As therefore in many other, so they have practised it in
this word *creare*: which being but of an even nature with
facere, or *producere,* they have laid a necessity upon it to Scot. 2.
30 signifie a *Making of Nothing*; For so is Creation defined. Sent. Dist.
But in this place neither the *Hebrew* nor *Greek* word afford 1. q. 5.
it; neither is it otherwise then indifferently used in the Pererius.
holy books. Sometimes of things of a preexistent matter,
He created man of Earth, and he created him a helper out of Sirach
35 *himself.* Sometimes of things but then revealed, *They are* 17. 1.
created now, and not of old. Sometimes of that, whereof God Isa. 48. 7.

---

[1] Eccles. *J*: Sirac. *1651.*   [2] *Pharisee;*] *Pharisee;*) 1651.
[3] 26. *J*: 6. *1651.*

is neither Creator, nor Maker, nor Concurrent, as of *Evill*;
faciens Pacem, et creans malum: And sometimes of that
which was neither created nor made by God, nor any
other, as *darkness*, which is but privation; *formans lucem,
et creans tenebras.* And the first that I can observe to have   5
taken away the liberty of this word, and made it to signify,
of *Nothing,* is our countryman *Bede* upon this place. For
Saint *Augustin* was as opposite and diametrall[3] against it,
as it is against truth. For he says, *facere est quod omnino non
erat; creare verò est, ex eo quod jam erat educendo constituere.* 10
Truly, it is not the power and victory of reason, that evicts
the world to be made of Nothing; for neither this word
creare inforces it, nor is it expressly said so in any Scripture.
When *Paul* says himself to be *Nothing*, it is but a diminution and Extenuation (not of himself, for he says there, *I* 15
am not inferior to the very chief of the Apostles, but) of Mankind. Where it is said to Man, *Your making is of Nothing,*
it is but a respective, and comparative undervaluing; as in
a lower descent then that before, *All Nations before God
are less then Nothing.* As in another place by a like extreme 20
extending it is said, *Deus regnabit in æternum et ultra*:
Only it is once said, *Ex nihilo fecit omnia Deus*; but in a
book of no straight obligation (if the matter needed
authority) and it is also well translated by us, *Of things
which were not.* But therefore we may spare Divine Autho- 25
rity, and ease our faith too, because it is present to our
reason. For, Omitting the quarelsome contending of *Sextus
Empiricus* the *Pyrrhonian,* (of the Author of which sect
Laertius says, that he handled Philosophy bravely, having
invented a way by which a man should determine nothing 30
of every thing) who with his Ordinary weapon, a two-
edged sword, thinks he cuts off all Arguments against pro-
duction of Nothing, by this, *Non fit quod jam est, Nec quod
non est; nam non patitur mutationem quod non est*; And
omitting those Idolaters of Nature, the *Epicureans,* who 35
pretending a mannerly lothness to trouble God, because
Nec bene promeritis capitur, nec tangitur ira, indeed out of

Marginal references:

Isa. 45. 7.[1]

Isa. 45.[2] 7.

Aq. 1.
q. 45.
ar. 1.
Aug. contr.
advers.
leg. et
proph.

2 Cor. 12.[4]
11.

Isa. 41. 24.

Isa. 40. 17.

Ex. 15. 18.
Machab.
2. 7. 28.

Ca. de
Ortu et
interit.

Lucret.

---

[1] 7. *J*: 5. *1651.*   [2] 45. *J*: 54. *1651.*
[3] diametrall] diamitrall *1651.*   [4] 2 Cor. 12. *J*: 1 Cor. 22. *1651.*

their pride are loth to be beholden to God, say, that we
are sick of the fear of God, *Quo morbo mentem concusse?* Horace.
Timore Deorum; And cannot therefore admit creation of
Nothing, because then *Nil semine egeret*, but *ferre omnes*
5 *omnia possent*, And *subitò exorirentur, incerto spacio*, with Lucret.
such other dotages. To make our approches nearer, and
batter effectually, let him that will not confess this Nothing, assign som⟨e⟩thing of which the world was made.
If it be of it self, it is God: and it is God, if it be of God;
10 who is also so simple, that it is impossible to imagine any
thing before him of which he should be compounded, or
any workman to do it. For to say, as one doth, that the Boet. de
world might be eternall, and yet not be God, because Consol. 5,
Gods eternity is all at once, and the worlds successive, will pros. 6.
15 not reconcile it; for yet, some part of the world must be
as old as God, and infinite things are equall, and equalls to
God are God. The greatest Dignity which we can give
this world, is, that the *Idæa* of it is eternall, and was ever
in God: And that he knew this world, not only *Scientiâ*
20 *Intellectus*, by which he knows things which shall never be,
and are in his purpose impossible, though yet possible and
contingent to us; but, after failing, become also to our
knowledg impossible, (as it is yet possible that you will
read this book thorow now, but if you discontinue it
25 (which is in your liberty) it is then impossible to your
knowledge, and was ever so to Gods;) but also *Scientiâ*
Visionis, by which he knows only infallible things; and
therefore these *Idæas* and eternall impressions in God,
may boldly be said to be *God*; for nothing understands
30 God of it self, but God; and it is said, *Intellectæ Jynges à* Zoroast.
patre, intelligunt et ipsæ: And with *Zoroaster* (if I miscon- Oracul. 4.
ceive not) *Jynx* is the same as *Idæa* with *Plato*. The
eternity of these *Idæas* wrought so much, and obtained so
high an estimation with *Scotus*, that he thinks them the
35 Essence of this world, and the Creation was but their
Existence; which Reason and *Scaliger* reprehend roundly,
when they do but ask him, whether the Creation were
only of accidents.
But because all which can be said hereof is cloudy, and

therefore apt to be mis-imagined, and ill interpreted, for, *obscurum loquitur quisque suo periculo*, I will turn to certain and evident things; And tell thee, O man, which art said to be the Epilogue, and *compendium* of all this world, and the *Hymen* and Matrimoniall knot of Eternal and Mortall *Picus.* things, whom one says to be *all Creatures*, because the Gospel, of which onely man is capable, is sent to be *Mar. 16. preached to all Creatures*; And wast made by Gods hands, not his commandment; and hast thy head erected to heaven, and all others to the Center; that yet only thy heart of all others, points downwards, and onely trembles. And, oh ye chief of men, ye Princes of the Earth, (for to you especially it is said, *Terram dedit filiis hominum*; for the sons of God have the least portion thereof; And you are so Princes of the Earth, as the Divell is Prince of the Air, it is given to you to raise storms of warr and persecution) know ye by how few descents ye are derived from Nothing? you are the Children of the Lust and Excrements of your parents, they and theirs the Children of *Adam*, the child of durt, the child of Nothing. Yea, our soul, which we magnify so much, and by which we consider this, is a veryer upstart then our body, being but of the first head, and immediately made of Nothing: for how many souls hath this world, which were not nothing a hundred years since? And of whole man compounded of Body and Soul, the best, and most spirituall and delicate parts, which are Honour and Pleasure, have such a neighbourhood and alliance with Nothing, that they lately were Nothing, and even now when they are, they are Nothing, or at least shall quickly become Nothing: which, even at the last great fire, shall not befall the most wretched worme, nor most abject grain of dust: for that fire shall be a purifier, not consumer to nothing. For to be Nothing, is so deep a curse, and high degree of punishment, that Hell and the prisoners there, not only have it not, but cannot wish so great a loss to themselves, nor such a frustrating of Gods purposes. Even in Hell, where if our mind could contract and gather together all the old persecutions of the first Church, where men were tor-

mented with exquisite deaths, and oftentimes more, by
being denyed that; And all the inhumanities of the Inquisition, where repentance encreaseth the torture, (for
they dy also, and lose the comfort of perseverance;) And
5 all the miseries which the mistakings, and furies, and sloth
of Princes, and infinity and corrosiveness of officers, the
trechery of women, and bondage of reputation hath laid
upon mankind, since it was, and distil the poyson and
strength of all these, and throw it upon one soul, it would
10 not equall the torment of so much time as you sound one
syllable. And for the *lasting*, if you take as many of *Plato's*
years, as a million of them hath minutes, and multiply
them by *Clavius* his number, which expresses how many
sands would fill the hollowness to the *first Mover*, you *In*
15 were so far from proceeding towards the end, that you *Sacrobos.*
had not described one minute. In Hell, I say, to escape
which, some have prayed to have *hils fall upon them*, and
many horrours shadowed in the Scriptures and Fathers,
none is ever said to have wished himself Nothing. Indeed,
20 as reposedly, and at home within himself no man is an
Atheist, however he pretend it, and serve the company
with his braveries (as Saint *Augustine* sayes of himself, that *Conf. l. 2.*
though he knew nothing was blameable but vice, yet he *cap. 3.*
seemed vicious, lest he should be blameable; and fain'd
25 false vices when he had not true, lest he should be despised
for his innocency;) so it is impossible that any man should
wish himself Nothing: for we can desire nothing but that
which seems satisfactory, and better to us at that time;
and whatsoever is better, is something. Doth, or can any
30 man wish that, of which, if it were granted, he should,
even by his wishing it, have no sense, nor benefit? To
speak truth freely, there was no such Nothing as this
before the beginning: for, he that hath refin'd all the old
Definitions, hath put this ingredient *Creabile*, (which can- *Picco-*
35 not be absolutely *nothing*) into his Definition of Creation: *lomin.*
And that *Nothing* which was, we cannot desire; for mans *Defin.*
will is not larger then Gods power; and since Nothing was *Creat.*
not a pre-existent matter, nor mother of this All, but
onely a limitation when any thing began to be; how

impossible is it to return to that first point of time, since
God (if it imply contradiction) cannot reduce yesterday?
Of this we will say no more; for this *Nothing* being no
creature, is more incomprehensible then all the rest: but
we will proceed to that which is *All, Heaven and Earth*.   5

PART 4

One sayes in admiration of the spirit and sublimenesse of
Picus. Abbot *Joachim* his Works, that he thinks he had read the
Book of life. Such an acquaintance as that should he need,
who would worthily expound or comprehend these words,   10
Heaven and *Earth*. And *Francis George* in his *Harmony*
sayes, That after he had curiously observed, that *the Ark
of Noah*, and *our body* had the same proportion and corre-
spondency in their parts, he was angry, when he found
after, that *St Augustine* had found out that before. So   15
natural is the disease of *Meum et Tuum* to us, that even
contemplative men, which have abandon'd temporall propriety, are delighted, and have their *Complacentiam*, in
having their spirituall Meditations and inventions knowne
to be theirs: for, *qui velit ingenio cedere, rarus erit*. But   20
because to such as I, who are but Interlopers, not staple
Merchants, nor of the company, nor within the commission of Expositors of the Scriptures, if any licence be
granted by the Spirit to discover and possesse any part,
herein, it is condition'd and qualified as the Commissions   25
of Princes, that we attempt not any part actually possess'd
before, nor disseise others; therefore of these words, so
abundantly handled, by so many, so learned, as no place
hath been more traded to, I will expositorily say nothing,
but onely a little refresh, what others have said of them,   30
and then contemplate their immensity. Al opinions about
these words, whether of Men too supple and slack, and so
miscarried with the streame and tide of elder Authority;
or too narrow and slavish, and so coasting ever within the
view and protection of Philosophy; or too singular, and so   35
disdaining all beaten paths, may fall within one of these
expositions. Either in these words *Moses* delivers roundly
the intire Creation of all, and after doth but dilate and

declare the Order; which is usually assign'd to *Chrysostome*
and *Basil*, govern'd by the words in *Gen. 2. 4. In the day
that the Lord God made the Earth and the Heavens*; and of
these, *He that liveth for ever made all things together*; and Sirach.
5 because the literall interpretation of successive dayes can- 18. 1.
not subsist, where there are some dayes mention'd before
the Creation of these Planets which made dayes. Or else,
(which *Augustine* authorizeth) the Heaven signifies Angels,
and the Earth *Materiam primam*, out of which all things
10 were produc'd; which *Averroes* hath call'd *Id ens quod* In 10 Phys.
mediat inter non esse penitus, et esse Actu. And another hath 7°.
afforded it a definition, which Divines have denied to
God: for he says, *Est nullum prædicamentum, neque Negatio*. Arist. 7.
And therfore that late *Italian* Distiller and Sublimer of Met.
15 old definitions hath riddled upon it, That it is first and Piccolom.
last; immortall and perishable; formed and formelesse; Mat.
One, four, and infinite; Good, bad, and neither; because primæ.
it is susceptible of all formes, and changeable into all. Or
else Heaven must mean that *Cælum Empyræum* (which
20 some have thought to be increate, and nothing but the
refulgence of God) which is exempt from all alteration
even of motion; and the Earth to designe the *first Matter*.
And in this channell came the tide of almost all accepted
Expositors, till later ages somwhat diverted it. For with,
25 and since *Lyra*, (of whom his Apologist *Dornike* says,
Delirat[1] *qui cum Lyra non sentit*) they agree much, that
Heaven and Earth in this place, is the same which it is
now; And that the substantiall forms were presently in it
distinctly, but other accidentall properties added succes-
30 sively. And therfore *Aquinas* having found danger in these [Summ.
words, *Præcessit informitas materiæ ejus formationem*, ex- Theol.]
pounds it, *Ornatum*, not *formam*. So that this *Heaven* and 1. q. 66.[2]
Earth, being themselves and all between them, is this Ar. 1.
World; the common house and City of Gods and men, in Nat.
35 *Cicero*'s words; and the corporeal and visible image and Deor. 2.
son of the invisible God, in the description of the *Academicks*; which being but one, (for *Universum est omnia
versa in unum*) hath been the subject of Gods labor, and

[1] *Delirat*] *Dilirat* 1651.   [2] 66. *J*: 65. *1651*.

providence, and delight, perchance almost six thousand
yeares; whose uppermost first moving Orbe is too swift
Gilbert. de for our thoughts to overtake, if it dispatch in every hour
Magn. l.6. three thousand times the compass of the Earth, and this
c. 3. exceeds fifteen thousand miles. In whose firmament are 5
scattered more *Eyes* (for our use, not their owne) then
any Cyphers can esteeme or expresse. For, how weake a
stomack to digest knowledge, or how strong and misgovern'd faith against common sense hath he, that is content to rest in their number of 1022 Stars? whose nearer 10
regions are illustrated with the Planets, which work so
effectually upon man, that they have often stop'd his
further search, and been themselves by him deified; And
whose navell, this Earth, which cannot stir, for every other
place is upwards to it, and is under the water, yet not sur- 15
rounded, and is mans prison and palace, yea man himself,
Conf. 12. (for *terra est quam calco, et terra quam porto*, says *Augustin*:)
⟨*c. 2*⟩ A world, which when God had made, *he saw it was very
good*; and when it became very bad, because *we* would not
repent, *he* did: and more then once; for he *repented that* 20
he made it, and then that he *destroyed* it; becoming for our
sakes, who were unnaturally constant (though in sinning)
unnaturally changeable in affection: And when we dis-
esteemed his benefits, and used not this world aright, but
rather chose Hell, he, to dignify his own work, left Heaven 25
it self, to pass a life in this world: Of the glory of which,
and the inhabitants of it, we shall best end in the words of
Ch. 43. 27. *Sirach*'s Son, *When we have spoken much, we cannot attain
unto them; but the sum of all is, that God is all.* But because,
Cha. 18. 6. as the same man says, *When a man hath done his best, he* 30
*must begin again; and when he thinks to come to an end, he
must go again to his labour*; let us further consider what
love we may bear to the world: for, to love it too much,
is to love it too little; as overpraysing is a kind of libelling.
For a man may oppress a favorite or officer with so much 35
commendation, as the Prince neglected and diminished
thereby, may be jealous, and ruine him. Ambassadours in
their first accesses to Princes, use not to apply themselves,
nor divert their eye upon any, untill they have made their

first Dispatch, and find themselves next the Prince; and
after acknowledg and respect the beams of his Majesty in
the beauties and dignities of the rest. So should our soul
do, between God, and his Creatures; for what is there in
5 this world immediately and primarily worthy our love,
which (by acceptation) is worthy the love of God? *Earth*
and *Heaven* are but the foot-stool of God: But *Earth it self*
is but the foot-ball of wise men. How like a Strumpet deales
this world with the Princes of it? Every one thinks he
10 possesseth all, and his servants have more at her hand then
he; and theirs, then they. They think they compass the
Earth, and a *Job* is not within their reach. A busie Wit *Mala-*
hath taken the pains to survey the possessions of some *guzzi.*
Princes: and he tells us that the *Spanish* King hath in *Theso.*
15 *Europe* almost three hundred thousand miles, and in the *par. 2.*
new world seaven millions, besides the borders of *Africk*, *fo. 60.*
and all his Ilands: And we say, the Sun cannot hide himself from his Eye, nor shine out of his Dominions. Yet let
him measure right, and the *Turke* exceeds him, and him
20 the *Persian*; the *Tartar* him, and him *Prete-Jan*. There
came an *Edict from the Emperour* (saith the Gospel) *that the* *Luk. 2. 1.*
whole world should be taxed: And when the Bishop of *Rome*
is covetous of one treasure, and expensive of another, he
gives and applies to some one the Indulgences *Urbis et*
25 *Orbis*. And alas, how many greater Kingdomes are there in
the world, which know not that there is such a Bishop or *ᵃ Jus-*
Emperour? Ambition rests not there: The *Turke*, and less *tinian.*
Princes, have stiled themselves *King of Kings*, and *Lord* *ᵇ Acacius*
of *Lords*, and *chosen to God*. Christian Princes, in no impure *l. 1. c. 6.*
30 times, have taken (nay given to themselves)ᵃ *Numen nos-* *Cassan.¹*
trum, and ᵇ*Divina Oracula*, and *Sacra Scripta* to their *Cat. glo.*
Laws. Of them also some speak so tremblingly, that they *P[ı]. 5.*
say, to dispute their Actions is sacriledg. And their ᶜ*Baldus* *Cons.*
says of him, *Est omnia, & super omnia, & facit ut Deus;* *24. 50.*
35 *habet enim cœleste arbitrium*. But more roundly the Canon- *ᶜ De nova*
ists of their Bishop, *Qui negat Dominum Deum nostrum* *forma fide-*
Papam, &c. which title the Emperour *Constantine* also long *Extra*
before afforded him. But alas, what are these our fellow- *Jo. 22 ca.*
cum Inter-
gloss.

¹ *Cassan.*] Chassanæus Bart. *J.*

Distin. 96.　ants, our fellow-durt, our fellow-nothings, compared to
l. Satis.　that God whom they make but their pattern? And how
And　little have any of these, compared to the whole Earth?
Martial to
Domitian,　whose hills, though they erect their heads beyond the
l. 8. 2.　Country of Meteors, and set their foot, in one land, and　5
　cast their shadow into another, are but as warts upon
　her¹ face: And her vaults, and caverns, the bed of the
Munster　winds, and the secret streets and passages of al rivers, and
l. 1. c. 16.　Hel it self, though they afford it three thousand great
　miles, are but as so many wrinkles, and pock-holes. A　10
　prince is Pilot of a great ship, a Kingdome; we of a pin-
　nace, a family, or a less skiff, our selves: and howsoever we
　be tossed, we cannot perish; for our haven (if we will) is
　even in the midst of the Sea; and where we dy, our home
　meets us. If he be a lion and live by prey, and wast amongst　15
　Cedars and pines, and I a mole, and scratch out my bed
　in the ground, happy in this, that I cannot see him: If he
　be a butterfly, the son of a Silkworm, and I a *Scarab*, the
　seed of durt; If he go to execution in a Chariot, and I in
　a Cart or by foot, where is the glorious advantage? If I　20
[Ecclus.]　can have (or if I can want) those things which the *Son of*
c. 39. 26.　*Sirach* calls principall, water, fire, and iron, salt and meal,
　wheat and hony, milk, and the blood of grapes, oyle, and
Horace.　clothing; If I can *prandere Olus*, and so need not Kings;
　Or can use Kings, and so need not *prandere Olus*: In one　25
Lombard.　word, if I do not *frui* (which is, set my delight, and affec-
l. 1.Dist. 1.　tion only due to God) but *Uti* the Creatures of this world,
Gen. 1. 28.　this world is mine; and to me belong those words, *Subdue*
　the Earth, and rule over all Creatures; and as God is pro-
　prietary, I am *usufructuarius* of this Heaven and Earth　30
　which God created in the beginning. And here, because
Auson.　*Nemo silens placuit, multi brevitate*, shall be the end.

⟨PRAYER⟩

O Eternall and Almighty power, which being infinite, hast
enabled a limited creature, Faith, to comprehend thee; And　35
being, even to Angels but a passive Mirror and looking-glasse,
art to us an Active guest and domestick, (for thou hast said, I

¹ her] our *1651, J.*

stand at the door and knock, if any man hear me, and open Rev. 3. 20.
the doore, I will come in unto him, and sup with him, and
he with me, *and so thou dwellst in our hearts; And not there*
only, but even in our mouths; for though thou beest greater,
5 *and more remov'd, yet[1] humbler and more communicable then*
the Kings of Egypt, *or* Roman *Emperours, which disdain'd*
their particular distinguishing Names, for Pharaoh *and*
Cæsar, *names of confusion; hast contracted thine immensity,*
and shut thy selfe within Syllables, and accepted a Name
10 *from us; O keep and defend my tongue from misusing that*
Name in lightnesse, passion, or falshood; and my heart, from
mistaking thy Nature, by an inordinate preferring thy Justice
before thy Mercy, or advancing this before that. And as,
though thy self hadst no beginning thou gavest a beginning to
15 *all things in which thou wouldst be served and glorified; so,*
though this soul of mine, by which I partake thee, begin not
now, yet let this minute, O God, this happy minute of thy
visitation, be the beginning of her conversion, and shaking
away confusion, darknesse, and barrennesse; and let her now
20 *produce Creatures, thoughts, words, and deeds agreeable to thee.*
And let her not produce them, O God, out of any contempla-
tion, or (I cannot say, Idæa, *but)* Chimera *of my worthinesse,*
either because I am a man and no worme, and within the pale
of thy Church, and not in the wild forrest, and enlightned with
25 *some glimerings of Naturall knowledge; but meerely out of*
Nothing: Nothing pre⟨e⟩xistent[2] in her selfe, but by power of
thy Divine will and word. By which, as thou didst so make
Heaven, as thou didst not neglect Earth, and madest them
answerable and agreeable to one another, so let my Soul's
30 *Creatures have that temper and Harmony, that they be not*
by a misdevout consideration of the next life, stupidly and
trecherously negligent of the offices and duties which thou
enjoynest amongst us in this life; nor so anxious in these, that
the other (which is our better business, though this also must
35 *be attended) be the less endeavoured. Thou hast, O God,*
denyed even to Angells, *the ability of arriving from one Ex-*
treme to another, without passing the mean way between. Nor

---

[1] *yet*] yet [being] *J.*
[2] *pre⟨e⟩xistent*] *prexistent* 1651: pre-existent *J.*

can we pass from the prison of our Mothers womb, to thy
palace, but we must walk (in that pace whereto thou hast
enabled us) through the street of this life, and not sleep at the
first corner, nor in the midst. Yet since my soul is sent imme-
diately from thee, let me[1] *(for her return) rely, not principally,* 5
but wholly upon thee and thy word: and for this body, made
of preordained matter, and instruments, let me so use the
matεriall means of her sustaining, that I neither neglect the
seeking, nor grudge the missing of the Conveniencies of this
life: And that for fame, which is a mean Nature between 10
them, I so esteem opinion, that I despise not others thoughts
of me, since most men are such, as most men think they be: nor
so reverence it, that I make it alwayes the rule of my Actions.
And because in this world my Body was first made, and then
my Soul, but in the next my soul shall be first, and then my 15
body, In my Exterior and morall conversation let my first and
presentest care be to give them satisfaction with whom I am
mingled, because they may be scandaliz'd, but thou, which
seest hearts, canst not: But for my faith, let my first relation
be to thee, because of that thou art justly jealous, which they 20
cannot be. Grant these requests, O God, if I have asked fit
things fitly, and as many more, under the same limitations, as
Sap. 16. *are within that prayer which (As thy* Manna, *which was*
20. *meat for all tasts, and served to the appetite of him which took*
it, and was that which every man would) includes all which 25
all can aske, Our Father which art, etc.

⟨BOOK II⟩

Exodus C. 1. V. 1.

Now these are the Names of the Children of Israel which
came into Egypt, &c.   30

Of *Exodus.* In this book our entrance is a *going out*: for *Exodus* is
Exitus.[2] The Meditation upon Gods works is infinite; and
whatsoever is so, is Circular, and returns into it selfe, and
is every where beginning and ending, and yet no where
either. Which the Jews (the children of God by his first 35

---

[1] *let me (for]* (*let me for* 1651.   [2] *Exitus] Excitus* 1651.

spouse the *Law*, as we are by *Grace*, his second) express'd
in their round Temples; for God himselfe is so much a
Circle, as being every where without any corner, (that is,
never hid from our Inquisition;) yet he is no where any
5 part of a straight line, (that is, may not be directly and
presently beheld and contemplated) but either we must
seek his Image in his works, or his will in his words; which,
whether they be plain or darke, are ever true, and guide
us aright. For as well the Pillar of *Cloud*, as that of *Fire*,
10 did the Office of directing. Yea, oftentimes, where fewest
Expositors contribute their helpes, the Spirit of God alone
enlightens us best; for many lights cast many shadows, and
since controverted Divinity became an occupation, the Contro-
Distortions and violencing of Scriptures, by Christians versies.
15 themselves, have wounded the Scriptures more then the
old Philosophy or *Turcism*. So that that is applyable to us,
which *Seneca* says of *Cæsars*[1] murderers, *Plures amici quam
inimici eum interfecerunt*. From which indulgence to our
own affections, that should somwhat deterr us, which
20 *Pliny* says of the same business, *Iisdem pugionibus quibus
Cæsarem interfecerunt, sibi mortem consciverunt*. For we
kill our own souls certainly, when we seek passionately to
draw truth into doubt and disputation.

I do not (I hope) in undertaking the Meditation upon Short
25 this verse, incur the fault of them, who for ostentation and Texts.
magnifying their wits, excerpt and tear shapeless and un-
significant[2] rags of a word or two, from whole sentences,
and make them obey their purpose in discoursing; The
Souldiers would not divide our Saviours garment, though
30 past his use and his propriety. No garment is so neer God
as his word: which is so much his, as it is *he*. His flesh,
though dignified with unexpressible priviledges, is not so
near God, as his word: for that is *Spiritus Oris*. And in the
Incarnation, the Act was onely of one Person, but the
35 whole Trinity speaks in every word. They therefore which
stub up these severall roots, and mangle them into chips,
in making the word of God not such, (for the word of God Literall
is not the word of God in any other sense then literall, Sense.

---

[1] *Cæsars*] *Csæars* 1651.   [2] unsignificant] insignificant *J*.

and[1] that also is not the literall, which the letter seems to
present, for so to diverse understandings there might be
diverse literall senses; but it is called literall, to distinguish
it from the Morall, Allegoricall, and the other senses; and
is that which the Holy Ghost doth in that place principally intend:) they, I say, do what they can this way, to
make God, whose word it is pretended to be, no God.
They which build, must take the solid stone, not the rub-
bish. Of which, though there be none in the word of God,
yet often unsincere translations, to justifie our prejudices[2]
and foreconceived opinions, and the underminings and
batteries of Hereticks, and the curious refinings of the
Allegoricall Fathers, which have made the Scriptures,
which are stronge toyles, to catch and destroy the bore
and bear which devast our Lords vineyard, fine cobwebs
to catch flies; And of strong gables,[3] by which we might
anker in all storms of Disputation and Persecution, the
threads of silkworms, curious vanities and excesses (for do
not many among us study even the Scriptures only for
ornament?) these, I say, may so bruse them, and raise so
much dust, as may blinde our Eyes, and make us see
nothing, by coveting too much. He which first invented
the cutting of Marble, had (says *Pliny*) *importunum ingenium*; a wit that would take no answer nor denyal. So
have they which break these Sentences, *importuna ingenia*,
unseasonable and murmuring spirits. When God out of
his abundance affords them whole Sentences, yea Chapters, rather then not have enough to break to their
auditory, they will attempt to feed miraculously great
Congregations with a loafe or two, and a few fishes; that
is, with two or three incoherent words of a Sentence. I
remember I have read of a General, who, having at last
carryed a town, yet not meerly by force, but upon this
article, That in sign of subjection they should admit him
to take away one row of stones round about their wall,
chose to take the undermost row, by which the whole
wall ruined. So do they demolish Gods fairest Temple, his

---

[1] literall, and] literall (and *1651*.   [2] prejudices] perjudices *1651*.
[3] gables] cables *J*.

Word, which pick out such stones, and deface the integrity
of it, so much, as neither that which they take, nor that
which they leave, is the word of God. In the Temple was
admitted no sound of hammer, nor in the building of this
5 great patriarchal Catholick Church, of which every one of
us is a little chappel, should the word be otherwise wrested
or broken, but taken intirely as it is offered and presented.
But I do not at this time transgress this rule, both because Of this
I made not choice of this unperfect sentence, but prose- Text.
10 cute my first purpose of taking the beginning of every
book: and because this verse is not so unperfect, but that
radically and virtually it comprehends all the book; which
being a history of Gods miraculous Mercy to his, is best
intimated or Epitomized in that first part, which is in-
15 sinuated in this verse, from how small a number he propagated so great a Nation. Upon this confidence, and
conscience of purposing good, I proceed in these Sermons; Unvocall
for they are such, in the allowance of him whom they have preaching.
stiled *resolutissimum et Christianissimum Doctorem*; for he Gers. de
20 says *Scriptor manu prædicat*. And that to write books, Scr.
though one gain and profit temporally by it, yet if the consid. 1ᵃ.
finall respect be the glory of God, is *latriæ veneratio*, and
more honorable to the Church, then the multiplication of
vocal prayers, *Imo, quam insolens Missarum inculcatio*. Did
25 the Author of that book, the *Preacher*, make vocal Sermons? Though these lack thus much of Sermons, that they
have no Auditory, yet as Saint *Bernard* did almost glory,
that Okes and Beeches were his Masters, I shall be content
that Okes and Beeches be my schollers, and witnesses of
30 my solitary Meditations. Therefore, after I shal have Division.
spoken a few words in generall of this book, I will proceed
to a neerer consideration of this verse; first, As it begins to
present a Register of their Names, whom God appointed
to be the foundation of his many great works; And then,
35 As it doth virtually comprehend those particular testi-
monies of Gods love to his people.
     In the first, we will look *Why God is willing, that those
through whom God prepares his miracles, should be named.*
Secondly, *why they are in divers places diversly named.*

Then, *why their number is expressed*; And *why that also diversly, in divers places*. And lastly, *whether there bee no Mystery in their Number, Seventy*.

In the second part, wherein out of this verse radically will arise to our consideration, all his favors to his chosen,   5 expressed in this book, we shall have occasion to contemplate *Gods Mercy*, and that, In bringing them into *Egypt*, In propagating them there, In delivering them from thence, and in nourishing them in the wilderness. Secondly his *Power*, Expressed in his many Miracles: Thirdly his 10 *Justice*, in their pressures in Egypt, and the wilderness: And lastly his *Judgments*, in affording them a law for their direction.

Exodus

Of Moses five Books. When this Book became a particular book, that is, when 15 *Moses* his book was divided into five parts, I cannot trace. Not only the first Christian Councells, which establish'd or declared the Canon of Scripture, and all the earlyest Expositors thereof, whether Christians or Jews, but the *Septuagint*, almost 300. years before Christ, acknowledge 20 this partition. Yet, that *Moses* left it a continued work, or at least not thus distributed, it seems evident, both because the Hebrew names of these books are not significant, but are only the first words of the book, (as we use to cite the Imperiall and the Canon laws) And because by 25 *Comment. in Pentat.* *Conradus Pellicanus* I am taught, that *Moses*, according to the 52. *Hebdomades*, distinguished the *Pentateuch* into so many sections, of which this is the 13. And *Josephus Simlerus* notes, that the first letter here, which ordinarily hath no use, but grace, hath in this place the force of a 30 conjunction. And so *Lyra*, and many others acknowledg, that this is but a continuing of the former History. Besides the reasons which moved those times to make this a singular Book, I may add this, That God, when he had in that part of *Moses* book which we call *Genesis*, expressed fully, 35 that by creating from Nothing, before *Nature* was, he needed not her to begin his glorious work; so in this he declares especially, that he hath not so assumed *Nature*

into a Colleagueship with himself, that he cannot leave
her out, or go besides[1] her, and neglect her, or go directly
against her when it pleases him: And therefore this book is,
more then any other, a Register of his *Miracles*. Of which
5 book this is notable, it consisting of the most particular
ceremoniall parts, wherein the Jews yet persist, and we
faithfully see already accomplished, and therefore likelyest
to minister matter of quarrell and difference between us,
of all other books in the Bible, is best agreed upon; and
10 fewer differences between ours and their Copies then in
any other book: so equally careful have al parties been to
preserve the Records of his Miracles intemerate.

PART I

I come now to the first Part: In which, the first Considera- Names.
15 tion is, *Why God would have them named? These are the*
Names, &c. *Josephus* delivering the same History, sayes, *Antiq.*
that he would not have ascribed the Names, because they *l. 2. c. 7.*[2]
are of an hard and unpleasant sound, but that some had
defamed the Nation, as *Egyptians*; and denyed them to
20 be *Mesopotamians*. It hath therefore one good use, to distinguish them from profane Nations: But the chiefest is,
That they are inserted into this Book for an everlasting
honour both to God and them. Amongst men, all Depositaries of our Memories, all means which we have trusted
25 with the preserving of our Names, putrifie and perish. Of
the infinite numbers of the Medals of the Emperors, some
one happy[3] Antiquary, with much pain, travell, cost, and
most faith, beleeves he hath recovered some one rusty
piece, which deformity makes reverend to him, and yet is
30 indeed the fresh work of an Impostor.

The very places of the *Obeliscs*,[4] and *Pyramides* are forgotten, and the purpose why they were erected. Books
themselves are subject to the mercy of the Magistrate:
and as though the ignorant had not been enemie enough
35 for them, the Learned unnaturally and treacherously contribute to their destruction, by rasure and mis-interpreta-

---

[1] besides] beside *J*.   [2] c. 7. *J*: c. 4. *1651*.
[3] happy] haypy *1651*.   [4] *Obeliscs*] *Obelises* 1651.

tion. *Caligula* would abolish *Homer*, *Virgil*, and all the
Lawyers Works, and eternize himself and his time in
Medals: The Senate, after his death, melted all them: Of
their brasse ⟨*Claudius*⟩[1] his Wife *Messalina* made the Statue
of her beloved Player; and where is that? But Names 5
honour'd with a place in this book, cannot perish, because
the Book cannot. Next to the glory of having his name
entred into the *Book of Life*, this is the second, to have
been matriculated in this Register, for an example or
instrument of good. *Lazarus* his name is enrolled, but the 10
wicked rich mans omitted. How often in the Scriptures is
the word *Name*, for *honour, fame, vertue*? How often doth
God accurse with abolishing the Name? *Thou shalt destroy
their Name*, Deut. 7. 24. And, *I wil destroy their Name de
sub cælo*, Deut. 9. 14. And, *Non seminabitur de Nomine tuo*, 15
Nah. 1. 14. With which curse also the civill *Ephesian* Law
punished the burner of the Temple, that none should
name him. And in the same phrase doth God expresse his
blessings to *Abraham, Gen.* 12. 2, and often elsewhere, *I
will make thy Name great*. Which, without God, those 20
vaine attempters of the Tower of *Babel* endeavoured: for
it is said, *Gen.* 11. 4. They did it, *to get themselves a Name*.
Whether *Nomen* be *Novimen*, or *Notamen*, it is still to
make one known: and God, which cannot be known by his
own Name, may nearlyest by the names and prosperity of 25
his. And therefore, for his own sake, he is carefull to have
Joh. 10. his servants named. *He calleth his own sheep by name*; And,
Scribe Nomen Diei hujus, says he to *Ezekiel*, c. 24. 2. Of all
Nations, the Jews have most chastly preserved that Cere-
Ethnick mony of abstaining from ethnick Names. At this time, 30
Names. when by their pressures they need most to descend to that
common degree of flattery, to take the names of the
Princes by whose leave they live, they do not degenerate
into it, when almost all Christendom hath straied into
that scandalous fashion, of returning to Heathen names, 35
as though they were ashamed of their Examples. And
almost in all their Names, the Jews have either testified
some event past, or prophecied or prayed for some good

---

[1] ⟨*Claudius*⟩ his *conject. Ed.* (see note): his *1651*.

to come: In no language are Names so significant. So that _{Significant}
if one consider diligently the sense[1] of the Names register'd _{Names.}
here, he will not so soon say, That the Names are in the
History, as that the History is in the Names. For, *Levi* is
5 *coupled to God*, which notes *Gods calling*. *Simeon, hearing*
and *obedient*, where their willingness is intimated. *Juda* is
confessing and *praising*, which results of the rest. *Zebulon*
is a *dwelling*, because they are established in God: in
whom, because they have both a Civill policy, and a
10 Military, *Dan* is a *Judgment*, and *Gad*, a *Garrison*. In
which, that they may be exercised in continual occasions
of meriting, *Naphthali* is a *wrestling*. And to crown all,
Asher is *complete blessedness*. The other Names have their
peculiar force, which will not come into this room: but
15 I entred the rather into this Meditation and opinion,
because I find the Scriptures often to allude to the Name,
and somtimes express it, as 1 Sam. 25. 25. *As his name is,*[2]
so is he, Nabal, a fool. And in Exod. 15. 23. *Therefore the*
name of the place was called bitter. And the *Romans* also had
20 so much respect to the ominousness of good Names, that
when in Musters every Souldier was to be called by Name, _{Cic. l. 1. de}
they were diligent to begin with one of a good and promis- _{Divinat.}
ing Name, which *Festus* reckons to be *Valerius, Salvius,*
Statorius, and such. And I have read in some of the
25 Criminalists, that to have an ill Name, in this sense, not
malæ famæ, was *Judicium ad torturam. Origen* exaggerat- _{Hom. 8. in}
ing pathetically the gradations of *Abraham's* sorrow at the _{Gen.}
immolation of his son, after he hath expostulated with
God why he would remember him of the Name *son,* and
30 why of *Beloved son,* rests most upon the last, that he would
call him by his *Name Isaac,* which signifies *joy,* in a commandement of so much *bitterness.* It may be then some
occasion of naming them in this place, that as these men
were instruments of this work of God, so their names did
35 sub-obscurely foresignifie it. For Reason, the common soul
to all lawes, forbids that either great punishments should
be inflicted otherwise then *Nominatim; Non nisi nominatim* _{Briss.}
liberi exheredandi: Or that great benefits should be in any _{form.}
_{fo.[3] 604.}

[1] sense] senes *1651.*   [2] *is,*] *is.* 1651.   [3] *fo.*] *so.* 1651: fol. *J.*

other sort conferr'd. For conformably to this case, which now we consider, of delivering persons from bondage, the law is, *Servis non nisi Nominatim libertas danda est.* Of this Honour to his servants, to be remembred by *Name*, God hath been so diligent, that somtimes himself hath imposed 5 the Name before the birth, and somtimes changed it to a higher signification, when he purposed to exalt the person. It is noted, that to *Abram's* Name he added a *letter*, whose number made the whole Name equall to the words, *Creavit Hominem.* So that the multiplying of his seed, was 10 a work not inferior to the Creation. And from *Sarai's* Name he took a letter, which expressed the number *ten*, and repos'd one, which made but *five*; so that she con- tributed that five which man wanted before, to shew a mutuall indigence and Supplement. How much Schis- 15 matick disputation hath proceeded from the change of *Simon's* Name into *Peter*? What a Majestick change had *James* and *John* into the *Sons of Thunder*? yet God not only forebore ever such vast Names, as *Pharaoh* gave *Joseph*, which is not only *Expounder of secrets*, but *Saviour of the* 20 *world*: which also the Roman Emperors assumed in many Coyns, (*Æternitas Cæsaris*, And *Cæsar salus*, And *Servator*, And *Restaurator Orbis*;) but (to my remembrance, and observation) he never added other Name, as a *prænomen*,[5] or *cognomen*, or such: To shew (I think) that man brought 25 not part of his Dignity, and God added; but that God, when he will change a man, begins, and works, and perfects all himself. For though corrupt custome hath authorised it now, And, *Gaudent prænomine*[6] *molles auriculæ*; yet the *Romans* themselves, from whom we have this burden of 30 many Names, till they were mingled with the *Sabins*, used but one Name. And before that Custom got to be noble, their slaves, only when they were manumitted, were forced to accept three names. In this Excess of Names the Chris- tians have exceeded their patterns: for to omit the vain 35 and empty fulness in *Paracelsus* Name, which of the

Lex Fus.[1]
Can.
Changed Names.

Fr. George pro. fo. 17.

Mat. 16.[2]
Mar. 3.[3]

Ge. 41. 45.[4]
Addition to Names.

Robortellus de Nominibus.
Politianus Miscel. c. 31.

---

[1] *Fus.*] Fur. *J.*   [2] 16.] 15. *1651.*   [3] Mar. 3.] Mar. 13. *1651.*
[4] Ge. 41. 45.] Ge. 41. 41. *1651.*   [5] *prænomen* J: *pronomen* 1651.
[6] *prænomine* J: *pronomine* 1651.

Ancients equalls that grave, wise Author, which writes
himself, *Pulmannus Anicius Manlius Torquatus Severinus
Boethius?* But God hath barely and nakedly, but permanently engrav'd these Names. Which shall never be subject
5 to that obscurity, which *Ausonius* imputes to one who was
Master to an Emperor, and rewarded with a Consulship,
but overswaid with his Colleague, that men were fain to
enquire, *Quibus Consulib. gesserit consulatum.* But wheresoever these Names shall be mentioned, the Miraculous
10 History shall be call'd to memory; And wheresoever the
History is remembred, their Names shal be refreshed.

Diversity in Names

Our next consideration is, *Why they are diversly named?
and not always alike,* in *Gen.* 46. and here, and in *Deutero-
15 nomy,* and the other places where they are spoken of? And
this belongs not only to this case, but to many others in
the Holy Bible. *Josua* and *Jesus* is all one. So is *Chonia,*[1]
and *Jechonias.* And how multinominous is the father in
law of *Moses?* And the name *Nebrycadrozor* is observ'd to
20 be written seven severall wayes in the Prophets. To change
the Name, in the party himself is, by many laws, *Dolus;*
and when a Notary doth it, he is *falsarius;* faults penall
and infamous. And therefore laws have provided, that in
instruments of contract, and in publick Registers, all the
25 Names, Sur-names and additions shall be inserted; and
they forbid *Abbreviations;* and they appoint a more con-
spicuous and more permanent Character to express them.
So necessary is a certainty and constancy in the Names.
Some late interpreters of the law, teach, that false Latin *Acacius de*
30 in Grammar, in Edicts or Rescripts from the Imperiall *privil.*
Chamber, or any other secular Prince or Court, doth not *Juris.*
annihilate or vitiate the whole writing, because all they
may be well enough presum'd not to understand Latine;
But the *Bulls* of the Popes, and decrees in the Court of
35 *Rome* are defeated and annulled by such a corruption,
because their sufficiency in that point being presumed,
it shall be justly thought subreptitious, what ever issues

[1] *Chonia*] Coniah *J.*

faulty and defective in that kind. So, though Error and variety in Names, may be pardonable in profane Histories, especially such as translate from Authors of other language, yet the wisdome and constancy of that one Author of al these books, the Holy Ghost, is likely to defend and estab- 5 lish all his instruments, chosen for building this frame of Scriptures, from any uncertaine wavering and vacillation.

The *Cabalists*, therfore, which are the Anatomists of words, and have a Theologicall Alchimy to draw soveraigne tinctures and spirits from plain and grosse literall matter, 10 observe in every variety some great mystick signification; but so it is almost in every Hebrew name and word. *Lyra*, who is not so refined, yet very Judaick too, thinks, that as with the Latin, *Cholaus*, *Choletus*, *Cholinus*, and *Nicolaus* is one Name; so it is in the variation of names in the Scrip- 15 tures. But oftentimes, neither the sound, nor letter, nor signification, nor beginning nor ending, nor roote, nor branch, have any affinity: as himselfe (though corruptly) says, that *Esau*, *Seir*, and *Edom* are one name. It may be some laziness to answer every thing thus, *It is so*, *because* 20 *God would have it so*; yet he which goes further, and asks, Why Gods will was so, inquires for something above God. For, find me something that enclines God, and I will worship that. Since[1] therefore this variety of Names fals out in no place, where the certainty of the person or History 25 is therby offuscate, I encline to think, that another usefull document arises from this admitting of variety; which seems to me to be this, that God in his eternall and ever-present omniscience, foreseeing that his universal, Christian, Catholick Church, imaged, and conceived, and be- 30 gotten by him in his eternall decree, born and brought to light when he travail'd and labored in those bitter agonies and throes of his passion, nourced ever more delicately[2] and preciously then any natural children (for they are fed with their Mothers blood in her[3] womb, but we with the 35 blood of our most Blessed Saviour all our lives,) fore-seeing, I say, that this his dearly beloved Spouse, and Sister, and

Gen. 36.

Difference in things not essentiall.

---

[1] that. Since] that. since *1651*.   [2] delicately] dilicately *1651*.
[3] her *Ed.*: their *1651*, *J*.

Daughter, the Church, should in her latter Age suffer
many convulsions, distractions, rents, schisms, and wounds,
by the severe and unrectified Zeal of many, who should
impose necessity upon indifferent things, and oblige all
5 the World to one precise forme of exterior worship,
and Ecclesiastick policie; averring that every degree, and
minute and scruple of all circumstances which may be
admitted in either beleif or practice, is certainly, constantly, expressly, and obligatorily exhibited in the Scrip-
10 tures; and that Grace, and Salvation is in this unity and
no where else; his Wisdome was mercifully pleas'd, that
those particular Churches, devout parts of the Universall,
which, in our Age, keeping still the foundation and corner
stone Christ Jesus, should piously abandon the spacious
15 and specious super-edifications which the Church of *Rome*
had built therupon, should from this variety of Names
in the Bible it selfe, be provided of an argument, *That an
unity and consonance in things not essentiall, is not so necessarily requisite as is imagined.* Certainly, when the Gen-
20 tiles were assum'd into the Church, they entred into the
same fundamentall faith and religion with the Jews, as
Musculus truly notes; and this conjunction in the roote
and foundation, fulfill'd that which was said, *Fiet unum* Joh.10.16.
Ovile, et unus Pastor, One fold, and one shepherd. For, by
25 that before, you may see that all Christs sheep are not
alwayes in one fold, *Other sheep have I also, which are not of
this fold.* So, all his sheep are of one fold, that is, *under one
Shepherd, Christ;* yet not of one fold, that is, not *in one
place,* nor form. For, that which was strayed and alone,
30 was his sheep; much more any flock which hearken together
to his voice, his Word, and feed together upon his Sacraments. Therefore that Church from which we are by Gods
Mercy escaped, because upon the foundation, which we
yet embrace together, Redemption in Christ, they had
35 built so many stories high, as the foundation was, though
not destroyed, yet hid and obscured; And their Additions
were of so dangerous a construction, and appearance, and
misapplyableness, that to tender consciences they seem'd
Idolatrous, and are certainly scandalous and very slippery,

and declinable into Idolatry, though the Church be not in circumstantiall and deduced points, at unity with us, nor it self; (for, with what tragick rage do the Sectaries of *Thomas* and *Scotus* prosecute their differences? and how impetuously doth *Molinas* and his Disciples at this day, 5 impugne the common doctrine of grace and freewill? And though these points be not immediately fundamentall points of faith, yet radically they are, and as neer the root as most of those things wherein we and they differ;) yet though we branch out *East* and *West*, that Church concurs 10 with us in the root, and sucks her vegetation from one and the same ground, *Christ Jesus*; who, as it is in the *Canticle* Cant. lies between the brests of his Church, and gives suck on 1. 12. both sides. And of that Church which is departed from us, disunited by an opinion of a necessity that all should be 15 united in one form, and that theirs is it, since they keep their right foot fast upon the Rock Christ, I dare not pronounce that she is not our Sister; but rather as in the same Cant. 8. 9. *Song of Solomon's*, *We have a little sister, and she hath no brests: if she be a wall, we will build upon her a silver palace.* 20 If therefore she be a wall, That is, *Because* she is a wall; for so *Lyra* expounds those words, as on her part, she shall be safer from ruine, if she apply her selfe to receive a *silver palace* of Order, and that Hierarchy which is most convenient and proportionall to that ground and state wherein 25 God hath planted her; and she may not transplant her self: So shall we best conserve the integrity of our own body, of which she is a member, if we laboriously build upon her, and not tempestuously and ruinously demolish and annull her; but rather cherish and foment her vitall 30 and wholsome parts, then either cut, or suffer them to rot or moulder off. As naturall, so politick bodies have *Cutem, et Cuticulam*. The little thin skin which covers al our body, may be broken without pain or danger, and may reunite it selfe, because it consists not of the chief and principiant 35 parts. But if in the skin it self, there be any solution or division, which is seldome without drawing of blood, no art nor good disposition of Nature, can ever bring the parts together again, and restore the same substance,

though it seem to the ey to have sodder'd it self. It will
ever seem so much as a deforming Scar, but is in truth a
breach. Outward Worship is this *Cuticula*: and integrity
of faith the skin it self. And if the first be touched with
5 any thing too corrosive, it will quickly pierce the other;
and so Schism, which is a departure from obedience, will
quickly become Heresie, which is a wilfull deflexion from
the way of faith.[1] Which is not yet, so long as the main skin
is inviolate: for so long that Church which despises another
10 Church, is it self no other[2] then that of which the *Psalm*
speakes, *Ecclesia Malignantium.*

Thus much was to my understanding naturally occasioned and presented by this variety of Names in the
Scriptures: For, if *Esau, Edom,* and *Seir* were but one man;
15 *Jethro* and *Revel,* etc. but one man, which have no consonance with one another, and might thereby discredit
and enervate any History but this, which is the fountain
of truth; so Synagogue and Church is the same thing, and
of the Church, *Roman* and *Reformed,* and all other dis-
20 tinctions of place, Discipline, or Person, but one Church,
journying to one *Hierusalem,* and directed by one guide,
Christ Jesus; In which, though this Unity of things not
fundamentall, be not absolutely necessary, yet it were so
comely and proportionall with the foundation it self, if it
25 were at Unity in these things also, that though in my poor
opinion, the form of Gods worship, established in the
Church of *England* be more convenient, and advantageous
then of any other Kingdome, both to provoke and kindle
devotion, and also to fix it, that it stray not into infinite
30 expansions and Subdivisions; (into the former of which,
Churches utterly despoyl'd of Ceremonies, seem to me to
have fallen; and the *Roman* Church, by presenting in-
numerable objects, into the later.) And though to all my
thanksgivings to God, I ever humbly acknowledg, as one
35 of his greatest Mercies to me, that he gave me my Pasture
in this Park, and my milk from the brests of this Church,
yet out of a fervent, and (I hope) not inordinate affection,
even to such an Unity, I do zealously wish, that the whole

[1] faith.] faith? *1651.*   [2] other] other church *J.*

catholick Church, were reduced to such Unity and agreement, in the form and profession Established, in any one
of these Churches (though ours were principally to be
wished) which have not by any additions destroyed the
foundation and possibility of salvation in Christ Jesus; 5
That then the Church, discharged of disputations, and misapprehensions, and this defensive warr, might contemplate Christ clearly and uniformely. For now he appears
to her, as in *Cant.* 2. 9. *He standeth behind a wall, looking
forth of the window, shewing himself through the grate.* But 10
then, when all had one appetite, and one food, one nostrill
and one purfume, the Church had obtained that which she
Cant. then asked, *Arise ô North, and come ô South, and blow on my*
4. 16.[1] *garden, that the spices thereof may flow out.* For then, that
savour of life unto life might allure and draw those to us, 15
whom our dissentions, more then their own stubborness
with-hold from us.

Of Number

As God Registers the *Names* of his Elect, and of his Instru-
ments, so doth he the *Number, He counteth the Number of* 20
Ps. 147. 4. *the Starrs, and calleth them by their Names,* says the
Psalmist; which many Expositors interpret of the Elect.
Of which Saint *John* expresses a very great Number, when
Rev. 7. 4.[2] he says, *I heard the number of them which were sealed*
144000. But after in the ninth verse, *A Multitude in white* 25
before the Lamb, which none could Number. In that place of
Gē. 14. 14. *Genesis,* when *Abram* took 318. to rescue *Lot* (which
Pererius. Number hath been, not unusefully[3] observed to accord
with the Number of the Fathers in the first *Nicene*[4] Councell, where Christianity was rescued from *Arius*) the *Sep-* 30
tuagint have *Numeravit,* and Saint *Ambrose* says, the
Hebrew word signifies *Elegit*; as though it were so connaturall in God, to number and to Elect, that one word
might express both. And because Christ knew how rigorous
Joh. 17. 12. an account God took of those whom he had made Gover- 35
nors of his, in his prayer, that they might be after pre-

---

[1] 16.] 10. *1651.*   [2] Rev. 7. 4.] Rev. 7. 6. *1651.*
[3] unusefully] unusually *J*   [4] *Nicene*] *Necene* 1651.

served, he says, *I have kept them, and none of them are lost,
except*, &c. How often doth God iterate this way also of
expressing his love to *Abraham*, that he *will multiply his
posterity*? *If a man can number the dust of the earth, then
shall thy seed be numbred, Gen.* 13. 16. And lest he should
have seemed to have performed that promise when he had
onely multiplyed their Number, and yet left them to be
trod under foot by the *Egyptians*, because that comparison
of *Dust* might import and insinuate so much; he chuses
after another of infinite Number and Dignity together;
*Tell the Starrs, if thou be able to number them: So shall thy
seed be, Gen.* 15. 5. *David*, to let them see what a blessing
their encrease in *number* was, bids them remember what
they were, *Cum essent Numero brevi*. And *Jeremy*, as Ps. 105. 12.
though they did not else concurr with God in his purpose
to restore them to greatnesse, when they were in *Babylon*,
sayes to them, *Nolite esse pauci Numero*. Upon this love of Jer. 29. 6.[1]
God to see his people prosper, sayes *Rabbi Solomon, Vt
homo habens peculium*: or, As a man which hath a Stock of
cattell which he loves, reckons them every day; so doth
God his people. Hence is it, that so many times God commands his people to be numbred. Insomuch, that that
which we call the *Fourth book of Moses*, in which Saint
Jerom saith are contained *totius Arithmeticæ Mysteria*, Prologo.
hath the denomination from *Numbering*. In the first
entrance whereof, God commands his to be numbred,[2]
and to be numbred by Name: And the number in that
place, when the old and young, and women are added to
it, one very curious, following those rules by which the
Hebrews have learned the number of the Angels in heaven, Fr. George
hath found to accord precisely with that number of Angels Prob. 376.
intimated in *Dan.* 7. This Order, of being first Named,
and then Numbred; or first Numbred, and then Named,
Antichrist perverts by Anticipation, and doing both at
once; for his Name is a Number. The Divel, who counter-
feits God, put a desire into *David* to number his people;
who was then only in his right Arithmetick, when he
prayed to finde the *number of his dayes*. But when *Satan* Psal. 39. 5.
⟨P.B.V.⟩

---

[1] Jer. 29] Jer. 26. *1651*.   [2] numbred] numbrd *1651*.

stood up against Israel, and provoked David to number his *people,* he entred a work of such glory and ostentation, that *Joab* was nine months and twenty dayes in doing that service. But *God* would number also; and because *David* would not attend his leisure, he changed his fashion, and 5 brought upon them that number, which he after threatens again in *Isaiah, Numerabo vos in gladio.*

For the Number registred in this History, As God had well provided for *their* Honour, by entring their Names in this everlasting record: so (I think) he provided for *his* 10 *own* Honour, of which he is ever jealous, in expressing the Number; that all posterity might be awakened to a reverent acknowledgment of his greatness and goodness, by seeing, from what a smal Number, in how short a time, how numerous a people, through how great pressures, and 15 straits, were by him propagated and established. For, since he is content to receive his Honour from us, (for although all cause of Honour be eternally inherent in himselfe, yet that Act proceeds from us, and of that Honour, which is *in* *Honorante,* he could have none, til he had made Creatures 20 to exhibit it:) his great work of Creation, which admits no arrest for our Reason, nor gradations for our discourse, but must be at once swallowed and devour'd by faith, without mastication, or digestion, is not so apt to work upon us, for the provoking of our Acts of Honour, as those other 25 miracles are, which are somewhat more submitted to reason, and exercise and entertain our disputation, and spiritual curiosity by the way, and yet at last go as far beyond reason, as the other; as all miracles do equally. Of that kind this is; because a mighty People is miracu- 30 lously made, not of Nothing, (upon which, Consideration can take no hold) but of a disproportionall, and incompetent littlenesse. And in these, where the smallnesse of the roote, or seed, is a degree of the miracle, the Spirit of God uses to be precise in recording it. And therefore, in the 35 greatest of that kind, which is the fulfilling and replenishing the world, after that great exinanition by the generall deluge, though *Moses* say twice or thrice, that *Noah*, and

Marginal notes:
1 Chr. 21. 1.
2 Sam. 24. 8.
Isa. 65.
12.[1]
Of this
Number.

[1] 12.] 11. *1651, J.*

his sonnes, and his and their wives went into the Ark, and
came out; yet, because the Miracle of propagating consists
in the Number, Almighty God is pleased, by his ordinary
way of expounding his word, (which is, to explicate and
5 assure one place by another) to teach us, that this Number
was but eight: for S[t]. *Peter* says, *In the Ark but few*, that 1 Pet. 3.
is, *but Eight were saved*. In like manner, I mean with like [20].
precisenesse, after the Miracle in *Mat*. 14. was precisely
recorded, how many *loafes*, how many *fishes*, how many
10 *Eaters*, how many *baskets* of fragments; In the next chapter, another Miracle of the same kind, being to be registred,
though it be lesse then the other, (for there[1] is more meat,
fewer eaters, and fewer fragments) yet God seems carefull
in the particular Numbers. This therefore I take to be
15 some reason of inserting this Number; which being somewhat discordantly, and differently set down, as the collation of places manifests, and the Spirit of God doing
nothing falsly, inordinatly, negligently, dangerously, or
perplexedly, to an humble and diligent[2] understanding;
20 we will in the next Section consider the *Variety* in this
Number.

Variety in the Number

Numbring is so proper and peculiar to man, who only
can number, that some philosophical Inquisitors have
25 argued doubtfully, whether if man[3] were not, there were
any Number. And error in Numbring is *De substantiali-
bus*, as lawyers say, and somtimes annuls, ever vitiates any
Instrument, so much, as it may not be corrected. Nothing
therefore seems so much to indanger the Scriptures, and
30 to submit and render them obnoxious to censure and   *August. in*
calumniation, as the apparance of Error in Chronology, or *Enchirid.*
other limbs and members of Arithmetick: for, since Error
is an approbation of false for true, or incertain[4] for certain,
the Author hath erred (and then the Author is not God)
35 if any Number be falsly delivered; And we erre, if we
arrest ourselves as upon certain truth (as we do upon all

---

[1] there *J*: their *1651*.   [2] diligent] deligent *1651*.
[3] man] men *J*.   [4] incertain] uncertain *J*.

the Scriptures,) when there is sufficient suspicion of Error,
(abstracting the reverence of the Author,) and a certain
confession and undeniableness of uncertainty. And as a
man delated juridically, or by fame, or by private information of any Crime, must, when Canonicall purgation is
required at his hands, not only sweare his own innocency
himself, but produce others of his neighbourhood and
friendship, to swear that they think he swears true; and
if they concurr'd not with him, this would have the nature
of a half-proof, and justifie a further proceeding to his
condemnation: so when any profane Historie rises up
against any place of Scripture, accusing it to Humane
Reason, and understanding, (for though[1] our supreme
Court in such cases, for the last Appeal be Faith, yet
Reason is her Delegate) it is not enough that one place
justify it self to say true, but all other places produced as
handling the same matter, must be of the same opinion,
and of one harmony. I have therefore wondered that
Althemerus, pretending to reconcile all apparant discor-
dances in the Scriptures, hath utterly pretermitted all
variety in Numbring: Of Examples whereof, the comparing of the Historicall books, would have afforded him great
plenty, and worthy of his travell. The generall reasons why
God admits some such diversities in his book, prevail also
for this place which is now under our consideration; which
are, first, To make men sharpe and industrious in the
inquisition of truth, he withdrawes it from present apprehension, and obviousness. For naturally great wits affect
the reading of obscure books, wrastle and sweat in the
explication of prophesies, digg and thresh out the words
of unlegible hands, resuscitate and bring to life again the
mangled, and lame fragmentary images and characters in
Marbles and Medals, because they have a joy and compla-
cency in the victory and atchievement thereof. Another
reason is, That as his elect children are submitted by him
to the malice and calumny of the Reprobate, and are not
only ragefully tempested with stormes of persecution, but
contemptuously and scornfully (which is oftentimes the

---

[1] though] though in *1651, J.*

greater affliction) insimulated of folly and silliness, are in
his knowledg, and often so declared in this world to
abound in the treasure of riches and wisdome: So he is
pleased that his word should endure and undergo the
5 opinion of contradiction, or other infirmities, in the eyes
of Pride (the Author of Heresie and Schism) that after all
such dissections, & cribrations, and examinings of Here-
ticall adventures upon it, it might return from the furnace
more refin'd, and gain luster and clearness by this vexa-
10 tion. But the most important and usefull reason is, that
we might ever have occasion to accustome our selves to
that best way of expounding Scriptures, by comparing one
place with another. All the doubts about this place determine in two. First, why the Number is in so many places
15 said to be *Seventy*, as *Gen*. 46. 27. and in this place of
Exodus, and in *Deut*. 10. 22. And yet *Gen*. 46. 26. the
Number is said to be but 66. And in all the process of time
from *Moses*'s to *Stephen*'s martyrdome, recorded *Act*. 7.
there could be no other doubt but this one, to them which
20 understood Hebrew, and were not misgoverned by the
translation of the *Septuagint*. And this first doubt is no
sooner offered, then answered; for in the 46. of *Gen*. the
26 verse speaks of 66, and considers not *Joseph* and his two
sons, which were already in *Egypt*, which[1] the 27. verse
25 doth, and adding *Jacob* himself, perfects the Number 70.
of which it speaks. So that here is no dissonance in the
Number, but only the Spirit of God hath used his liberty,
in the phrase, reckoning some born in *Egypt* among the
soules which came into *Egypt*. The other Doubt, which
30 hath more travelled the Expositors, is, why *Stephen*, refer-   Act. 7.
ring to *Moses*, should say, they were 75. The occasion of
this mistaking (for so I think it was) was given by false
Copies of the *Septuagint's* translation, then in most use.
For the Hebrew text was long before so farr out of ordinary
35 use, that we see our Saviour himself, in his allegations,
follows the *Septuagint*. And in my mind, so much reverence
is due to that translation, that it were hard to think, that
they at first added five to *Moses* Number. For, that which

[1] which] in which *1651*.

is said for that opinion (though by Saint *Hierome*) which is, that they comprehend some nephews of *Joseph*, hath no warrant; and all the rest of the brethren were likely to have nephews at that time also. And against this opinion it prevails much with me, that, by Saint *Hieromes* testi- 5 mony, that translation in his time, in the other place, *Deut.* 10. 22. had but 70, conform to *Moses*: And any reason which might have induced them to add 5 in *Genesis*,

L. 1. Par. 92. had been as strong for *Deuteronomy*. *Junius*, scarce exceeded by any, in learning, sharpness, and faith, thinks that 10 *Stephen* neither applyed his speech to that account of those that were issued from *Jacob*'s loyns, which were indeed but 66, nor to the addition of the three in *Egypt*, which, with *Jacob* himself accomplish'd the number of 70; but that, insisting precisely upon *Moses* syllables, he related so 15 many as were expressed by name by *Moses* in that Chapter, to have been of *Jacob*'s Family; which were *Jacob*'s four wives, and the two sons of *Judah*, which make up 75. But with that modesty wherein he asks leave to depart from the Fathers, I must depart from him: for *Joseph* could not 20 cause these two sons of *Judah* to be brought into *Egypt*, (as appears in the Text he did, for all the number there intended) since they were dead in *Canaan* before, as is evident, *Genes.* 46. Others therefore have thought, that Saint *Luke* reported not the words out of *Stephen*'s mouth, 25 but by view of *Moses* his text, and that but in the Transla- tion; because being but a Proselite, he had no perfection, nor was accustom'd to the *Hebrew*. And others, that indul- gently he descended to that text which was most familiar, and so most credible to them. For, though this be either 30 an apparant Error in the *Septuagint* at first, (which is hard to allow, if we beleeve half of that which uses to be said, in proof[1] that the Holy Ghost assisted them) Or a corrup- tion insinuated after, (as it is easie, when Numbers are expressed by numerant letters,) yet that translation, so 35 corrupted, had so much weight, that all then followed it; and it maintained that authority so long, that even in *Lyra*'s time the Latin obeyed it. For he reads in this place

[1] proof *J*: proof; *1651*.

of *Exodus*, 75. though he there confess the Hebrew hath
but 70. This in my understanding may safelyer be admitted, then to decline so farr as Master *Calvin* doth, who
thinks it possible that Saint *Luke* repos'd the true Number
5 70; but some other exscriber, ignorant of *Hebrew*, and
obedient to the *Septuagint*, reformed it deformly since his
writing; for this seems to me to open dangerously a way
to the infringing, or infirming many places of Scripture.
The Number being then certainly 70, since by the hard-
10 ness and insolence of the Phrase, there seems some violence
and force, to raise the Number to 75. (for it may seem
hard, that *Joseph*, which sent for these 70, should be called
one of the 70 which came; And that his two Sons already
in *Egypt*, should be two[1] of them which came into *Egypt*;
15 And that *Jacob* should be one of these 70 which issued
out of *Jacobs* loins;) in a few words we will consider,
whether any Mystery reside in that chosen Number; Of the
the rather because very many remarkable things, and *Number*
passages in History, seeme to me to have been limited in 70.
20 that Number, which therefore seems more Periodick then
any other.
    But because any overcurious and Mysterious considera-
tion of this Number 70. though it be composed of the two
greatest Numbers (for *Ten* cannot be exceeded, but that
25 to express any further Number you must take a part of it
again; and *Seven* is ever used to express infinite,) be too
Cabalistick and Pythagorick for a vulgar Christian, (which
I offer not for a phrase of Diminution or Distrust, that
such are unprovided of sufficient defences for themselves,
30 or are ignorant of any thing required in such as they,
for salvation; But that there is needed also a Meta-
theology, and super-divinity, above that which serves our
particular consciences, in them, who must fight against
Philosophers and Jews) because I am one, and in a low
35 degree, of the first and vulgar rank, and write but to
my equals, I will forbear it, as mis-interpretable; since
to some palates it may taste of Ostentation; but to some,
of distraction from better contemplations, and of super-

[1] be two] betwo *1651*.

stition to others: yet, we may, as well with reverence to
the things, as respect to the Number, rest a little upon
those works of God, or his Servants, which this Number,
at least, reduces to our memory.

First therefore, Those Fathers of the world, to whom 5
God affords a room by name in the 10th of *Gen.* from whom
70. *Patri-*
archs. are derived all Nations, all extinguish'd and forgotten, all
now eminent and in actions, and all yet undiscovered, and
unbeing; They to whose Sons he hath given the earth,
utterly wasted before, and hath reserved rooms in Heaven, 10
from whence their betters are dejected, are reckoned there
to be 70. After, when the children of *Israel's* murmuring
70. *Elders.* kindled *Moses* zeal to expostulate with God thus, *Have*
I conceived all this people, or have I begotten them, that I
should bear this? I am not able to bear all this alone; there- 15
fore, if thou deal thus with me, if I have found favour in thy
sight, I pray thee kill me, that I behold not my misery. When
by this importunity *Moses* had extorted from God another
form of policy, the Number amongst which God would
divide *Moses's* labour, and *Moses's* spirit, was 70. The bar- 20
70. *Kings* barous cruelty of *Adonibezek*, confess'd by himself, was
slain. then accomplish'd, and ripe for God's vengeance, when
Judg. 1.7.[1] he had executed it upon 70. Kings. *Moses*, though his
70. *years* words, *Gen.* 6. *Mans dayes shall be* 120 *years*, are by many,
our life. and may well be expounded to be the ordinary term of 25
mans life after the floud, (though ordinarily they are said
to designe the years from that speech to the floud.) And
though at that time when he writ the 89th. *Psalm*, (for he
writ the *Pentateuch* first, and that after his going out of
Egypt) he was more then 80 years old,[2] yet in that *Psalm*, 30
In 70. he pitches the limits of mans life 70 years. Though *David*
David were not Author of that *Psalm*, he was an Example of it;
died. for, though in a Kingdom which had but newly taken that
form, and was now translated to *David's* Family, and
vexed with the discontentments of *Saul's* friends, and his 35
own son's ambitions, a longer life, and longer raign might
seem to many to have been requisite, yet he ended his
years in 70. *David was thirty when he began to raign, and*

[1] 1. 7. *J*: 6. 1. *1651.*   [2] old, *J*: old) *1651.*

he raigned forty; After he had seen the anger of God, 2 Sam. 5. 4.
punishing his confidence in the number of his men, by 70 000. of the plague.
diminishing them, limit and determine it self in 70 thou-
sand. And in that great Captivity of *Babylon*, in which 2 Sam. 24. 15.1
5 (as many think) the word of God himself, the Text of 70. years in Baby-lon.
Scriptures perished, that great and pregnant Mother, and
Daughter of Mysteries, (for how many Prophesies were
fulfill'd and accomplish'd in that, and how many conceived
but then, which are not yet brought to light?) the chosen
10 people of God, were *trodden down 70. years*. To which
forraign sojourning, for many concurrences, and main
circumstances, many have assimilated and compared the 70. in Avignon.
Roman Churches straying into *France*, and being em-
pounded in *Avignon* 70. years; And so long also lasted 70. the Goths in Italy.
15 the Inundation of the *Goths* in *Italy*. In that dejection
and bondage in *Babylon*, God afforded to *Daniel* that
vision and voice, then which nothing is more mysterious,
nothing more important for our assurance, nothing more
advantageable against the *Jews*, which is the seventy 70. Heb-domad.
20 *Hebdomades*. Then, those Disciples, supplyers and fellow-
workers with the Apostles, equall to them in very many 70. Dis-ciples.
things (and, men dispute, whether not in all) whom our
most Blessed Saviour instituted, were also of this Number, Luk. 10. 1.
70. And so having refresh'd to your memory, upon this
25 occasion of the Number 70. these stories out of the Bible,
we will end with this observation, that when God moved
Ptolomeus to a desire of having the Bible translated, he Septua-gint.
accited from *Jerusalem* 72, for that glorious and mystick
work; And these, though they were 72, either for affection
30 to conform themselves to a number so notorious, or for
some true mysterie in it, or for what else, God knowes;
have ever retained the name of *Septuagint*.

And so having delivered what by Gods grace I received,
of this book in generall, and of the reason of registring the
35 names, and why there is therein some variety. Why also
they are summ'd and numbred up; and why variously;
And lastly, noted those speciall places, which the Number
70. presented; I will now passe to that which I destin'd

¹ 15.] 31. *1651*.

for a second Part, because it is radically and contractedly
in that first *verse*, but diffused and expansively through the
whole book; The *Mercy, Power, Justice,* and *Judgement*
of God: of which, if nothing can be said new, nothing can
be said too often.   5

PART 2

Though God be absolutely simple, yet since for our sakes[1]
in his Scriptures he often submits himself to comparisons
and similitudes, we may offencelesly[2] (since there is nothing
but himself, so large as the world) thus compare him to 10
the world: That his eternall *Prescience* is the *Cœlestiall*
world, which admits no alteration, no generation of new
purposes, nor corruption of old; and those four, *Mercy,
Power, Justice, Judgment,* are the *Elementary* world, of
which all below is composed, and the Elemented world 15
are his particular extrinsick actions: In which, though they
be so complexioned, that all are[3] mingled equally, yet in
every one of them, every one of these four concur. For,
in every work of God there is mercy and justice, so, as they
presuppose one another. And as in his created Elements, 20
so in these there is a condensing and a rarifying, by which
they become and grow into one another. For often that
action which was principally intended for a work of Justice
against one Malefactor, extends it self to an universall
Mercy, by the Example. And the children of God know 25
how to resolve and make liquid all his Actions. They can
spie out and extract Balmes, and Oyles from his Vinegers;[4]
and supple, and cure with his corrosives. Be he what he
will, they will make him Mercifull, if Mercy be then
wholsomest for them. For so that brave *Macabee* inter- 30
preted Gods daily afflicting them; *The Lord doth not long
wait for us, as for other nations, whom he punisheth when
they come to the fulness of their sins; but he never withdraweth
his Mercy from us.* And in like manner out of his Mercies

*Composi-
tion in
Gods
actions.*

*Aq.⟨1⟩.qu.
21. ar. 4.*

---

[1] sakes] saks *1651.*
[2] offencelesly] (offencelesly *1651.*
[3] all are] they are all *J.*
[4] Vinegers] vinegar *J.*

they can distil Justice, when presumption upon Mercy
needs such a corrective. For so says Saint *Ambrose, Cain* De Para-
indignus judicatus est, qui puniretur in peccato; because he diso.
was not so much spared, as reserved to a greater condemna- De pœnit.
dist. 1.
5 tion. And upon like reason, the Emperiall laws forbid a Serpens.
servant in an Inne to be accused of incontinency, because
(in those times) custome had made them all such, and
therefore unworthy of the laws cognisance. Yet of all these
four Elements *Mercy* is the uppermost and most Embrac- Of Mercy.
10 ing. *Miserationes ejus super omnia opera ejus.* And, *Quanta* Psal. 144.
Magnitudo, as great as his greatness (which is infinite) is [Vulg.]
Eccl[us].
his Mercy. And as great as his power, which is omnipotent: 2. 23.[1]
for it is therefore said, *Misereris omnium, quia omnia potes.* Sap. 11.
Before there was any subject of his mercy, he was merci- [24].
15 full; for Creation it self is one of the greatest of his
Mercies. And it is *Misericordia Domini, quia non sumus* Thre.
consumpti; so that our preservation is also from mercy. 3. 22.[2]
And therefore will the *Lord wait that he may have mercy* Isa. 30. 18.
upon you; and, *miserans miserabitur*, in the next verse. God
20 is the Lord of Hostes, and this world a warfare. And as
the Emperiall Armies had three *Signa Militaria* to be Veget. l. 3.
given them, so hath Gods mercy afforded us. They had cap. 5.
Signa Vocalia, the express word of the Commander, which
office the word of God doth to us; And *Semivocalia*, which
25 were the sound of trumpets and other instruments, and
such to us are traditions and Sermons, partaking of God
and man: And they had *Signa muta*, which were the
Colours and Ensignes, and such to us are the Creatures and
works of God. His Mercy is infinite in Extent: for it is in
30 all places; yea, where there is no place: And it is infinite
in Duration; For as it never begun, (for the Ideating of this
world, which was from everlasting, was a work of mercy)
and as the interruptions which by acts of Justice it seemes
to suffer here, discontinue it not, (for though God say,
35 *For a moment in mine anger I hid my face from thee*; yet he Isa. 54. 8.
adds there, *yet with everlasting Mercy have I had compas-*
sion on thee;) so also is it reasonable to think, that it shall

---

[1] Eccl[us]. 2. 23.] Eccl. 2. 17. *1651: J substitutes* [Ps. ciii. 11. ?].
[2] Thre. 3. 22.] Thre. 9. *1651*: Lam. iii. 22. *J*.

never have end. And because in heaven there can be no distinct and particular act of Mercy from God, because there shall be no demerit in us, nor possibility of it, after judgment; Therefore, and from the *Psalm, Non continebit in ira sua misericordias suas,* some (but too licenciously) 5 have concluded a determination and ending of the pains of the damned; and others learned and pious, and accused by no body for this opinion, evict from hence, certain *intervalla,* and relaxations in the torments of Hell, after the generall Judgment, as all confesse a diminishing of the 10 pains there, and that the punishment is *citra condignum,* by the benefit of the passion of our Blessed Saviour. That which is *Mercy* in God, in us is *Compassion.* And in us, it hath two steps. To rest upon the first, which is but a sadnesse, and sorrow for anothers misery, is but a dull, 15 lazy, and barren compassion. Therefore it is elegantly expressed in the Psalm, *Jucundus homo, qui miseretur, et commodat;* for that is the second and highest step in Compassion, Alacrity, and Chearfulnesse to help. And as God, delighting most in mercy, hath proposed to himselfe most 20 wayes for the exercise thereof, so hath he provided man of most occasions of that vertue. Every man contributes to it, by being Agent, or Patient. Certainly, we were all miserable, if none were; for we wanted the exercise[1] of the profitablest vertue. For though a Judg may be just, though 25 none transgresse; and we might be mercifull, though none wanted, by keeping ever a disposition[2] to be such, if need were; yet what can we hope would serve to awake us then, which snort[3] now under the cries of the wretched, the testimony of our own consciences, the liberall promises of 30 reward from God, and his loud threatnings for such omissions? Amongst the Rules of State, it is taught and practis'd for one, That they which advance and do good, must do it immediately from themselves, that all the Obligation may be towards them: But when they will destroy or do 35 hurt, they must do it instrumentally by others, to remove

Lomb. l. 4. Dist. 46. ex August.

Ps. 111. [5]. [Vulg.]

---

[1] exercise] excercise *1651.*
[2] disposition] disposion *1651.*
[3] snort] snore *J.*

and alienate the envy. Accordingly, when Princes com-
municate to any *Jura Regalia*, by that they are authorized
to apprehend, accuse, pursue, condemne, execute, and
dispoil, but not to pardon. God doth otherwise; for, for
5 our first sin, himselfe hath inflicted death, and labour upon
us. And, as it were to take from us all occasion of evill, he
doth all the evill of which his nature is capable, which is
but *Malum pœnæ.* But of the treasures of his mercy, he
hath made us the Stewards, by dispensing to one another.
10 For first, he hath redeemed man by man, and then he hath
made *Hominem homini Deum.* And proportionall to this
treasure, he hath made our necessities and miseries infinite.
So much, that an *Egyptian* King forbad *Hegesias* the *Val. Max.*
Philosopher to speak publickly of humane misery, least l. 8. c. 9.
15 every one should kill himself. All consists of givers and
receivers: and to contract it closer, every man is both
those; and therefore made so, because one provokes the
other: for, *Homo indigus,*[1] *misericors est.* And it is there- *Prov. 19.*
fore that *Aquinas* sayes, that old men, and wise men, are [22].
20 aptest to this vertue, because they best fore-see a possi- 2ª. 2æ.
bility of needing others compassion. And if thou hadst *q. 30. ar. 2.*
nothing to give, or knewest no want in any other, thou
hast work enough within doors; *Miserere animæ tuæ.* But *Ecclus.*[2]
towards our selves or persons almost our selves, there is 30. [24.
25 not properly mercy, but grief; therfore we must go to Vulg.]
seek guests. And to such a chearfull giver, God gives him- *Aqu.* ibid.
self; *Et quid non possidet, qui ipsum possidet possidentem?* *Paulinus:*
sayes a contemplative wise man. And for such a giver to *Homil. de*
work upon, God makes others needy; *Fecit miseros, ut* *Gazophi-*
lactio.
30 *agnosceret misericordes,* sayes the same man, in the same l. 4. c. 5.
Book. In the first constitution of the *Roman* Empire, by
the generall corruption of all men, which is to give more
to them which abound, they easily fore-saw, that men
would soon decline and stray into a chargeable and sump-
35 tuous worship of their Gods; And therefore they resisted
it with this law, *Deos frugi colunto.* This moderated their
sacrifices, but yet withheld them not from the superfluous

---

[1] *indigus*] *indigens* J (see note).
[2] Ecclus. J: Eccles. *1651.*

adorning the Temples and Images of their Gods. But in
our reformed Christian Religion, which is the thriftiest
and cheapest that ever was instituted, (for our Sacrifices
grow within us, and are our owne creatures, prayer and
praise; and since our Blessed[1] Saviour hath given himself 5
for us, we are now as men which had paid a great fine, and
were bound to no other rent, then acknowledgements and
services) now that we have removed the expensive dignifying[2] of images, and relicks, what other exercise is there left
for our charity, then those nearer images both of God, and 10
of our selves, the poore? *Be mercifull then, as your Father
in heaven is mercifull.* And how is he? *homines et jumenta
salvabis, Deus,* Psal. 35. and by *jumenta* are understood
men not yet reduced to the knowledg of God. Give then
thy counsel to the ignorant, thy prayers to the negligent, 15
but most thy strength to the oppressed and dejected in
heart; for surely, *oppression maketh a wise man mad,*
Eccl. 7. 7.[3] how tempestuously[4] will it then work upon a
weaker? let no greatness retard thee from giving, as though
thou wert above want. Alas, our greatness is Hydroptick, 20
not solid: we are not firm, but puffed, and swoln; we are
the lighter, and the lesser for such greatness. *Alcibiades*
bragg'd how he could walk in his own ground; all this was
his, and no man a foot within him; and *Socrates* gave him
a little map of the world, and bid him show him his terri- 25
tory there; and there an Ant would have overstrid it. Let
no smalnesse retard thee: if thou beest not a Cedar to help
towards a palace, if thou beest not Amber, Bezoar, nor
liquid gold, to restore Princes; yet thou art a shrub to
shelter a lambe, or to feed a bird; or thou art a plantane, 30
to ease a childs smart; or a grasse to cure a sick dog. Love
an asker better then a giver: which was good *Agapetus*
counsel to *Justinian*: Yea rather, prevent the asking; and
do not so much joyn and concur with misery, as to suffer
it to grow to that strength, that it shall make thy brother 35
ask, and put him to the danger of a denyall. Avoid in

*Ælian.
l. 3. c. 28.*

---

[1] Blessed] Bessed *1651.*
[2] dignifying *J*: dignising *1651.*
[3] Eccl. 7. 7] Eccl. 7. 9. *1651.*   [4] tempestuously] impetuously *J.*

giving, that which the Canonists expresse by *Cyminibilis*, which is a trifling giver. And give not (as *Seneca* cals them) *panes lapidosos*; which are benefits hardly drawn, which have onely the shape, not the nourishment of benefits:
5 But give as thou wouldst receive. For thou givest not, but restorest, yea thou performest another duty too, thou lendest. Thou dost not waste, but lay up; and thou gainest in losing. For to this giving most properly squares *Plato's* definition of liberality, that it is, *studium lucrandi ut decet.*
10 I need not much fear that any man is too much inflamed to a wastfull charity by this; yet it is an affection capable of sin. And therefore, as waggoners in steep descents, tie the teame behind, not to draw it up, but to stop sodaine precipitations downward, so, onely to prevent such slipery
15 downfals, I say, That as the Holy Ghost forbids, *Eccl. 7. 18.*
Be not just overmuch, so one may be charitable overmuch. His aptnes to give, may occasion anothers sloth, and he may breed the worms which shall eat him; and produce the lean kine, which shall devoure the fat. And so, as *Ad*
20 *Paulinus* says, *In charitatem de charitate peccat.* And in *Severum.* another place, *Multa charitas pæne[1] delirum, et pietas* *De Mona-* *stultum fecit.* For, God would not, saith Saint *Ambrose,* *chatu.[2]* that we should pour out, but distribute our wealth. So *De Officiis.* that for precise Moderation herein precept will not serve;
25 but that prayer of that most devout Abbot *Antony* (of *De Doc-* whom Saint *Augustine* says, that without knowledge of *trina* letters, he rehearsed, and expounded all the Scriptures) *Christiana.* *Deus det nobis gratiam Discretionis.* For, the same B. *Dorothæus* which says wisely, God requires not that you *Doctrin.*
30 should fly, but that you should not fall, sayes also devoutly, *14.* That they which do what they are commanded of Christ, *Doctrin. 1.* pay their tribute justly,[3] but they which performe his counsels, bring him presents. But in this we may insist no longer: wee shall best know what wee should do, by con-
35 sidering what God hath done, and how hee express'd his mercies towards his *Israelites.*

---

[1] *pæne*] *pene* 1651.
[2] *Monachatu* J: *Monachata* 1651.
[3] tribute justly] tribut justly *corr. 1651*: tribute july *1651 originally.*

His Mercy
in bring-
ing them
to Egypt.
He brought them *into the Land of Egypt*. For though in
the Scriptures, when God would excite his children, he
uses to remember them that he is *that God which brought
them out of the Land of Egypt*; yet, that he brought them
into that Land, was more simply, absolutely, and intirely
a work of Mercy. For, in the other he exercised his *Justice*
upon *Pharaoh*; and his *Power* in *Miracles*. And Miracles
must not be drawne into consequence; No man may argue
to himself, God hath miraculously preserved me, therefore he will do so still. Miracles are to our apprehension incoherent and independent things with the rest of Nature.
They seem none of the links of that great chaine of providence, and connexion of causes. Therefore he which hears
them, beleeves them but so far as he beleeves the reporter;
and he which sees them, suspects his sense in the appre-
hending, and his judgment in the inquisition and pursuite
of the causes; or goes more roundly to work, and imputes
it all to the Divell. But this work of bringing them *into
Egypt*, was only a work of a familiar and fatherly *Providence*: and, though it were greater then the other (for in
coming from Egypt they were but redeemed from *serving*,
here from *perishing*) yet there is nothing in the History,
which a meer naturall man would grudg to beleeve. From
what kind of Destruction did he then deliver them? From

Famine. famine; One of those three afflictions, which God in a
diligent and exquisite revenge presented to *David*'s choice.
And one of those two, in comparison whereof, *David* chose
a pestilence of uncertain lasting and intenseness. An affliction so great, as God chooses that comparison to express

Amos. his greatest affliction of all, which is a famine of his word.
An affliction which defeats all Magistracy; for in it one
may lawfully steal. All propriety; for in it all things return
to their primitive[1] community. All naturall affection; for
in it fathers may sell their children, by humane laws; and
divine books have Examples where they have eaten them.

Sueton.
Calig. 26. An affliction, which *Caligula*, to exceed his predecessors
and his own Examples, studied out, when to imitate the
greatest power of all, *præclusis horreis, indixit populo*

[1] primitive] primative *1651*.

famem. An affliction with which our law revenges her self
when a delinquent which had offended her before, doth
after in contempt of her stand mute at the bar. It is a
Rack, without either Engine or Executioner; a devouring
5 poyson, and yet by substraction; and a way to make a man
kill himself by doing nothing. Such are all extreme famines,
and such was this. For it was no particular curse upon one Gen.
country; for famine was in all the Land, says the text. And 41. 54.
all Countryes came to *Egypt* to buy corn. It was no naturall ver. 57.
10 disease or infirmity in the earth or aire: but as the Psalmist Ps. 105.
expresses it, *God* had *called a famine upon the land, and* 16.
utterly brake the staffe of bread. Egypt herself, which uses
to brag, *Nihil se imbribus cœloque debere*, and whose in- Paneg.
undations are fertilities, felt the barreness, though by Plin. in
15 *Josephs providence* it felt not the penury. In this affliction, Traia-
in this distress, the sons of *Jacob* must go into a strange num.[1]
land, where they had no friend whom they knew, but (to
speak humanely) an enemy whom they knew not. And yet
God, as though their malice against their brother *Joseph*,
20 and as though this curse upon the whole land had been
ordained by him for their advantage, (for so it may seem
by those words of *Joseph*, *You sent me not hither, but God;* Gen. 45. 8.
and in the Psalm, *God sent a man before them*) appears to Psal. 105.
Jacob, perswades the journey, assures him[2] his safe going,
25 great propagation, and safe return.

 Propagation is the truest Image and nearest representa- His Mercy
tion of eternity. For eternity it self, that is, the Deity it in propa-
self seems to have been ever delighted with it: for the gating
producing of the three Persons in the Trinity, which is a Egypt.
30 continuing and undeterminable work, is a propagation of Propaga-
the Deity. And next to this contemplation, that God, tion of
which is full, and perfect, and All, should admit a propaga- God.
tion, it may deserve a second place to consider, that that
which is meerly and utterly Nothing, which is *Sin*, (for it Of Sin.
35 is but privation) hath had the greatest propagation that
can be. And between these two extreme Miracles, A propagation in that which is already All, and a propagation
in that which is always Nothing, we may wonder at a

 [1] *Traianum*] *Iracund*. 1651. [2] him *J*: him and *1651*.

propagation in that which is but one halfe; which is, those
Of re- Religious Orders, and devout professions, which multiply
ligious without Mothers. Of which (not to speak of late times,
Orders. when that profession was become a disease and contagion,
and so no wonder though they infected, and possessed, 5
and devoured whole ter⟨r⟩itories; but in their primitive
institution and practice, how infinite was the propagation?
we cannot discredit those stories (for being dis-interested
in our late-sprung Controversies they could not speak pre-
judicially) which reckon 5000. in some one Monastery; 10
and 500 Monasteries under one Abbot. These who had no
wives, had infinite spirituall children; and having nothing
in the world, had a great part of it. Within one mile of
Alexandria, there were 500 Monasteries *pæne*[1] *contigua*.
So that, it is truly said of them, they had *Oppida extra* 15
Azor.l.12. *Mundum*. And when the only tribe of the *Benedictins* was
in full height, it had not many lesse then 40000 Monasteries. And not only the Christian Church, the easiness of
whose yoke might invite them to these counsails, but the
Jews under an insupportable law, would ever super-erro- 20
L. 5. c. 17. gate in this kinde. Of whose one sect, the *Esseni*, *Pliny*
says, *per multa seculorum millia, gens æterna, in qua nemo
nascitur*; and he gives no other mother to such an increase
then this, *Tam fœcunda illis aliorum vitæ pœnitentia*. Of
these men, (if they will accept that name,) (except such 25
of them as being all born to sail in the same ship as we,
and to suffer with us, have so sublimed their wits with a
contempt of ours, that they steal from us in a *Calenture*; or
so stupified themselves, that they forsake their partnership
in our labours and dangers, in a lazy Scurvie,) I dare not 30
conceive any hard opinion: For though we be all Gods
tenants in this world, and freeholders for life, and are so
bound amongst other duties, to keep the world in repara-
tion, and leave it as well as we found it, (for, *ut gignamus
geniti*) yet since we have here two employments, one to 35
conserve this world, another to increase Gods Kingdome,
none is to be accused, that every one doth not all, so all do
all. For as, though every particular man by his diet and

[1] *pæne*] *pene* 1651.

temperance, should preserve his own body, and so observe
it by his own experience of it, that he might ordinarily be
his own Physician; yet it is fit, that some sepose all their
time for that study, and be able to instruct and reform
5 others; So, though every one should watch his own steps,
and serve God in his vocation; yet there should be some,
whose Vocation it should be to serve God; as all should
do it, so some should do nothing else. But, because, our
esse must be considered before our *bene esse*, and to our
10 *esse* properly conduce all things which belong to our preservation here, (for, the first words that ever God said to
man, were, *Bring forth, and multiply, and fill the earth*, Gen. 1.28.
which was *propagation*; And then presently, *subdue it, and
rule*, which is *Dominion*. And then, *Every thing which hath
15 life, shall be to you for meat*; which is not only *sustenance*,
but lawfull abundance and delicacy.) Therefore to advance
propagation, lawes have been diligent and curious. Some
have forbidden a man to divide himselfe to divers women,
because, though God in his secret ends have somtimes
20 permitted it to the Patriarchs, and though (being able to
make contraries serve to one end) he threatens in another
place, that *ten women shall follow one man*; yet ordinarily
this liberality of a mans self, frustrates propagation, and
is in it selfe a confession, that he seeks not children. And
25 therefore the *Panegyrick* justly extols that Emperour, who Maxi-
married young, *Novum jam, tum miraculum, juvenis uxorius.* miniano, et
And some lawes in the *Greek* States enforced men to Constan-
marry: and the *Roman* law pretended to have the same [c. iv.]
ends, but with more sweetnesse, by giving priviledges to
30 the married: but ever increasing them with their number
of children, of which to have had none, threw a man back
again into penalty; for of the estate of such, a tenth part
was confiscate; for to have children, is so much of the
essence of the lawfulnesse of that act, that Saint *Augustine*
35 sayes, *Si prolem ex conditione vitant, non est matrimonium*; for De bono
that is a condition destroying the nature of matrimony; of Conjugali.
which, and of the fruits thereof, how indulgent the *Romans*
were, this one law declares; That to *Minors* they allowed
so many years more then they had, as they had children.

Of this *propagation*, which is our present contemplation,
many think devoutly, that the smalnesse of the first number, and the shortnesse of the time, are the remarkable and
essentiall parts. To advance their devotion, I will remember them, that the number of 430. years divers times
spoken of, is from *Abraham's* coming to *Canaan*; for the
time of this propagation in *Egypt*, was but 215. years. And
the number of men, which is 600000. is[1] only of fighting
men, which cannot well be thought a fift part of all the
souls. The whole number *Josephus*, proportioning 10. to
a paschal lamb, as the *Rabbins* do, brings to be 3700000.
yet to me these seem no great parts of Gods exceeding
Mercy in this History; for from so many, in such a space,
God, without miracle, by affording twins, and preserving
alive, might ordinarily have derived more men then ever
were at once upon the whole earth. But whether his decree
have appointed a certain number which mankind shall not
exceed, (as it seems to be a reasonable conjecture of the
whole, because in the most famous parts it is found to
have held; *Rome*, and *Venice*, and like States never exceeding that number to which they have very soon arrived:)
Or that the whole earth is able to nourish no more, without doubt it is evident, that the world had very long since
as many souls as ever it had, or may be presumed to have
ever hereafter. And it is a very probable conjecture, that
the reason, why, since wolves produce oftner, and more
then sheep, and more sheep are killed then wolves, yet
more sheep remain, is, because they are cherished by all
industry. For only there men increase, where there is
means for their sustentation. That therefore which God
did mercifully in this, was, that he propagated them to
such numbers under such oppressions and destructions:
for the *Egyptians* cruelly caused them to serve, and made
them weary of their lives by sore labour, with all manner
of bondage: yea, their devotion was scornfully mis-inter-
preted, *Because you are idle, you say, let us go offer to our
Lord*. And yet, the more they vexed them, the more they
grew; *and hee made them stronger then their oppressors*; And

Marginal notes:
Of this propaga-tion.

Exod. 12. 41.

Numb. 1.

Exod. 1.

Exod. 5. 8.[2]

Ps. 105. 24.

---

[1] is] and is *J.*   [2] Exod. 5. 8] Exod. 12. *1651.*

this, though that desperate law of destroying all their male children, had been executed among them.

Now follows his bringing them *from Egypt*: And though His Mercy that were properly a work of *Justice*, because it was the in bring-5 performance of God's promise, yet that promise was rooted ing them from in Mercy: And though hee brought them out *In Manu* Egypt. *forti*, as it is very often repeated, and by effect of miracles, and so show'd his power, (for it is written, *he saved them* Ps. 106. 8.¹ *for his Names sake, that he might make his power to be* Exo. 14. 4. 10 *knowne*. And in another place, *I will get me honour upon Pharaoh*,² *and upon all his host*) yet respecting the time when he did it, (to which his promise had not limited him) and for whom he did it, we can contemplate nothing but *Mercy*. For in the same place, it is said, *Our Fathers under-*15 *stood not thy wonders in Egypt, neither remembred the multi-tude of thy Mercies*: so that, diversly beheld, the same Act might seem all *Power*, and all *Mercy*. And at this time we consider, not that those plagues afflicted *Egypt*, but ⟨that⟩³ the land of *Goshen* felt none: and we hear not now the 20 cryes and lamentations for the death of the first-born, but we remember, that *not a dog opened his mouth against the* Exod. 11. *children of Israel*. He delivered them then from such an oppressor, as would neither let them go, nor live there. From one who increased their labours, and diminished 25 their numbers. From one who would neither allow them to be Naturals, nor Aliens. So ambiguous and perplex'd, and wayward is humane policy, when she exceeds her limits, and her subject. But God, though his mercy be abundantly enough for all the world, (for since he swet, 30 and bled Physick enough for all, it were more easie for him, to apply it to all, if that conduced to his ends,) yet because his children were ever froward, and grudged any part to others in this their Delivery, pours out all his sea of Mercy upon them, and withdraws all from the Egyptians. There-35 fore he is said to have *hardned Pharaoh's heart*. Which Indura-because it is so often repeated (at least nine times) was tion. done certainly all those ways by which God can be said to

¹ Ps. 106. 8.] Ps. 106. 7. *1651*.   ² *Pharaoh*] *Pharoah* 1651.
³ but that *J*: but *1651*.

harden us. Either *Ad captum humanum*, when God descends to our phrase of speech, and serves our way of apprehend-

Corn. Cel.
l. 5. 3.
ing; Or *permissively*, when God, as it were looks another way, and agrees with that counsell of the Physician, It is a discreet mans part to let him alone, which cannot be cured; Or *substractively*, when he withdrawes that spirituall food, which, because it is ordained for children, must not be cast to dogs; Or *Occasionally*, when he presents grace proportioned to a good end, in its own nature and quality, which yet he knows the taker will corrupt and envenom it, (for so, a Magistrate may occasion evill, though neither he may, nor God can cause any;) Or els *Ordinately* and instrumentally, when God, by this Evill, workes a greater good; which yet was not Evill where it first grew, in the Paradise of Gods purpose and decree (for so no simple is Evill) but becomes such, when it comes to our handling, and mingling, and applying. Yea, that very Act which God punished in *Pharaoh*, which was the oppression, pro-

Ps. 105. 25.
ceeded from God. For the Psalmist says, *He hardned their heart to hate his people, and to deal craftily with his servants.*

Pererius
[in] Ex. 1.
That so by this Violence and this Deceit, they might have a double title to possess themselves of the Egyptians treasure. And accordingly for all their pressures, he brought

Ps. 105. 37.
them away sound; and rich, for all their deceit: *He brought them forth with silver and gold, and there was none feeble in their tribes.* Yea it is added, *Egypt was glad at their depart-*

Exo. 11. 1.
ing; which God intimated, when he said, *when he letteth you go, he shall at once chase you hence.* Only to paraphrase the History of this Delivery, without amplifying, were furniture and food enough for a meditation of the best perseverence, and appetite, and digestion; yea, the least word in the History would serve a long rumination. If this be in the bark, what is in the tree? If in the superficiall grass, the letter; what treasure is there in the hearty and inward Mine, the Mistick and retired sense? Dig a little deeper, O my poor lazy soul, and thou shalt see that thou, and all mankind are delivered from an Egypt; and more miraculously then these. For, Almightiness is so naturall to God, that nothing done by his power, is very properly

miracles, which is above all[1] Nature. But God delivered us,
by that which is most contrary to him; by being *impotent*;
by being *sin*; by being *Dead*. That great *Pharaoh*, whose
Egypt all the world is by usurpation, (for *Pharaoh* is but
5 *exemptus* and *privilegiatus*; and that Name, (I hope not
the Nature) is strai'd into our word *Baro*) whom God hath
made *Prince of the air*, and *Prince of Darkness*; that is, of
all light and aiery illusions, and of all sad and earnest
wickedness, of Vanity, and of sin; had made us fetch our
10 own straw, that is, painfully seek out light and blasing
Vanities; and then burn his brick, which is, the clay of our
own bodies with concupiscences and ambitions, to build
up with our selves his Kingdome; He made us travell more
for hell, then would have purchased Heaven; He enfeebled
15 us from begetting or conceiving Male children, which are
our good thoughts, and those few which we had, he
strangled in the birth: And then, camest thou, O Christ,
thine own *Moses*, and deliveredst us; not by doing, but
suffering; not by killing, but dying. Go one step lower,
20 that is higher, and nearer to God, O my soul, in this
Meditation, and thou shalt see, that even in this moment,
when he affords thee these thoughts, he delivers thee from
an Egypt of dulness and stupiditie. As often as he moves
thee to pray to be delivered from the Egypt of sin, he
25 delivers thee. And as often as thou promisest him not to
return thither, he delivers thee. Thou hast delivered me,
O God, from the Egypt of confidence and presumption,
by interrupting my fortunes, and intercepting my hopes;
And from the Egypt of despair by contemplation of thine
30 abundant treasures, and my portion therein; from the
Egypt of lust, by confining my affections; and from the
monstrous and unnaturall Egypt of painfull and wearisome
idleness, by the necessities of domestick and familiar cares
and duties. Yet as an Eagle, though she enjoy her wing
35 and beak, is wholly prisoner, if she be held by but one
talon; so are we, though we could be delivered of all habit
of sin, in bondage still, if Vanity hold us but by a silken
thred. But, O God, as mine inward corruptions have made

Acacius de privilegiis.

[1] all] *om. J.*

me mine own *Pharaoh*, and mine own *Egypt*; so thou, by the inhabitation of thy Spirit, and application of thy merit, hast made me mine own Christ; and contenting thy self with being my Medicine, allowest me to be my Physician.

Lastly, descend, O my Soul, to the very Center, which 5 is the very Pole, (for in infinite things, incapable of distinction of parts, Highest and lowest are all one) and consider to what a land of promise, and heavenly *Hierusalem* God will at last bring thee, from the *Egypt* of this world, and the most Egyptiacal part, this flesh. God is so abun- 10 dantly true, that he ever performes his words more then once. And therefore, as he hath fulfilled that promise, *Out of Egypt have I called my Son*; So will he also perform it in every one of his elect; and as when *Herod* dyed, his Angell appeared to *Joseph in Egypt in a dream*, to call him thence; 15 So when our persecutor, our flesh shall dy, and the slumber of death shall overtake us in this our *Egypt*, His Angels, sent from Heaven, or his Angels newly created in us, (which are good desires of that dissolution), or his Ministeriall Angels in his militant Church, shall call and invite 20 us from this *Egypt* to that *Canaan*. Between which (as the Israelites did) we must pass a desert; a disunion and divorce of our body and soul, and a solitude of the grave. In which, the faithful and discreet prayers of them which stay behind, may much advantage and benefit us, and themselves, 25 if therby God may be moved to hasten that judgment which shall set open Heavens greater gates, at which our Bodyes may enter, and to consummate and accomplish our salvation.

The next place is, to consider his *Mercy in their pre-* 30 *servation in the Desert*. For God hath made nothing which needs him not, or which would not instantly return again to nothing without his special conservation: Angels and our Souls are not delivered from this dependancy upon him. As therefore Conservation is as great a work of Power 35 as Creation; so the particular[1] wayes of Gods preserving

---

[1] particular] particuliar *1651*.

those special people in the Wilderness, are as great works
of *Mercy*, as the Delivery from *Egypt*. And though this
book of *Exodus* embrace not all those, yet here are some
instances of every kinde; as well of preservation from
5 extrinsick violences of *War*, as intrinsick of *Famine*; and
mix'd, of *infirmities and diseases*. And because Gods purpose had destined them to an *offensive* War at last, let us
mark by what degrees he instructed and noursed them to
it. They had been ever frozen in slavery, without use of
10 Arms, or taste of Honour, or Glory, or Victory. And
because they were therfore likely to forsake themselves,
and dishonour him, God (saith the History) *carried them* Exod. 13.
not by the way of the Philistims[1] *Country, though that were* 17.
nearer, lest they should repent when they see Warr, and turn
15 *again into Egypt.* But presently after, when he had contracted himself to them, and affirmed and affianced his
preference by the Sacrament of the *Pillar*, he was then
content that they should see an Army pursuing them;
which was not so much terrible to them as they were
20 *Enemies*, as that[2] they were their *Masters*. For then they
exclaimed to *Moses, Hast thou brought us to die in the* Exod. 14.
wilderness, because there were no graves in Egypt? Did not 11.
we say, let us be in rest, that we may serve the Egyptians? So
soon did a dejection make them call their former *bondage*,
25 *rest*; and sink down to meet and invite death, when the
Lord of life upheld them. And at this time, God used not
their swords at all, yet gave them a full victory. But when
this had warm'd them, as soon as the *Amalekites* made
towards them, they fear'd not, murmur'd not, retir'd not;
30 nay, they expected not: but saith *Moses* to *Joshuah, Chuse* Exod.
us men, and go, fight with Amalek. Which victory, lest they 17. 9.
should attribute to themselves, and so grow too forward
in exposing themselves, and tempting God; the lifting up,
or falling down of *Moses*'s hands in prayer, that day,
35 sway'd and govern'd the battell. Which therfore God was
especially carefull that the souldier should know; for so
he commanded *Moses, Write that for a remembrance in the* Exod. 17.
book, and rehearse it to Joshuah. To their other wars this 14.

---

[1] *Philistims*] Philistines' *J*.   [2] as that *J*: as that that *1651*.

book extends not: but is full of examples of his other
mercies towards them, though they murmur'd; yea, by
the words it may well seem, they were done because they
murmur'd: *In the Morning ye shall see the glory of God,*
(says Moses to them) for, he hath heard your grudging 5
against him. And again, *At evening shall the Lord give you*
flesh; for the Lord hath heard your murmuring. They mur-
mur'd for water, saying, What shall we drink? and then
God presented water; but lest they should attribute all
that to the nature of the place, those waters were too 10
bitter to be drunk. Then God would sweeten them; yet
not by *Miracle*; but to encline them to a reverence of
Moses, he inform'd him, what would do it *naturally*; as
it appears in another place, where the Art of physick is
extoll'd: *Was not the water made sweet with wood, that men* 15
might know the vertue thereof? And yet, the next time that
they murmur'd for water, he gave it them miraculously
from the rock; to shew, that though *Moses* was enabled to
all naturall works, yet he withdrew not his miraculous
presence from them. And then, when they murmur'd des- 20
perately for meat, *Oh that we had dyed in the Land of*
Egypt, when we sat by fleshpots, etc. the Lord, as though
nothing in use, or in nature, had been precious enough for
them, rained down such fowles, as no Naturalist since can
tell what they were: and such a grain, as though it abide 25
the interpretation of *panis fortium,* and *panis Angelorum,*
yet, saith a curious observer of those subtilties, the name
signifies, *Quid est hoc?* which is easily gathered from the
very Text, *When they saw it, they said to one another, it is*
Man; for they wist not what it was. In which, the same 30
Problemist[2] observes this wonder, that every man took a
like proportion, and all were alike satisfied, though all
could not be of a like appetite[3] and digestion. And a
greater wonder, and by a better Author is observed in it,
That it was meat[4] for all tasts, and served to the appetite of 35
him which took it, and was that which every man would. Yet
this heavenly food they injured with a wearinesse of it; and

Exod.
16. 7.
Ver. 8.
Exod. 15.
24.

Eccl[us].
38. 5.

Exo. 16. 3.[1]

Fra. Geor.
problem.
fol. 45.
Exod. 16.
15.
Probl. 351.

Sap. 16. 20.

---

[1] 3.] 2. *1651*.   [2] Problemist] Problamist *1651*.
[3] a like appetite *J*: alike appetite *1651*.   [4] *meat*] food *J*.

worse, with their comparisons; for they cried, *We remember the flesh we ate in Egypt for nought, the cucumers, pepons, leeks, onions, and garlick.* As though that had been lesse worth, or they had paid more for it. If then they could

5 chide him into mercy, and make him mercifull not only to their sin, but for their sin, where or when may we doubt of his mercy? Of which, we will here end the consideration; not without an humble acknowledgment, that it is not his least mercy, that we have been thus long possessed

10 with the meditation thereof: for thus long we have been in the Harbour, but we launch into a main and unknown Sea, when we come to consider his *Power*.

Of all the wayes in which God hath expressed himselfe towards us, we have made no word which doth lesse signifie

15 what we mean, then *Power*: for *Power*, which is but an ability to do, ever relates to some future thing: and God is ever a present, simple, and pure Act. But we think we have done much, and gone far, when we have made up the word *Omnipotence*, which is both wayes improper; for it

20 is much too short, because *Omnipotence* supposes and confesses a matter and subject to work upon, and yet God was the same, when there was nothing. And then it overreaches, and goes down-wards beyond God: for God hath not, or is not such an Omnipotence, as can do all things;

25 for though squeamish and tenderer men think it more mannerly to say, *This thing cannot be done*, then, *God cannot do this thing*; yet it is all one: And if that be an Omnipotence, which is limited with the nature of the worker, or with the congruity of the subject, other things may

30 incroach upon the word *Omnipotent*; that is, they can do all things which are not against their nature, or the nature of the matter upon which they work. *Beza* therefore might well enough say, That God could not make a body without place; And *Prateolus* might truly enough infer upon that,

35 that the *Bezanites* (as he calls them) deny omnipotence in God; for both are true. And therefore I doubt not, but it hath some mysterie, that the word *Omnipotence* is not found in all the Bible; nor *Omnipotent* in the New Testament. And where it is in the Old, it would rather be interpreted

Num. 11. 5.

Verbo Bezanitæ.

All-sufficient, then *Almighty;* between which there is much difference. God is so *Al-sufficient,* that he is sufficient for all, and sufficient to all: He is enough, and we are in him able enough to take and apply. We fetch part of our wealth, which is our faith, expresly from his Treasury: 5 And for our good works, we bring the metall to his Mint, (or that Mint comes to us) and there the Character of Baptisme, and the impression of his grace, makes them currant, and somewhat worth, even towards him. God is *all-efficient:* that is, hath created the beginning, ordained 10 the way, fore-seen the end of every thing; and nothing else is any kind of cause thereof. Yet, since this word *efficient,* is now grown to signifie infallibility in God, it reaches not home to that which we mean of God; since man is efficient cause of his own destruction. God is also 15 *all-conficient:* that is, concurs with the nature of every thing; for indeed the nature of every thing is that which he works in it. And as he redeemed not man as he was God, (though the Mercy, and Purpose, and Acceptation were only of God) but as God and man; so in our repentances and 20 reconciliations, though the first grace proceed only from God, yet we concurr so, as there is an union of two Hypostases, *Grace,* and *Nature.* Which, (as the incarnation of our Blessed Saviour himself was) is conceived in us of the Holy Ghost, without father; but fed and produced by us; 25 that is, by our will first enabled and illumined. For neither God nor man determine mans will; (for that must either imply a necessiting therof from God, or else *Pelagianisme)* but they condetermine it. And thus God is truly *all-conficient,* that is, concurrent in all; and yet we may not 30 dare to say, that he hath any part in sin. So God is also *all-perficient:* that is, all, and all parts of every work are his intirely: and lest any might seem to escape him, and be attributed to Nature or to Art, all things were in him at once, before he made Nature, or she Art. All things 35 which we do to day were done by us in him, before we were made. And now, (when they are produced in time, as they were foreseen in eternity,) his exciting grace provokes every particular good work, and his assisting grace perfects it. And yet we may not say, but that God begins many things which we frustrate; and calls when we come not. So that, as yet our understanding hath found no word, which is well proportioned to that which we mean by *power of God*; much less of that refined and subtil part thereof, which we chiefly consider in this place, which is the absolute and transcendent *power of Miracles*, with which this History abounds. For whatsoever God did for his Israelits, beside Miracles, was but an extension of his Mercy, and belongs to that Paragraph which we have ended before.

Nature is the *Common law* by which God governs us, and *Miracle* is his *Prerogative*. For Miracles are but so many *Non-obstantes* upon Nature. And Miracle is not like prerogative in any thing more then in this, that no body can tell what it is. For first, Creation and such as that, are not Miracles, because they are not (to speak in that language) *Nata fieri per alium modum*. And so, only that is Miracle, which might be done naturally, and is not so done. And then, lest we allow the Divell a power to do Miracles, we must say, that Miracle is *contra totam Naturam*, against the whole order and disposition of Nature. For as in Cities, a father governs his family by a certain Order, which yet the Magistrate of the City may change for the Cities good, and a higher Officer may change[1] the Cities Order; but none, all, except the King: so, I can change some naturall things (as I can make a stone fly upward) a Physician more, and the Divell more then he; but only God can change all. And after that is out of necessity established, that *Miracle* is against the whole *Order* of Nature, I see not how there is left in God a power of Miracles. For, the Miracles which are produced to day, were determined and inserted into the body of the whole History of Nature (though they seem to us to be[2] but interlineary and Marginall) at the beginning, and are as infallible and certain, as the most Ordinary and customary things. Which is evicted and approved by that which *De vera* *Lactantius* says, and particularly proves, that all Christs *Sap.* c. 15.

---

¹ change] change for *J.*   ² to be] *om. J.*

Miracles were long before prophecied. So that truly
nothing can be done against the Order of Nature. For,
Cont. Saint *Augustine* says truly, That is Naturall to each thing,
Faustum which God doth, from whom proceeds all Fashion, Num-
l. 26. c. 3. ber and Order of Nature: for that God, whose Decree is 5
the Nature of every thing, should do against his own
Decree, if he should do against Nature. As therefore if we
understood all created Nature, nothing would be *Mirum*
to us; so if we knew Gods purpose, nothing would be
Miraculum. For certainly, those Miracles which *Moses* did, 10
after God had once revealed to *Moses*, that he would do
them, were not Miracles to him, no more then the works
of the Conjurers, which *ex Ratione Rei*, were as true as his.
But the expressing of his power at this time was, that in
the sight of such understanders and workmasters, as the 15
Magi were, he would do more without any Instrument
conducing to those ends, then they could do by their best
instrument, the Divell; and so draw from them that confession, *Digitus Dei hic est*: for else who could have distinguished between his and their works, or denied the 20
name of *Miracle* to theirs? for they (not to depart at this
time from vulgar Philosophy; not that I bind your faith
to it, but that if we abandon this, it is not easie and ready
to constitute another so defensible) by their power of
locall Motion, and Application of Active and passive 25
things, could oppose matter to heate, and so produce
frogs truly; yea, when such things are brought together by
such a workman, he can by them produce greater effects
then nature could. As an Axe and timber being in the
hand of a Statuary, he can make an Image; which they 30
two, or a less skilfull Agent could not do. But God wrought
Adversus not so: But, as *Arnobius* says, he did them, *Sine vi car-*
Gent. l. 1. *minum, sine herbarum aut graminum succis, sine ulla observa-*
De vera *tione sollicita*: but *verbo, et jussione*, as *Lactantius* notes.
sap. c. 15. By which means *Arnobius* pronounces, none of the Philo- 35
Adv. gent. sophers could cure an Itch; *Nemo Philosophorum potuit*
l. 2. *unquam scabiem, unâ*[1] *interdictione sanare.* Another express-
ing[2] of his power, was in this, that when he would, he

---

[1] *unâ* corr. 1651: *unû* 1651 originally.   [2] expressing] expression *J.*

intercepted their power; which was, when they attempted
to make *Cyniphs*. For that is a kind of treason, and clipping
God's coyn, to say, that they were hindered by naturall
causes: for if those *Cyniphs* were lice, (as many Transla-
5 tions call them) and if sweat be the matter of them, and
the Divel could not ordinarily provide store of that, yet
I say, their credit stood not upon the story, but the fact:
And then the Divel knew natural means, to warm and
distill multitudes of men into sweats: And last, if they
10 were such vermine, yet they are agreed to be of that kind
which infest dogs; and they never sweat. And if by *Cyniph*
be express'd some flie, not made till then, and then of
putrefaction (for it were too much to allow creatures of a
new Species,) certainly, the Divell can produce all such.
15 Either then the creature being meerly new, the Divell
understood not of what it was composed; Or God changed
the form of Dust into another form, which the Divell
could never do; or else, God manacled his hand in the
easiest thing, to confound him the more; for after this,
20 it appears not that the *Magi* attempted to do any more
Miracles. To discountenance then their deceits, and withall to afflict the Land of Egypt, was the principall purpose
of God in these Miracles: not to declare himself, or beget
faith; for he doth not alwayes bind miracles to faith, nor
25 faith to miracles. He will somtimes be believed without
them; and somtimes spend them upon unbelievers; lest
men should think their faith gave strength to his power.
For though it be said, *Christ could do no great works in his* Mark 6. 5.
own countrey, for their unbeliefe: yet he did some there; *Ema. Sâ,*[1]
30 which Saint *Hierom* sayes, was done, lest they should be *in hunc*
excusable, having seen no Miracle: And he did not *many*, *Locum.*
least, as *Theophylact* sayes, he should after many Miracles
resisted, have been forced in justice to a severer punishment of them. But because the danger of beleeving false
35 miracles is extreamly great, and the essentiall differences
of false and true, very few, and very obscure, (for what
humane understanding can discern, whether they be
wrought immediately, or by second causes; And then for

¹ *Ema. Sâ*] *Ema. Sacrâ* 1651: Apud Em. Sâ *J*.

the end to which they are addressed, what sect of Christians, or what sect departed from all Christians, will refuse
Deut. to stand to that law? *If there arise a Prophet, and he give a*
13. 1. *wonder, and the wonder come to passe, saying, let us go after*
other Gods, that Prophet shal be slaine.) I encline to think, 5
that God for the most part, works his miracles rather to
shew his Power, then Mercy, and to terrifie enemies, rather
then comfort his children. For miracles lessen the merit
Mat. 12. of faith. And our Blessed Saviour said to the Pharisees, *An*
39.¹ *Evill and adulterous generation seeketh a sign,* And *John* 10
Joh. 10. Baptist, in whom there seems to have been most use of
[41]. Miracles, did none. And though in this delivery from
Egypt, for *Pharaoh's* hardness, God abounded in Miracles,
yet in their delivery from *Babylon,* (of which in respect of
Jer.² 16. this, the Prophet says, *The day shall come, saith the Lord,* 15
[14, 15]. *that it shall no more be said, The Lord liveth, that brought*
his sons out of the land of Egypt; But the Lord liveth, that
brought his sons out of the land of the North) God proceeded
without Miracles. And though in propagation of Christian
Religion in the new discoveries, the Jesuites have recorded 20
Jo. Acosta. infinite Miracles, yet the best amongst them ingenuously
de procur. deny it; And one gives this for a reason, why Miracles are
Ind.³ sal. not afforded by God now, as well as in the primitive
l. 2. c. 9. Church, since the occasion seems to be the same, That
then ignorant men were sent to preach Christianity 25
amongst men armed and instructed against it, with all
kindes of learnings and philosophies; but now learned men
are sent to the ignorant; and are superiour to them in
Reason and in Civility, and in Authority; and besides,
present them a Religion less incredible then their own. I 30
speak not thus, to cherish their opinion, who think God
doth no Miracle now: that were to shorten his power, or
to understand his counsels; but to resist theirs, who make
Miracles ordinary. For, besides that it contradicts and
destroyes the Nature of Miracle, to be frequent, God at 35
first possest his Church, (*Fortiter*) by conquest of Miracles;
but he governs it now, (*suaviter*) like an indulgent King,

¹ 39] 38 *1651.*   ² Jer. *J*: *Herc.* 1651.
³ *Ind.*] *Jud.* 1651: Indorum *J*.

by a law which he hath let us know. God forbid I should
discredit or diminish the great works that he hath done
at the tombs of his Martyrs, or at the pious and devout
commemoration of the sanctity and compassion of his
5 most Blessed Mother. But to set her up a Banke almost in
every good Town, and make her keep a shop of Miracles
greater then her Sons, (for is it not so, to raise a childe, *Miracula*
which was born dead, and had been buried seventeen days, *B. Virg.*
to so small end ?) (for it died again as soon as it was carried *ab. Anno*
10 from her sight) is fearfull and dangerous to admit. God *1581 ad*
forbid, I should deny or obscure the power and practice *1605. fo.*
of our blessed Saviour, and his Apostles, in casting out *150.*
Divels in the primitive Church: but that the Roman
Church should make an Occupation of it, and bind Ap-
15 prentices to it (for such are those little boys whom they
make Exorcists) and then make them free when they
receive greater Orders, and yet forbid them to set up, or
utter their ware but where they appoint, is scarce agreeable to the first Examples, I dare not say, Institution; for
20 I see not that this Order had any. Why we do not so, the
reason is, because *non fuit sic ab initio*: And no hardnesse
of heart is enough to justifie a toleration of these *devout
deceits* and *holy lyes*, as they are often called amongst themselves. The Power of God, which we cannot name, needs
25 not our help. And this very History (in expounding of
which *Pererius* inculcates so often, *Non multiplicanda
miracula*) which seems the principallest record of Gods
Miracles, though literally it seem to be directed to his
enemies, by often expressing his power; yet to his children
30 it insinuates an Admonition, to beware of Miracles, since
it tels them how great things the Divel did: And that his
giving over in no great thing, but the least of all, shows,
That that was not a cancelling of his Patent, which he had
in his Creation, but onely a *Supersedeas* not to execute it
35 at that time. For, (excepting the staying of the Sun, and
carrying it back (if it be cleer that the body of the Sun was
carried back, and not the shadow only) and a very few
more) it appears enough, that the Divell hath done oftner
greater Miracles, then the children of God: For God

delights not so much in the exercise of his *Power*, as of his
Mercy and *Justice*, which partakes of both the other: For
Mercy is his *Paradise* and garden in which he descends to
walk and converse with man: *Power* his *Army* and *Arsenel*,
by which he protects and overthrows: *Justice* his *Ex-*   5
chequer, where he preserves his own Dignity, and exacts
our Forfeitures.

Even at first God intimated how unwillingly he is drawn
to execute *Justice* upon transgressors; for he first exercised
all the rest: *Mercy*, in purposing our Creation; *Power*, in   10
doing it; and *Judgment*, in giving us a Law: Of which the
written part was in a volume and character so familiar
and inward to us (for it was written in our hearts, and by
Nature) as needed no Expositor: And that part which was
vocall, and delivered by Edict and Proclamation, was so   15
short, so perspicuous, and so easie (for it was but pro-
hibitory, and exacted nothing from Man) as it is one of the
greatest strangenesses in the Story, that they could so soon
forget the Text thereof, and not espy the Serpents additions and falsifications. And then at last God interposed   20
his *Justice*; yet not so much for *Justice* sake, as to get
opportunitie of *new Mercy*, in promising a Redeemer; of
new Power, in raising again bodies made mortall by that
sin; and of *new Judgments*, in delivering, upon more com-
munications, a more particular law, apparelled with Cere-   25
monies, the cement and mortar of all exterior, and often
the inflamer of interior Religion. So that almost all Gods
Justice is but Mercy: as all our Mercy is but Justice; for
we are all mutuall debtors to one another; but he to none.
Yea, both his *Nature*, and his *will* are so condition'd, as he   30
cannot do Justice so much as man can. For, for his *will*,
though he neither will nor can do any thing *against* Justice,
he doth many things *beside* it. Nothing unjustly, but many
things not justly: for he rewards beyond our Merits, and
our sins are beyond his punishments. And then, we have   35
exercise as well of Commutative Justice as Distributive;
God only of the later, since he can receive nothing from
us. And indeed, Distributive Justice in God, is nothing
but Mercy. So that there is but one limb of Justice left to

God, which is Punishment; And of that, all the degrees
on this side finall condemnation, are acts of Mercy. So that Pierius
the *Vulture*, by which some of the Ancients figured *Justice*, li. 18.
was a just symbole of this Justice; for as that bird prayes
5 onely upon Carcasses, and upon nothing which lives; so
this Justice apprehends none but such as are dead and
putrified in sin and impenitence.

To proceed then: All ordinary significations of *Justice*
will conveniently be reduced to these two, *Innocence*,
10 which in the Scriptures is every where called Righteous-
nesse: or else *Satisfaction* for transgressions, which, though
Christ have paid aforehand for us all, and so we are rather
pardoned then put to satisfaction; yet we are bound at
Gods tribunall to plead our pardon, and to pay the fees
15 of contrition and penance. For, since our justification now
consists not in a pacification of God, (for then nothing
but that which is infinite could have any proportion) but
in the application of the merits of Christ to us, our contrition (which is a compassion with Christ, and so an in-
20 corporating of our selves into his merit) hath *aliqualem*
proportionem to Gods Justice; and the passion of Christ
had not *æqualem*, but that Gods acceptation (which also
dignifies our contrition, though not to that height) ad-
vanced it to that worthinesse. To enquire further the way
25 and manner by which God makes a few do acceptable
works; or, how out of a corrupt lumpe he selects and
purifies a few, is but a stumbling block and a tentation:
Who asks a charitable man that gives him an almes, where
he got it, or why he gave it? will any favorite, whom his
30 Prince only for his appliableness to him, or some half-
vertue, or his own glory, burdens with Honours and
Fortunes every day, and destines to future Offices and
Dignities, dispute or expostulate with his Prince, why he
rather chose not another, how he will restore his Coffers;
35 how he will quench his peoples murmurings, by whom
this liberality is fed; or his Nobility, with whom he equalls
new men; and will not rather repose himself gratefully in
the wisdome, greatness and bounty of his Master? Will
a languishing desperate patient, that hath scarce time

enough to swallow the potion, examine the Physician, how
he procured those ingredients, how that soyle nourished
them, which humor they affect in the body, whether they
work by excess of quality, or specifically; whether he have
prepared them by correcting, or else by withdrawing their 5
Malignity; and for such unnecessary scruples neglect his
health? Alas, our time is little enough for prayer, and
praise, and society; which is, for our mutuall duties. Morall
Divinity becomes us all; but Naturall Divinity, and Meta-
physick Divinity, almost all may spare. Almost all the 10
ruptures in the Christian Church have been occasioned by
such bold disputations *De Modo*. One example is too much.
That our Blessed Saviours body is in the Sacrament, all
say; The *Roman* Church appoints it to be there by *Transubstantiation*. The needless multiplying of Miracles for 15
that opinion hath moved the *French* and *Helvetick* reformed Churches to find the word Sacramentally; which,
because it puts the body there, and yet no nearer then
Heaven to Earth, seems a riddle to the *Saxon* and such
Churches; whose modesty (though not clearness) seems 20
greatest in this Point; since beleeving the reall being of it
there, they abstain generally (though some bold adven-
turers amongst them also do exorbitate) from pronouncing
De Modo. The like tempests hath the inquisition *De Modo*,
rais'd in the article of Descent into Hell, even in our 25
Church; and of the conveyance of Gods grace (which was
the occasion of this digression) in the *Roman* at this day.
But to decline this sad contemplation, and to further our
selves in the Meditation of Gods justice declared in this
History, let me observe to you, that God in his Scriptures 30
hath Registred especially three symbols or Sacraments,
of use in this matter. One in *Genesis*, of pure and meer
Justice, vindicative, and permanent; which is, The *Cheru-
bim and fiery sword* placed in Paradise, to *keep out*, not only
Adam, but his *Posterity*. The second in *Exodus*, of *pure* 35
and *only Mercy*, which is the modell and fabrick of the
Mercy seate, under the shadow of two Cherubims wings.
The third, partaking of both *Mercy* and *Justice*, and a
Memoriall and seal of both, is the *Rainebow* after the

Cha. 3. 22.

Ch. 25. 17.

Gen. 9. 14.

Deluge. The first of these, which is of *meer Justice*, is so figurative, and so mystick, and so unfit for Example or consequence, and so disputable whether it lasted long, or ever were literally, that it seems God had no purpose to 5 deliver any evident testimony of so severe and *meer Justice*. But that of *meer Mercy*, he made so familiar, that only devising the form himself, he committed the making of it to man: and so affiancing and binding his Mercy to mans work, did, as it were, put his Mercy into our hands. Yet 10 that also is long since translated from us: and there remains only the middle one, more convenient, and proportionall, and usefull. For, as it betokens his Justice in the precedent deluge, or his Mercy in assuring us from any future; so is it made of naturall and well known causes, 15 (and thereby familiar to us) and yet became a Sacrament by Gods speciall institution then. And though it should be true which *Chrysostome* says, That it was a new miracle *Hom.* 28. then, and never appeared before; yea, though that could *in Gen.* be true which *Ambrose*, somewhat against the text, and *De Noe* 20 directly against the other Expositors, says, That the *Bow* *et Arca,* mentioned there was not a *Rainbow*, but that *A bow in the* *cap.* 27. *clouds*, signifies only, *The power of God in persecution*, and thereupon he observes, that God says, *A Bow*, but says not *Arrows*, to inflict terror, not wounds; Every way, I say, it 25 doth the office of remembring Gods Justice and Mercy together. And accordingly, in this large and particular History of Gods Justice and Persecution, both towards his children, and his enemies, if we consider their laborious waste and maceratings of their bodies by hot and intem- 30 perate labour; All their contempts, and scorns, and aviling, and annihilating in the eye of the Egyptians; All their Orbity, and enfeebling their race by the Edict of destroying their male children; All their deviations and strayings forty years, in a passage of a few dayes; and all their 35 penuries and battels in that journey; And then for the Egyptians, if we looke upon all their afflictions, first of plagues hatefull to their senses, then noisome to their fruites, then to their cattel, then to their bodies, then to their posterity, then to their lives, excepting only the

drowning of the Egyptians in the sea, and the killing
of the Israelites by their own hands in their guiltinesse of
Idolatry with the Calfe, it will scarce be found that any
of the afflictions proceeded from meer Justice, but were
rather as Physick, and had only a medicinall bitternesse in 5
them. It remains, for determination of this Meditation,
that we speake a little of Gods Judgements.

And at this time, (as by infinite places in the Scriptures
we are directed) we call Gods Judgements, all those lawes
and directions by which he hath informed the Judgements 10
of his children, and by which he governes his Judgements
with or against them. For otherwise this word *Judgement*
hath also three profane, and three Divine acceptations. Of
the first sort, the first serves contemplations only, and so,
Judgement is the last act of our understanding, and a con- 15
clusive resolution: which both in private studies, and at
Counsail tables, many want, though endued with excellent
abilities of objecting, disputing, infirming, yea destroying
others allegations; yet are not able to establish or propose
any other from themselves. These men, whether you con- 20
sult them in Religion, or State, or Law, onely when they
are joyned with others, have good use, because they bring
doubts into disceptation; else, they are, at least, unprofitable: and are but as Simplicists, which know the venom
and peccant quality of every herbe, but cannot fit them to 25
Medicin; or such a Lapidary, which can soone spie the
flaw, but not mend it with setting. Judgement in the
Second acceptation serves for practice, and is almost synoni-
mous with Discretion; when we consider not so much the
thing which we then do, as the whole frame and machine 30
of the businesse, as it is complexioned and circumstanced
with time, and place, and beholders:[1] and so, make a thing,
which was at most but indifferent, good. The *third* way,
Judgment serves not only present practice, but enlightens,
and almost governs posterity; and these are Decrees 35
and Sentences, and Judgments in Courts. The phrase of
Divinity also accepts Judgment three wayes; for somtimes
it is severe and meer Justice, as, [*Judgment must begin at*

1 Pet. 4. 17.[2]   [1] beholders] behoders *1651*.   [2] 1 Pet. 4. 17.] 1 Pet. 4. 7. *1651*.

the house of God,] And many such. And Judgment in this
sense, is deep and unsearchable. For, though *Solomon* pronounce, [*There is a just man that perisheth in his justice*, Eccl. 7.
and there is a wicked man that continueth long in his malice;] 15.¹
5 yet he enquires for no reason of it; For, [*Gods righteousness* Ps. 36. 6.
is like the mountains] eminent and inviting our contemplation towards Heaven; but, [*his Judgments are like a great
deep*,] terrible and bottomless, and declining us towards
the center of horrour and desperation. *These judgments* we
10 cannot measure nor fathome; yet, for all that, we must
more then beleeve them to be just; for the Apostle says,
We know the Judgement of God is according to truth. But Rom. 2. 2.
yet oftentimes Judgement signifies not *meer Justice*, but
as it is attempred and sweetned with Mercy. For, by the
15 phrase of the Psalmist, [*Judicabit populum in Justitia, et* Ps. 72. 2.
pauperes in Judicio] and many such, the Cabalists (as one Reuch. de
which understood them well, observes) have concluded, *Arte*
that the word *Judgment* applyed to *God*, hath every where *Cabal. l. 1.*
a mixt and participant nature, and intimates both *Justice*
20 and *Mercy*. And thirdly the *Talmudists* have straitned the
word, and restrain'd *Judgment* to signifie only the *Judiciall*
part of the law: and say, the Holy Ghost so directed them,
in *Deut.* [*These are the commandments, and the Ceremonies,
and the Judgments, which the Lord commanded.*] And they
25 proceeed further; for, Because Gods Covenant and his ten Deu. 4. 13.
Commandements are said simply to be given them, and
without any limitation of time or place, they confess, they
are bound to them ever, and every where; but, because
his Ordinances and his law, (which in the Original is,
30 *Ceremonies and Judgments*) are thus delivered, [*You shall* Ver. 5.
keep them in the Land which you go to possesse] they there- *Galatinus,*
fore now cut off Ceremonies and Judgements, from the *l. 11. c. 3.*
body of the law, and in their dispersion bind not themselves to them, but where they may with convenience
35 enough. But here we take the word *Judgment* intirely, to
signifie *all* the law: for, so the Psalmist² speaks, [*He showes* Ps. 147. 19.
*his word unto Jacob, his Statutes and his Judgments unto
Israel; he hath not dealt so with every Nation, nor have they*

¹ Eccl. 7. 15.] Eccl. 7. 17. *1651*.   ² Psalmist] Psalmists *1651*.

known his Judgements]. For here *Judgements* are as much
as *all* the rest. And God himself in that last peice of his,
Deut. which he commanded *Moses* to record, that Heavenly
32. 4. Song which onely himself compos'd, (for though every
other poetick part of Scripture, be also Gods word, and 5
so made by him, yet all the rest were Ministerially and
instrumentally delivered by the Prophets, onely inflamed
by him; but this which himself cals a Song, was made
immediately by himself, and *Moses* was commanded to
deliver it to the Children; God choosing this way and 10
conveyance of a Song, as fittest to justifie his future severi-
ties against his children, because he knew that they would
ever be repeating this Song, (as the Delicacy, and Elegancy
therof, both for Divinity and Poetry, would invite any
to that) and so he should draw from their own mouthes a 15
confession of his benefits, and of their ingratitude;) in this
Song, I say, himself best expresses the value of this word
thus, [*All my wayes are Judgement.*]

　　The greatness of this benefit or blessing of giving them
a law, was not that salvation was due to the fulfilling of it; 20
nor were they bound to a perfect fulfilling of it upon
damnation; for, Salvation was ever from a faith in the
promise of the *Messias*; and accordingly the Apostle
Gal. 3. 17. reasons strongly, [*The promise of Christ to Abraham was
430 years before the law, and therefore this cannot dis-annull* 25
that] and yet this to *Abraham* was but an iteration of the
promise formerly given, and iterated often. But one benefit
of the Law was, that it did in some measure restore them
towards the first light of Nature: For, if man had kept
that, he had needed no outward law; for then he was to 30
himself a law, having all law in his heart; as God promiseth
for one of the greatest blessings under the Gospel, when
Jer. 31. the Law of Nature is more cleerly restored: [*I will make
33.¹ a new Covenant, and put my law in their inward parts and
write it in their hearts:*] So that we are brought neerer 35
home, and set in a fairer way then the Jews; though their
Tho.[Aq.] and our Law differ not as diverse in species; but as a
2ᵃ.²q.60.³

5.　　¹ Jer. 31. 33.] Jer. 13. 31. *1651.*　　　　　² 2ᵃ.] 12ᵃ. *1651.*
　　　³ q. 60. J: q. 51. *1651.*

perfect and grown thing from an unperfect and growing:
for to that first Law all Laws aspire. As we may observe
in the Jews, who, after the Law of Nature was clouded
and darkened in man by sin, framed to themselves many
5 directive laws, before the promulgation of this Law in the
Desert. For we may easily trace out, besides Circumcision, Bertram.[1]
(which was commanded) Sabboths, Sacrifices of divers De politia[2]
sorts, Expiatory and Eucharisticall, Vows, Excommunica- Judaica.
tion, Buriall and Marriage, before the written Law. But c. 2.
10 these had but half the nature of Law; they did direct, but
not correct; they did but counsell, not command: and
they were not particular enough to do that office fully; for
they shew'd not all. Therefore Saint *Paul* sayes of *Moses's*
Law, and the sufficiency of it, *By the Law comes the know-* Ro. 3. 20.
15 *ledge of sin.* And in another place, *Where no Law is, there* Ro. 4. 15.
is no transgression: And again, *When the Commandement* Rom. 7. 9.
came, sin revived; that is, it revived to his understanding
and conscience: For, that sin was before any written commandement, himself cleers it; *Unto the time of the Law was* Ro. 5. 13.[3]
20 *sin in the world; but sin is not imputed when there is no law.*
Not that God imputes it not; (for there is always enough
within us for him to try us by; and his written Laws are
but Declaratory of the former;) but we impute it not to
our selves, by confession and repentance. This therefore is
25 the benefit of the Law, that (as *Calvin* upon this place
sayes) *Arguit, objurgat, et vellicando nos expergefacit.* We
read in *Leviticus, That a Blasphemer was stoned,* and after Lev. 24.
his execution a law was made against Blasphemers: If it had 10.
been made before, perchance he had not perished. Often-
30 times lawes, though they be ambiguous, yea impossible,
avert men from doing many things, which may, in their
fear, be drawn within the compass of that Law. Not to
go far for Examples; without doubt, our Law which makes
Multiplication Felony, keeps many from doing things
35 which may be so called, for any thing they know, though
perchance no body know what *Multiplication* is. And our
Law, which makes it Felony to feed a Spirit, holds many

---

[1] *Bertram* J: *Bretram* 1651.   [2] *politia* J: *politica* 1651.
[3] Ro. 5. 13.] Ro. 3. 15. *1651.*

from that melancholick and mischievous beleef of making
such an express Covenant with the Divell, though every
body know[1] it is impossible to feed a spirit. Another benefit
of the law, (taking the law at large, for all the Scriptures,
Galat. 4. as the Apostle doth, [*Tell me, you that are under the law,*
[21]. *have you not read in the law,* etc.] and then cites a place out
of *Genesis*, before the law was given; And as Saint *John*
Joh. 15. 25. says, [*It is written in the law*] and then cites the 35 *Psalm*)
is, that it hath prepar'd us to Christ, by manifold and
evident prophesies. Which use the Apostle makes of it
Gal. 3. 24. thus, [*Before faith came* (that is to say, the fulfilling of
faith, for faith was ever) *we were kept under the law, and
shut up unto the faith which should after be revealed: wherefore the law was our schoolmaster to bring us to Christ.*]
Lastly, the law benefits us thus, that it wrastles with that
other law which St Paul found himselfe not only subject
Rom. 7. to, but slave to, [*I am Captive to the law of sin.*] And, [*I
23.*[2] *serve in my flesh the law of sin.*] These then were the advan-
tages of the law; And had it any disadvantages? It is true,
the laws were many; for, as the frame of our body hath
Fra. Geor. 248 bones, so the body of the law had so many affirmative
To. 2. precepts; and of the same number consisted *Abrahams*
prob. 8. name, to whose seed the *Messias*, to whose knowledg all
the law conduced, was promised. It hath also 365 negative
precepts; and so many sinews and ligatures hath our body,
and so many dayes the year. But, not to pursue these
curiosities, besides that, multiplicity of laws, (because
thereby little is left to the discretion of the Judg) is not
so burdenous as it is thought, except it be in a captious,
and entangling, and needy State; or under a Prince too
indulgent to his own Prerogative: All this great number of
Galatinus. lawes are observed by one, who (*Capnio* says) was breath'd
l. 11. c. 4. upon by the Holy Ghost, to have been reduced by *David*
to 11, by *Esay* to 6, by *Micheas* to 3, and by *Abacuc* to one.
The Lawgiver himself reduced them in the *Decalogue* to
ten, and therefore the Cabalists marke mysteriously, that
Fra. Geor. in the Decalogue there are just so many letters, as there
ibid. are precepts in the whole law. Yet certainly the number

¹ know] knows *J.*   ² Rom. 7. 23.] Rom. 7. 13. *1651.*

and intricacy and perplexity of these laws, (for their later Bux-
Rabins, which make the Orall law their rule, insist upon dorfius
many both contradictions and imperfections in the letter Synag.
of this law,) was extremely burdenous to the punctuall c. 4. fo. 44.
5 observers thereof. Yet, to say peremptorily that it could
not be observed, seems to me, hasty. Though Calvin,
citing Saint Hierome, [Si quis dixerit, impossibile esse ser- Marlorate
vare legem, Anathema sit] say wisely and truly, that Hierom in hunc
must not prevail so much as he which says, Why tempt locum.
10 you God, to lay a yoke upon the Disciples necks, which neither Act. 15.
our Fathers nor we are able to bear? Yet that place in 10.
Deut. 30. 8. hath as much Authority as this [Do all the
Commandements which I command thee this day;] therefore
they might be done. And in another verse it is said of all
15 the Commandments, laws and Ordinances together, [This
Commandement is not hid from thee, nor far off; It is not
in heaven, that thou shouldest say, who shall go up, and bring
it down; nor beyond sea, that thou shouldst say, who shal go
beyond sea and fetch it: but it is near thee, in thy mouth, and
20 in thy heart.] For, though the Prophet in Gods person say,
Dedi eis præcepta non bona; it was but in comparison of the Eze.20.25.
laws of the Gospel: As our Saviour calls his Apostles evill
comparatively; [Yee which are evill, can give good things.] Mat. 7. 11.
For simply, the law was good; And, as Chrysostome says, so Homil. ad
25 easie, that they were easier things which were commanded Rom. 13.
by the written law, then by the law of Nature: As, to my in ver. 25.
understanding, in the point of concupisence it is evident; Rom.
which in the first Law of Nature, and now in the Gospel,
is prohibited, but was not so in the letter of the written
30 law. So much therefore as was required of them, (for so
Calvin says) that is, to make the law a bridle, and a direc- Ibid.
tion to them, was possible to them: and he concludes this
point, and I with him, That even the regenerate do but
half that themselves, the grace of God perfecting the rest.

FINIS

PRAYERS

⟨1⟩

O Eternall God, as thou didst admit thy faithfull servant
Abraham, *to make the granting of one petition an incourage-*
ment and rise to another, and gavest him leave to gather upon
thee from fifty to ten; so I beseech thee, that since by thy
grace, I have thus long meditated upon thee, and spoken of 5
thee, I may now speak to thee. As thou hast enlightned and
enlarged me to contemplate thy greatness, so, O God, descend
thou and stoop down to see my infirmities and the Egypt in
which I live; and (If thy good pleasure be such) hasten mine
Exodus *and deliverance, for I desire to be dissolved,[1] and be* 10
with thee. O Lord, I most humbly acknowledg and confess
thine infinite Mercy, that when thou hadst almost broke the
staff of bread, and called a famine of thy word almost upon
all the world, then thou broughtest me into this Egypt, where
thou hadst appointed thy stewards to husband thy blessings, 15
and to feed thy flock. Here also, O God, thou hast multiplied
thy children in me, by begetting and cherishing in me reverent
devotions, and pious affections towards thee, but that mine
own corruption, mine own Pharaoh *hath ever smothered and*
strangled them. And thou hast put me in my way towards thy 20
land of promise, thy Heavenly Canaan, *by removing me from*
the Egypt of frequented and populous, glorious places, to a
more solitary and desart retirednes, where I may more safely
feed upon both thy Mannaes, *thy self in thy Sacrament, and*
that other, which is true Angells food, contemplation of thee. 25
O Lord, I most humbly acknowledg and confess, that I feel
in me so many strong effects of thy Power, as only for the
Ordinariness and frequency thereof, they are not Miracles.
For hourly thou rectifiest my lameness, hourly thou restorest
my sight, and hourly not only deliverest me from the Egypt, 30
but raisest me from the death of sin. My sin, O God, hath not
onely caused thy descent hither, and passion here; but by it
I am become that hell into which thou descendedst after thy
Passion; yea, after thy glorification: for hourly thou in thy

[1] *be dissolved] be, disolved* 1651.

Spirit descendest into my heart, to overthrow there Legions of spirits of Disobedience, and Incredulity, and Murmuring. O Lord, I most humbly acknowledg and confesse, that by thy Mercy I have a sense of thy Justice; for not onely those afflic-
5 *tions with which it pleaseth thee to exercise mee, awaken me to consider how terrible thy severe justice is; but even the rest and security which thou affordest mee, puts me often into fear, that thou reservest and sparest me for a greater measure of punishment. O Lord, I most humbly acknowledg and confesse,*
10 *that I have understood sin, by understanding thy laws and judgments; but have done against thy known and revealed will. Thou hast set up many candlesticks, and kindled many lamps in mee; but I have either blown them out, or carried them to guide me in by and forbidden ways. Thou hast given*
15 *mee a desire of knowledg, and some meanes to it, and some possession of it; and I have arm'd my self with thy weapons against thee: Yet, O God, have mercy upon me, for thine own sake have mercy upon me. Let not sin and me be able to exceed thee, nor to defraud thee, nor to frustrate thy purposes:*
20 *But let me, in despite of Me, be of so much use to thy glory, that by thy mercy to my sin, other sinners may see how much sin thou canst pardon. Thus show mercy to many in one: And shew thy power and al-mightinesse upon thy self, by casting manacles upon thine own hands, and calling back those*
25 *Thunder-bolts which thou hadst thrown against mee. Show thy Justice upon the common Seducer and Devourer of us all: and show to us so much of thy Judgments, as may instruct, not condemn us. Hear us, O God, hear us, for this contrition which thou hast put into us, who come to thee with that watch-*
30 *word, by which thy Son hath assured us of access.* Our Father which art in Heaven, *etc.*

⟨2⟩

O Eternal God, who art not only first and last, but in whom, first and last is all one, who art not only all Mercy, and all Justice, but in whom Mercy and Justice is all one; who in the
35 *height of thy Justice, wouldest not spare thine own, and only most innocent Son; and yet in the depth of thy mercy, would'st not have the wretched'st liver come to destruction; Behold us,*

O God, here gathered together in thy fear, according to thine ordinance, and in confidence of thy promise, that when two or three are gathered together in thy name, thou wilt be in the midst of them, and grant them their petitions. We confess, O God, that we are not worthy so much as to confess; less to be heard, least of all to be pardoned our manifold sins and transgressions against thee. We have betrayed thy Temples to prophaness, our bodies to sensuality, thy fortresses to thine enemy, our soules to Satan. We have armed him with thy munition to fight against thee, by surrendring our eyes, and eares, all our senses, all our faculties to be exercised and wrought upon, and tyrannized by him. Vanities and disguises have covered us, and thereby we are naked; licenciousness hath inflam'd us, and thereby we are frozen; voluptuousness hath fed us, and thereby we are sterved, the fancies and traditions of men have taught and instructed us, and thereby we are ignorant. These distempers, thou only, O God, who art true, and perfect harmonie, canst tune, and rectify, and set in order again. Doe so then, O most Mercifull Father, for thy most innocent Sons sake: and since he hath spread his armes upon the cross, to receive the whole world, O Lord, shut out none of us (who are now fallen before the throne of thy Majesty and thy Mercy) from the benefit of his merits; but with as many of us, as begin their conversion and newness of life, this minute, this minute, O God, begin thou thy account with them, and put all that is past out of thy remembrance. Accept our humble thanks for all thy Mercies; and, continue and enlarge them upon the whole Church, etc.

⟨3⟩

O Most glorious and most gracious God, into whose presence our own consciences make us afraid to come, and from whose presence we cannot hide our selves, hide us in the wounds of thy Son, our Saviour Christ Jesus; And though our sins be as red as scarlet, give them there another redness, which may be acceptable in thy sight. We renounce, O Lord, all our confidence in this world; for this world passeth away, and the lusts thereof: Wee renounce all our confidence in our own merits, for we have done nothing in respect of that which we might have

done; neither could we ever have done any such thing, but
that still we must have remained unprofitable servants to thee;
we renounce all confidence, even in our own confessions, and
accusations of our self;[1] for our sins are above number, if we
5 would reckon them; above weight and measure, if we would
weigh and measure them; and past finding out, if we would
seek them in those dark corners, in which we have multiplied
them against thee: yea we renounce all confidence even in our
repentances; for we have found by many lamentable experi-
10 ences, that we never perform our promises to thee, never perfect
our purposes in our selves, but relapse again and again into
those sins which again and again we have repented. We have
no confidence in this world, but in him who hath taken possession of the next world for us, by sitting down at thy right
15 hand. We have no confidence in our merits, but in him, whose
merits thou hast been pleased to accept for us, and to apply to
us, we have: no confidence in our own confessions and repentances, but in that blessed Spirit, who is the Author of them,
and loves to perfect his own works and build upon his own
20 foundations, we have: Accept them therefore, O Lord, for
their sakes whose they are; our poor endeavours, for thy
glorious Sons sake, who gives them their root, and so they are
his; our poor beginnings of sanctification, for thy blessed
Spirits sake, who gives them their growth, and so they are his:
25 and for thy Sons sake, in whom only our prayers are acceptable to thee: and for thy Spirits sake which is now in us, and
must be so whensoever we do pray acceptably to thee; accept
our humble prayers for, etc.

⟨4⟩

O Eternal and most merciful God, against whom, as we
30 know and acknowledg that we have multiplied contemptuous
and rebellious sins, so we know and acknowledg too, that it
were a more sinfull contempt and rebellion, then all[2] those, to
doubt of thy mercy for them; have mercy upon us: In the
merits and mediation of thy Son, our Saviour Christ Jesus, be
35 mercifull unto us. Suffer not, O Lord, so great a waste, as the
effusion of his blood, without any return to thee; suffer not the

<hr />

[1] our self] ourselves J. [2] all] in all J.

expence of so rich a treasure, as the spending of his life, without any purchace to thee; but as thou didst empty and evacuate his glory here upon earth, glorify us with that glory which his humiliation purchased for us in the kingdom of Heaven. And as thou didst empty that Kingdome of thine, in a great part, by the banishment of those Angels, whose pride threw them into everlasting ruine, be pleased to repair that Kingdom, which their fall did so far depopulate, by assuming us into their places, and making us rich with their confiscations. And to that purpose, O Lord, make us capable of that succession to thine Angels there; begin in us here in this life an angelicall purity, an angelicall chastity, an angelicall integrity to thy service, an Angelical acknowledgment that we alwaies stand in thy presence, and should direct al our actions to thy glory. Rebuke us not, O Lord, in thine anger, that we have not done so till now; but enable us now to begin that great work; and imprint in us an assurance that thou receivest us now graciously, as reconciled, though enemies; and fatherly, as children, though prodigals; and powerfully, as the God of our salvation, though our own consciences testifie against us. Continue and enlarge thy blessings upon the whole Church, etc.

FINIS

SOURCES OF THE ESSAYS IN DIVINITY

Donne drew his material from different sources, of which the most important were the Scriptures, including the Apocrypha, the Fathers, and the Renaissance commentators. His wide knowledge of the Scriptures is evident in the first two essays, in which he begins with Genesis, passes at once to the book of Revelation, then to St. Matthew, Proverbs, Daniel, 1 Corinthians, Deuteronomy, Ezekiel, Revelation, St. John, Ecclesiasticus, Isaiah, Romans, and Exodus. He quotes these from the Vulgate or from the Geneva Version, not from the Hebrew or Greek, or from the Authorized Version. This last point is particularly noticeable in the quotations from Ecclesiasticus, where Donne uses the Geneva, which is widely different from the Authorized Version.[1]

It is difficult to decide how much material he drew directly from the Fathers, and how much from the great commentaries of Pererius, Paraeus, Calvin, and others,[2] who summarized the opinions of the Fathers on doubtful points. He certainly knew Augustine at first hand, and quoted him at considerable length. After Donne's ordination he studied the Latin Fathers assiduously, but at this early stage he may well have relied chiefly on the commentaries. The one to which Donne refers most often is the fine four-volume *Commentaria et disputationes in Genesim* of the Spanish Jesuit, Benedictus Pererius. This was popular with Protestants as well as with Catholics, and Raleigh made extensive use of it in the first five chapters of his *History of the World*, published in 1614. There is a certain resemblance between his first three chapters and the early sections of the *Essays*, which is due to Raleigh's and Donne's common dependence on Pererius. To him

[1] See note on p. 110.
[2] See Arnold Williams, *The Common Expositor: An Account of the Commentaries on Genesis, 1527–1633*, University of North Carolina Press, 1948, pp. 7–19.

they both owe their allusions to Orpheus, Linus, Zoroaster, Hermes Trismegistus, and the like, as possible rivals in antiquity as authors to Moses. Donne makes no secret of his debt to Pererius, though he sometimes questions the soundness of the latter's arguments. Thus he remarks: '*Pererius* seems peremtory that no Author is elder ⟨then Moses⟩. . . . But if we shall escape this, that *Abraham*'s booke *De formationibus* is yet alive, by suspecting and pronouncing it supposititious . . . how shall we deliver our selves from *Zoroasters* Oracles? whom *Epiphanius* places in *Nembrots* time, and *Eusebius* in *Abraham's*.'[1] Pererius is quoted again on pages 10, 19, 27, 52, 74.

Donne also made use of the great medieval commentary of Nicholas de Lyra, and of the fifteenth-century commentary of Tostatus, as well as of the sixteenth-century commentaries of Calvin, Buntingus, Drusius, Paraeus, and Pellicanus.

As for the Schoolmen, he drew freely on the great work of St. Thomas Aquinas, the *Summa Theologiae*, with which he had long been familiar. He also made use of the works of Duns Scotus.

Certain Christian Cabalists of the Renaissance, such as Pico della Mirandola, Francis George (F. Zorgi), and the German humanist Reuchlin, are often quoted or referred to by Donne. Among writers on science he mentions Paracelsus, who had evolved a new system of medicine, William Gilbert, who had written on terrestrial magnetism, and he alludes to Galileo's invention of the telescope. He also mentions the work of the Jesuit mathematician Clavius.

The *Essays* are enlivened by a number of allusions to classical Latin authors such as Lucretius, Horace, Martial, Juvenal, Cicero, Seneca, and Diogenes Laertius. Donne had long been familiar with most of these, and quotations

---

[1] *Supra*, pp. 11–12. Donne's argument is unsound in this particular instance, but it is an interesting example of his independence of mind. On p. 15 he again rejects the opinion of Pererius. On pp. 17, 18, 32, 60, 72, 83, 89 Pererius, though not mentioned by name, is evidently the authority on whom Donne is drawing.

from them would come quickly to his mind, but I believe
that Lucretius is quoted nowhere else in his works. Probably Donne found his two short citations from the first
two books of the *De Rerum Natura* in one or other of the
commentaries or *Florilegia*.

An alphabetical list of the less well-known authors
quoted in the *Essays*, with a few biographical details, is
appended for the convenience of readers. It does not
include classical writers, nor any of the Fathers. For the
information contained in it I am considerably indebted
to Miss Ramsay's biographical lists in *Les Doctrines médiévales chez Donne*, but I have also used encyclopaedias,
French, German, and Italian, as well as English.

ACACIUS (Georg Enenckel, Baron von Hoheneck, late sixteenth and
early seventeenth century), an antiquary whose *De privilegiis
juris civilis* (Frankfort, 1606) was used by Donne here and in
Biathanatos.

ACOSTA (José, 1539?–1600), a Spanish Jesuit who helped to evangel-
ize the American Indians. Donne quotes his book *De promulgando
evangelio apud Barbaros, sive de procuranda Indorum salute* (1588).

ALTHEMERUS (André Althamer, 1498–1540), a Lutheran pastor,
also known as Andreas Brentius. Donne quotes his *Diallage, sive
conciliatio locorum scripturae* (1528).

ARCHANGELUS (Pozzo Archangelo da Borgo-Nuovo) wrote *Cabali-
starum selectiora obscuraque dogmata* (1569) and *Apologia pro de-
fensione doctrinae caballae* (1600).

AZORIUS (Juan Azor, 1533–1603), a Spanish Jesuit, whose *Institutiones Morales* is quoted also in *Biathanatos* (pp. 84, 130) and the
Sermons.

BALDUS (1327–1400), professor of law at Bologna. Donne refers to
him also in *Biathanatos*, *Pseudo-Martyr*, and the *Sermons*.

BERTRAM (Bonaventure-Corneille, 1531–94), a French scholar who
retired to Geneva and taught Hebrew there, and at Lausanne
(M. P. Ramsay).

BIBLIANDER (Buchmann, *c.* 1504–64), a Protestant theologian and
orientalist, who with Melanchthon produced an edition of the
Koran.

BUNTINGUS (H. Bunting, 1545–1606), a German Protestant theologian, wrote a number of books on the Scriptures, among them being *Harmonia Evangelistarum* and *De Monetis et Mensuris Scripturae Sacrae* (1583).

BUXDORFIUS (Johann Buxdorf, 1564–1629), a German Hebrew scholar, wrote *Synagoga Judaica* (1603) and other books on Jewish subjects. He is quoted in *Biathanatos* (p. 95) and the *Sermons*.

CAJETAN (Thomas de Vio, 1470–1534), a Dominican who became General of the Order, and finally a Cardinal. He wrote biblical commentaries to which Donne has many references in the *Sermons*.

CANISIUS (De Hondt, 1520–97), a Dutch Jesuit, who took part in the Council of Trent. Donne quotes his *Summa Doctrinae Christianae* and his *Institutiones Christianae Pietatis* (Ramsay).

CASTRENSIS (Alfonso, 1495–1558), a Spanish Franciscan. Donne quotes his *De justa haereticorum punitione* and *De Sortilegis*. He is mentioned in *Biathanatos* (p. 68).

CATHARINUS (Ambrosius, 1487–1553), bishop of Naples, a prolific author, who wrote commentaries on Genesis and the epistles of St. Paul, and other theological works to which Donne alludes in the *Sermons*.

CHASSANAEUS or CASSANAEUS (Barthélemy de Chasseneux, 1480–1541), a French lawyer whose *Catalogus gloriae mundi* is quoted also in *Biathanatos*.

CHEMNITIUS (Martin Chemnitz, 1522–86), who wrote *Examen Concilii Tridenti* (1585) and a number of other works.

CLAVIUS (Christopher, 1537–1612), a Jesuit mathematician who worked at the reform of the calendar. He wrote a commentary on the *De Sphaera* of Sacrobosco, which went through many editions. Coffin (*John Donne and the New Philosophy*, p. 88) gives reason for thinking that Donne's reference to it here must be to the 1607 edition.

COMITOLUS (Paolo, 1545–1626), an Italian Jesuit whose *Consilia, seu Responsa Moralia* (1609) is quoted by Donne.

CUSANUS (Nicholas de Cusa, 1401–64), Cardinal, mathematician, and neo-platonist. Donne quotes him also in *Pseudo-Martyr*.

DANAEUS (Lambert Daneau), a French Calvinist theologian whose *Opuscula Omnia Theologica* were collected in 1583.

DONATUS (Marcellus, sixteenth century, dates uncertain), a Florentine whose notes on Suetonius are quoted by Donne.

DRUSIUS (Jan van der Driesche, 1550–1616), a Dutchman who taught oriental languages at Oxford and Leyden. He wrote a commentary on the Pentateuch, and also *Tetragrammaton, seu de Nomine Dei proprio* (1604).

FESTUS (Rufus), a Latin historian of the fourth century A.D. Donne refers to his *De Victoriis et Provinciis Populi Romani*, first published in 1472.

GALATINUS (Petrus), a Jew, who after his conversion to Christianity became a Franciscan friar. In the tenth book of his *De Arcanis Catholicae Veritatis* (1572), to which Donne here alludes, he attempted to prove that the sacraments of Baptism, Penance, and the Eucharist, as well as the doctrine of Transubstantiation, were predicted in the Talmud.

GEORGE, Francis (Franciscus Georgius Venetus, or F. Zorgi), whose *De Harmonia Mundi totius cantica* (1525) was a medley of neo-Pythagorean and cabalistic ideas, is also mentioned in *Biathanatos* and *Catalogus Librorum*.

GERSON (Johannes, 1363–1429), Chancellor of the University of Paris, author of *De Auferibilitate Papae, De Laude Scriptorum*, and many other works. Donne quotes him also in *Biathanatos* and the *Sermons*.

GILBERT (William, 1540–1603) made an important contribution to the scientific literature of his time by his book on terrestrial magnetism, *De Magnete* (1600).

GOROPIUS (Becanus, or Becannus, van Gorp, 1518–72), an eccentric Flemish scholar who tried to prove that High Dutch, or German, was the original language of Adam in Paradise. Richard Verstegen (Rowlands) in *A Restitution of Decayed Intelligence* (1605) gave currency in English to his speculations. Ben Jonson made fun of them in *The Alchemist*, II. i. 85–86.

HEURNIUS (Otho van Heurn, born 1577) wrote *Antiquitatum Philosophiae Barbariae libri II* (1600), in which the oracles of Zoroaster are discussed. Donne quotes it also in *Biathanatos* (pp. 55, 106).

HUNNIUS (Aegidius, 1550–1603), a German Protestant theologian, wrote many controversial works, including *Articulus de SS. Trinitate per Quaestiones et Responsiones . . .* (1592). About 1596 he had a controversy with Paraeus.

LYRA, Nicholas of (1270–1340), professor at Paris, was famous for his great commentary on the whole Bible, which became a standard work of reference. Donne has many allusions to it in *Biathanatos* (pp. 158, 184, 203) and the *Sermons*. When he resigned his Readership at Lincoln's Inn he presented the Benchers with a six-volume copy of *Biblia Sacra cum Glossa Ordinaria et Postillis Nicholai Lyrani*, which is still in the Library.

MARLORATUS (Auguste Marlorat, 1506–63), a French Protestant, translated the New Testament and wrote a number of theological works. Donne refers to him in *Biathanatos* (pp. 103, 121, 134).

MARTYR, Peter (Vermigli, 1500–62), a Florentine, who became one of the most learned of the Calvinists. He wrote a commentary on the Bible, and various treatises which were published as *Locorum communium theologicorum tomi III* (1580–3). He is quoted also in *Biathanatos* (pp. 103, 104).

MELANCHTHON (Philip Schwarzerd, 1497–1560), one of the leaders of the Reformation. He is often quoted in the *Sermons* for his *Loci communes rerum theologicarum* (1521). Here in the *Essays* Donne refers to the volume of treatises on the Koran which Bibliander and Melanchthon issued together in 1550.

MÜNSTER (Sebastian, 1489–1552), a German mathematician and Hebrew scholar. Donne alludes to his *Cosmographia Universalis* here and in the *Sermons*.

MUSCULUS (Wolfgang Mösel, 1497–1563), a Benedictine monk who became a Lutheran. Donne refers to his treatise *De abominabile usura*, and in the *Sermons* to his commentaries on Genesis.

PARAEUS (David Wängler, 1548–1622), a Calvinist theologian whose commentary on Genesis was published at Frankfort in 1609 and went through several editions.

PATRICIUS (Francesco Patrizzi, 1529–97) was a professor of philosophy first at Ferrara, then at Rome. He wrote many books, but the one to which Donne alludes here is probably *Nova de Universis Philosophia, libris L comprehensa . . . quibus postremo sunt adjecta Zoroastris Oracula CCCXX ex platonicis collecta. Hermetis Trismegisti libelli et fragmenta . . . Asclepii discipuli tres libelli . . .* 1591.

PAULINUS DE NOLA (353–431), a pupil of Ausonius and a friend of St. Ambrose and St. Jerome.

PELLICANUS (Conrad Kurschner, 1478–1556), a Swiss Reformer who wrote many books, among them being a commentary on the Pentateuch. He is quoted also in the *Sermons*.

PERERIUS (Benedictus or Bento Pereyra, 1535–1610), a Jesuit who taught theology and philosophy at Rome, wrote commentaries on Genesis, Exodus, and certain other books of the Bible. Donne quotes him frequently here and in the *Sermons*.

PICCOLOMINI (Francesco, 1520–1604), an Italian scholar and philosopher, whose *De arte definiendi* is quoted here by Donne.

PICUS (Pico della Mirandola, 1463–94), a brilliant Italian scholar and Platonist, a friend and pupil of Ficino, who studied oriental languages and the Jewish Cabala. He is quoted also in *Biathanatos*, p. 49, and in the *Sermons*.

PRATEOLUS (Gabriel Dupréau, 1511–88), a controversialist who wrote much against the Protestants. He is mentioned also in *Biathanatos* (pp. 68, 69).

REUCHLIN (Johann, 1455–1522), a great German humanist and student of Hebrew. He was interested in the Jewish Cabala, and wrote *De Verbo Mirifico* (1494) and *De Arte Cabbalistica* (1517). Donne alludes to him also in *Catalogus Librorum*, *Biathanatos*, and the *Sermons*.

ROBORTELLO (Francesco, 1516–67), an Italian who wrote *De Facultate Historica* (1548) and *De Vita et Victu Populi Romani* (1567), and edited some classical authors.

ROSELLIS (Antonio di, died in 1466) studied law at Bologna, Siena, and Rome. His works included *De Legitimatione* and *Monarchia, seu de Potestate Imperatoris et Papae* (Venice, 1483–7).

SÂ (Emmanuel, 1530–96), a Jesuit, who wrote *Scholia in quattuor Evangelia*, *Notationes in totam sacram Scripturam*, and *Aphorismi Confessariorum*. He is quoted also in *Biathanatos* (pp. 122, 126, 128).

SACROBOSCO (John of Holywood, died about the middle of the thirteenth century), an English mathematician who wrote a treatise *De Sphaera*, which went through many editions.

SEBUNDUS (Raymond of Sebund), a Spanish philosopher of the late fourteenth and early fifteenth centuries, wrote *Liber Naturae sive Creaturarum*, to which Donne here alludes. See also the reference in *Catalogus Librorum*, Item 14 (*The Courtier's Library*, pp. 46, 64). It was probably from Montaigne's 'Apologie pour Raymond de Sebonde' in his *Essais* that Donne derived his initial impulse towards the study of Sebund.

SEXTUS SENENSIS (1520–69), of Siena, a Jew converted to Christianity, who became a celebrated Dominican preacher. Donne quotes his *Bibliotheca Sacra* (1586) here, and also in *Biathanatos* and the *Sermons*.

SMILERUS (Josias Smiler, 1530–76), a Swiss theologian and mathematician. Donne quotes his commentary on Exodus (1605).

TOSTATUS (Alonso Tostado, 1400–55), bishop of Avila in Spain. He wrote many biblical commentaries which Donne quotes here and in his *Sermons*.

VERCELLUS, probably Johannes de Vercellis, a Dominican who taught canon law at Paris and became General of his order. He died in 1283. He left some sermons and epistles (M. P. Ramsay).

NOTES

p. 4, *l.* 15. *Printed from an exact copy, under the Authors own hand.* This explains the excellence of the text of the *Essays*, as compared with the extremely corrupt text of *Paradoxes, Problems, Essays, Characters.* The younger Donne was a careless editor, who reproduced the text with fair exactitude when he had his father's manuscript before him, but made no attempt to ascertain the true reading when he had to depend on copy produced by ignorant scribes.

p. 4, *l.* 17. *When he had many debates betwixt God and himself, whether he were worthy,* &c. These words have generally been taken to mean that the *Essays* were written shortly before Donne's ordination, and should therefore be dated about the end of 1614. They would, however, apply equally well to the whole period from the publication of *Pseudo-Martyr* in 1610 up to the end of 1614. The theological matter of the *Essays* anticipates that of the *Sermons* and *Devotions*, but there is a difference of tone which suggests that the *Essays* may have preceded Donne's ordination by a year or more. Donne shows a preoccupation with occult literature which is not evident in the *Sermons*, and he quotes a number of authors whose names appear in *Biathanatos, Pseudo-Martyr, Ignatius his Conclave,* and *Catalogus Librorum.*

In the cancelled dedication (printed *supra*) to Sir Henry Vane, the younger Donne had written of the *Essays*: '. . . they come (Sir) with the greater confidence, because being writ when the Author was obliged in Civill business, and had no ingagement in that of the Church, the manner of their birth may seem to have some analogie with the course you now seem to steer; who being so highly interested in the publick affairs of the State, can yet allow so much time to the exercise of your private Devotions.' Donne was not engaged in 'Civill business' in December 1614 and January 1615, the period to which Gosse (*Life and Letters of Donne,* ii. 321) assigned the *Essays*, but he was a member of the Parliament which sat from March to June 1614, and his attendance on Sir Robert Drury's embassy in 1611–12 might also be considered as public business.

GENESIS

p. 5, *l.* 5. *He which is holy . . . openeth.* After quoting the text from Genesis on which he is to meditate, Donne turns at once to the last book of the Bible, the Revelation of St. John. This passage from Revelation iii. 7 on the Key of David was a favourite of his. He used it again in a sermon preached on Easter Day, 1629: *'The key of David opens, and no man shuts.* The Son of *David,* is the key of *David,* Christ Jesus; He hath opened heaven for us all . . .' (*LXXX Sermons,* p. 241). The Church uses this verse in the antiphon *O Clavis David,* which is one of the seven in the *O Sapientia* series sung at the end of Advent.

p. 5, l. 10. *Lyra.* Nicholas de Lyra (1270–1340) was famous for his biblical commentary, of which Donne makes use in his sermons. See *LXXX Sermons*, 5. 50; 50. 555, also *Biathanatos*, p. 198.

p. 5, l. 19. *Saint Augustine enlarges it well. Sermo* 69, 2. (al. 10 *de verbis Dom.*) (J.)

p. 5, l. 28. *Humility, and Studiousnesse.* Aquinas, *Summa Theol.*, II. ii. 161, art. 4, and quaest. 166. art. 2. (J.)

p. 5, l. 32. *Vir Desideriorum.* 'A man of desires', the Vulgate reading, where A.V. has 'a man greatly beloved', though it gives the former reading in the margin.

p. 6, l. 32. *I give eternall things*, &c. This and the following verses are taken from the Geneva Bible, which followed the Vulgate in this passage, whereas A.V. reads 'I therefore being eternal, am given to all my children which are named of him . . . . They that eat me shall yet be hungry, and they that drink me shall yet be thirsty . . . . All these things are the book of the Covenant of the most high God, even the Law which Moses commanded . . .'. The verse numbers here given are also those of the Geneva Bible, not those of A.V. Even after his ordination Donne continued to use the Geneva version to a certain extent, side by side with the Authorized, but in the *Essays* he does not seem to have used the latter at all. This indicates an earlier date than the end of 1614 for the *Essays*; see above, p. 109.

p. 7, l. 1. *And as our orderly love to the understanding this Book of life*, &c. *The Litanie*, stanza xiii:

> Both bookes of life to us (for love
> To know thy Scriptures tells us, we are wrote
> In thy other booke). . . .

p. 7, l. 18. *Propriety.* Ownership, property.

p. 8, l. 5. *Trismegistus.* The works attributed to the fabled Hermes Trismegistus attracted much notice in the sixteenth and seventeenth centuries on account of their supposed antiquity and Egyptian origin. In reality they belong to the fourth (or, at the earliest, the third) century A.D. and are evidently the work of a Neoplatonist. The book which Donne quotes here and later in his sermons is *Hermetis Trismegisti Asclepius sive de Natura Deorum Dialogus*, which was often reprinted during the Renaissance. Jessopp states that it was probably from the *Nova de Universis Philosophia, libris L comprehensa* of Patricius (Fran. Patrizzi, 1529–97) that Donne derived his knowledge, and refers the present passage to fol. 126 of the 1593 edition of that work.

p. 8, l. 33. *Suspicious, and crasie.* Questionable and unsound.

p. 8, l. 36. *Obnoxious.* Open to attack or censure. Cf. *Pseudo-Martyr*, *p.* 118. 'Our corruption is now more obnoxious and apter to admitte and inuite such poysonous ingredients.'

p. 8, l. 36 n. *Epist. Pii secundi.* Jessopp quotes, from p. 84 of the third volume of Tracts printed with the Koran in 1550 by Bibliander and Melanchthon, a passage from the letter of Pius II attacking Origen's error in asserting that devils might be saved. This is followed by the words 'Hunc secutus est Mahometes, qui salvandos per Alcoran malos angelos affirmat'.

p. 8, *l.* 39. *Cusanus.* 'The *Cribratio Alcorani* of Nicholas de Cusa is in the second volume of Tracts mentioned above.' (J.)

p. 9, *l.* 25. *The Emperour Maximilian.* Maximilian I (1459–1519) was urged by Reuchlin in his *Augenspiegel* or *Speculum Oculare* (1511) not to agree to the confiscation and burning of Jewish books, including the Talmud, for which the Dominicans of Cologne had asked. See Johannes Maius, *Vita Jo. Reuchlini* (Frankfort, 1687), pp. 258–69.

p. 9, *l.* 31. *By Gods own finger.* 'Donne adopts here an assertion, of which he takes elsewhere more particular notice, maintained by Chemnitz . . . " nullum igitur dubium est . . . ut Deus Decalogum prius scripserit in tabula quam Moses suos libros conscriberit, &c." *Exam. Conc. Trid.* Franc. fol. 1596, p. 8.' (J.)

p. 10, *l.* 4 n. *Irenæus. Tertul.* Jessopp supplies the references: 'Irenæus, lib. iii, c. xxi, §2; Tertullian, *De Cultu Fœmin.* lib. i, c. 9; Clemens Alex., *Strom.* lib. i, c. xxi; Hieron. *Adv. Helvid.* § 7.' From the form of Donne's reference, however, it seems clear that he is merely following the commentaries.

p. 10, *l.* 26. *Of Moses.* Donne took much of the material for this chapter from Pererius, *Commentarium in Genesim*, Praefatio, where in section 23 there will be found 'Animadversio in Picum Mirandulanum'.

p. 10, *l.* 27. *In which number, compos'd of the first even, and first odd.* Compare Donne's poem *The Primrose*, lines 28–30:

> Since all
> Numbers are odde, or even, and they fall
> First into this, five, . . .

The whole of the poem turns on the symbolical value of 'this mysterious number'. M. P. Ramsay quotes Chaignet's summary of the ideas of Nicomachus of Gerasa on the symbolical value of the number five: 'C'est le symbole du centre, du milieu . . . , le plus parfait et le plus naturel des nombres. Car il se lie deux termes extrêmes du nombre naturel, à l'unité comme à son point de départ, à la décade comme à son point d'arrivée. Or, le monde, qui a sa racine dans l'unité, s'achève et se manifeste par la décade' (*Psychologie des Grecs*). Donne was familiar with such ideas through 'the Harmony of Francis George' to which he here alludes.

p. 10, *l.* 31. *The Harmony of Francis George.* Franciscus Georgius Venetus (F. Zorgi) wrote a treatise *De Harmonia Mundi totius cantica* (1525). This was a mixture of Neoplatonic and Cabalistic doctrines with some speculations of his own. Though Donne here calls him 'that transcending wit', the reference to him in *Catalogus Librorum* is much less complimentary (*The Courtier's Library*, p. 44).

p. 11, *l.* 2. *Solutionem continui.* Cf. p. 50: 'But if in the skin it self, there be any solution or division, which is seldome without drawing of blood.' Jessopp quotes Quincy's *Phys. Dict.* (1719), 'Solution of continuity is a term used by surgeons for every division of the parts made by wounds or any other cause.'

p. 11, *l.* 5. *the Cabal.* The name Kabbalah, anglicized as *Cabal*, was originally given to the oral law of the Jews as opposed to the written law. But from the beginning of the thirteenth century it was applied to a metaphysical mysticism which was far removed from orthodox Judaism. Isaac the Blind was the leader of the early cabalists, but the system did not find its full development till the appearance of the *Zohar.* Its adherents claimed that this work was derived from Rabbi Simon ben Jochai, who lived at the end of the first century A.D. and who was supposed to have collected and written down the tradition of the doctrines given by God to Adam in Paradise. It was, however, largely the work of the Spanish Jew, Moses ben Leon, who may have incorporated in it some much older material. In the fifteenth and sixteenth centuries it had considerable influence on the thought of the Renaissance, owing to the use made of it by Ficino and Pico della Mirandola. Through Reuchlin the knowledge of it spread to Germany. For fuller accounts of it see M. P. Ramsay, op. cit., pp. 61–62, note 3, from which much of the above has been summarized, and Denis Saurat, *Milton, Man and Thinker,* p. 281, and *Literature and the Occult Tradition,* pp. 145–6.

Donne was apparently familiar with cabalistic ideas when he wrote *The Progresse of the Soule* in 1601. The doctrine of the transmigration of souls is found in the *Zohar,* which taught that the soul of a male could in a later existence animate a female, and that it could also pass into the body of an animal. The *Zohar* also speaks of souls as emanating from 'the Tree of Knowledge'.

p. 11, *l.* 6. *Paracelsian Phisick of the understanding.* Donne took a keen interest in the debate which raged during his lifetime between the Galenist and Paracelsian schools of medicine. He possessed a copy of the *Chirurgia Magna* of Paracelsus, and in one of his letters (*Letters,* 1651, pp. 14–15) he discusses at some length the differences between the two schools. For a discussion of possible allusions in the *Poems* see W. A. Murray, 'Donne and Paracelsus', *R.E.S.,* xxv. 115–23.

p. 11, *l.* 7 n. *Archangelus Apol. Cabal.* 'Burgonovensis Apologia pro Doctrina Cabalae contra Petrum Garziam (Basel, 1600) p. 67.' (J.) See below, note on p. 12.

p. 11, *l.* 17. *Rabbi Moses, call'd the Egyptian, but a Spaniard.* Maimonides, 1135–1204, the greatest Jewish philosopher of the Middle Ages. Donne quotes him in *LXXX Sermons,* 7. 63: '. . . sayes the saddest and soundest of the Hebrew Rabbins' (margin, R. Moses); see also pp. 66, 608.

p. 11, *l.* 37. *So is the booke of the Battails of the Lord.* Pererius, op. cit., Praefatio, § 10: 'Non esse libros Pentateuchi, ut nunc sunt, ita scriptos à Mose, quidam eo argumento colligunt, quod in cap. 21 libri Numerorum citatur liber Bellorum Domini . . . .'

p. 12, *l.* 2. *Linus, Orpheus, and all Greeke learning.* Ibid., §4: 'Nec verò Moses priscos tantum gentilium Poëtas, et Theologos Orpheum, Linum, et Musaeum, Homero atque Hesiodo longe antiquiores . . . .'

p. 12, *l.* 4. *Abraham's booke De formationibus.* This is the *Sephir Yezirah* or *Jezireh,* the *Book of Creation,* a Hebrew treatise falsely ascribed to

Abraham. A Latin translation under the title *Liber Iezireh, sive formationis mundi*, by Guil. Postellus, appeared in Paris in 1552.

p. 12, l. 7. Francis George often vouches it. See p. 10 n. Jessopp supplies the reference: '*Problemata*, to. i, sect. i, Prob. 3, and in the *Harmonia Cantica* 1, Tonus 7.'

p. 12, l. 8. Zoroasters Oracles. This passage should be compared with Raleigh, *History of the World*, Book I, ch. ii, pp. 202–3: '. . . it seemeth that *Zoroaster* was exceedingly learned. . . . For in his *Oracles* hee confesseth God to bee the Creatour of the Vniuersal: he beleeueth of the *Trinitie*, which he could not inuestigate by any naturall knowledge . . . which *Oracles* of his, *Psellus, Ficinus, Patritius*, and others haue gathered and translated.' Raleigh's marginal note on p. 202 quotes the passage which Donne quotes here, with one slight verbal difference: 'Toto in mundo lucet Trias, cuius Monas est princeps.' It is obvious that Raleigh and Donne are drawing on the same source.

p. 12, l. 15. From whence shall we say that Hermes Trismegistus sucked his not only Divinity, but Christianity? Raleigh (op. cit., 11. vi. 319–20) is equally enthusiastic about Hermes and his wonderful foreknowledge of Christian doctrine. Since the real author of the Hermetic books lived in the third or fourth century A.D. it is not surprising that he was influenced by Christian ideas.

p. 12, l. 31. Buntingus in his Chronology. 'Henrici Buntingi *Chronologia Catholica* in anno Mundi 2261, fol. 28b, Magd. 1608.' (J.)

p. 13, l. 1. As in violent tempests, when a ship dares bear no main sayl. Donne's *Essays*, like his *Sermons*, contain many nautical metaphors which remind us that he had served as a gentleman volunteer in the Cadiz expedition of 1596 and the 'Islands Voyage' of 1597, when the fleet encountered a great storm. See his poem, *The Storme* (Grierson, *Poems*, i. 175–7), and also the letter which he wrote from Plymouth (E. M. Simpson, *A Study of the Prose Works of John Donne*, Oxford, 1948, pp. 303–4). For other nautical passages in the *Essays* see p. 20 with its comparison of men who seek God by reason to the 'Mariners which voyaged before the invention of the Compass, which were but Costers, and unwillingly left the sight of the land', whereas those who seek Him by faith are like the sailors who by means of the compass 'have found out a new world richer then the old'. There is also the passage on p. 36, where a prince is described as pilot of a great ship, the kingdom, and 'we of a pinnace, a family, or a less skiff, our selves'. On p. 40 the Scriptures are strong cables by which we can anchor in all storms of dispute and persecution. Certain men who retire into monasteries are compared to seamen afflicted with the calenture who fling themselves into the sea (p. 70). When Donne has finished his consideration of God's mercy he says: 'thus long we have been in the Harbour, but we launch into a main and unknown Sea, when we come to consider his *Power*' (p. 79).

p. 13, l. 9. Hulling. Lying a-hull, or drifting to the wind with sails furled. Cf. *Fifty Sermons*, 18. 150 (misnumbered as 158): 'It is well for us, if, though we be put to take in our sayls, and to take down our masts, yet we can hull it out . . . He is a good Christian that can ride out, or board out, or hull out a storm, that by industry, as long as he can, and by patience, when he can do no more, over-lives a storm, and does not forsake his ship for it, that is not scandalized with that State, nor that Church, of which he is a member, for those abuses that are in it.'

p. 13, l. 18. The Divine and learned book of Job. Donne was particularly fond of the book of Job, and preached a number of sermons on texts taken from it (*LXXX Sermons*, nos. 13, 24; *Fifty Sermons*, nos. 14, 30, 31). I do not know why he considers that 'indeed it hath somwhat a Greek taste', since it is characteristically Hebrew in tone. Probably the statement reflects Donne's ignorance of Greek literature, except in Latin translations.

p. 13, l. 20. For to confess, that it was found by Moses in Madian. Cf. Raleigh, op. cit., II. iii, § 4: 'That *Moses*, in this time of his abode at *Madian*, wrote the Booke of *Iob*, as *Pererius* supposeth, I cannot iudge of it, because it is thought, that *Iob* was at that time living.'

p. 13, l. 30. His firebrands of Contention, and curiosity. In *The Litanie*, 71–72, Donne speaks of 'excesse In seeking secrets'. In the *Sermons* he has many warnings against inquiring beyond what God has revealed. See *LXXX Sermons*, 6. 57 and 79. 807.

p. 13, l. 35. Sir Thomas More. It is curious that the 1651 edition should have the misprint '*John*' for '*Thomas*'. Probably Donne wrote the name in the abbreviated form 'Tho' which was mistaken for 'Jho'. More was an ancestor of Donne, whose great-grandmother, Elizabeth Rastall, was More's sister.

p. 13, l. 36. Pursuing the rules of Cabal, &c.
Here Donne shows his knowledge, through Pico, of some of the essential doctrines of the Cabala. In that system God Himself is unknown and inaccessible. The inaccessible Deity gives forth an emanation, identified by the Christian Cabalists, such as Pico, with God the Son, the Logos. Next in the scale of being, according to the Cabala, comes the Head, which Donne identifies with heaven, and fire, which he identifies with the air. The relevant passage in the *Zohar* states 'The white Head wished to glorify his Name, it caused to issue from the primary light a spark . . . . From this spark issued a pure and buoyant air. In the middle of this air rose a powerful head which spread itself out in the four directions of the world. Thus this pure air, formed of the spark, surrounds the Head. This air is surrounded by fire and air; the pure air lies above the fire and the ordinary air. The fire in question here is not an ordinary fire, but the fire with which the world is charged, and which gives light to two hundred and seventy worlds.' De Pauly's translation of the *Zohar*, v. 356, quoted by D. Saurat in *Literature and Occult Tradition*, p. 80.

p. 14, l. 19. Accited. Cited, quoted, from the late Latin form, *accitatus*. See also p. 61, l. 28.

p. 14, l. 21. Seposed. Set apart. Cf. *Letters*, 1651, p. 111: 'God seposed a seventh of our time for his exterior worship.'

p. 14, l. 24. There are marked an hundred differences in mens Writings concerning an Ant. This is the first of many parallels between the *Essays* and Donne's two *Anniversaries.* Cf. *The second Anniversary,* 281–2:

> Wee see in Authors, too stiffe to recant,
> A hundred controversies of an Ant.

> (Grierson, i. 259.)

Donne owned a copy of Wilde's *De Formica,* Hamburg, 1615, which is now in the Library of Chichester Cathedral. See *Cambridge Bibliog. Soc.,* 1. i. 68 (1949).

p. 15, *l.* 3. *I . . . have before engaged my selfe to accompany Chemnitius . . . And leave Pererius.* Donne is much more frank in his acknowledgement of his indebtedness to the commentators, such as Pererius, than were Raleigh and Sir Thomas Browne (see A. Williams, *The Common Expositor,* pp. 35–37). Here he deserts Pererius, whom he has been following fairly closely, in favour of Chemnitius.

p. 15, *l.* 12. *Reclining the Jews from Egypt.* For this obsolete use of *recline* in the sense of 'to turn (a person) from something' compare *Biathanatos,* p. 215: 'they would utterly recline and avert our nature from it'.

p. 15, *l.* 21. *In the Beginning whereof,* &c. By the use of inverted commas for the whole of this long paragraph, Donne implies that the passage is taken from the *Confessions* of St. Augustine, to which reference is made in the margin. It is a paraphrase and summary of the first four chapters of Book I, with a detailed translation of one passage from Book XI, chapter iii. Donne's fondness for Augustine is apparent throughout the *Sermons.*

p. 16, *l.* 14. *Minerall.* Deeply buried, recondite. The *O.E.D.* records only this passage from Donne for this meaning of the word.

p. 16, *l.* 14. *Centrick.* Belonging to the centre. Cf. *Loves Alchymie,* 1, 2. In both passages it seems to be used of the 'centre', i.e. the earth.

p. 16, *l.* 15. *That it is an Article of our Belief, that the world began.* Aquinas, *Summa,* I, xlvi. 2: 'Utrum mundum incoepisse sit articulus fidei (Affirm.).' Here Christian philosophy parts company with Aristotle, who held that the world was eternal.

p. 16, *l.* 31. *Old, well disciplined Armies punished more severely the loss of this.* Jessopp refers to Plutarch, *Apophth. Lacon. Demarati,* ii, p. 220 A, and Lysias, *Or.,* x, p. 117.

p. 22, *l.* 8. *Out of this proceeded Dea febris, and Dea fraus, and Tenebræ.* Cicero enumerates among the deities worshipped 'Amor, Dolus, Metus, Labor, . . . Mors, Tenebrae, Fraus' (*De Natura Deorum,* III. xvii), and writes a little later 'Febris enim fanum in Palatio . . . et aram Malae Fortunae Esquiliis consecratam videmus' (ibid., III, xxv). The reading *Tenebris,* instead of *Tenebrae,* in *1651* must be due to the printer's eye seeing *febris* in the line just above. For parallel passages in Donne's poems and sermons, see above, Introduction, p. xiv.

p. 22, *l.* 10. *The Egyptians . . . were from thence said to have Gods grow in their gardens.* Jessopp points out the reference to Juvenal, *Sat.,* xv. 10, 11: 'O sanctas gentes quibus haec nascuntur in hortis Numina.'

p. 22, l. 15. A great Greek generall. Themistocles, who pressed the Andrians for money. Herodotus, viii, c. 111. Donne probably took the story from Plutarch's *Life* of Themistocles.

p. 22, l. 26. Determining. Coming to an end.

p. 23, l. 14. An enormous pretending Wit. Like Jessopp, I have been unable to discover the person to whom Donne refers. Bacon often mentions Adam's naming of the animals according to their properties (*Of the Interpretations of Nature*, ed. Ellis and Spedding, iii. 219; *De Augment. Sc.*, Ellis and Spedding, i. 434). *Enormous* is evidently used here in the common Elizabethan sense of 'irregular, disordered', and need not imply any great eminence in the person mentioned.

p. 23, l. 21. So that it is truly said . . . except God could be named. Donne took this passage and amplified it later in an undated sermon on Psalm vi. 1. See above, Introduction, pp. xx–xxi, where the two parallel passages are quoted in full.

p. 24, l. 9. Communicable with Princes. According to the *O.E.D.* this use of *communicable* to mean 'pertaining in common' is rare.

p. 24, l. 17. The Pythagorean oath, by the number of four. 'See the passages from Plutarch and Lucian, given in Menagius's note to Diog. Laert. viii. 22.' (J.) The Pythagoreans held that the sum of the first four numbers $(1 + 2 + 3 + 4 = 10)$ was the root or source of all creation, and introduced it into their most solemn oath. In addition to the passages mentioned by Jessopp see Hierocles, *Comment.* 20.

p. 24, l. 30. One says (marg. *Reuclin,*). For Donne's knowledge of the great German humanist and Hebrew scholar, Reuchlin (1455–1522), see *Biathanatos*, p. 118, and *Catalogus Librorum* (*The Courtier's Library*, pp. 45, 60).

p. 24, l. 35. This is the Name, which the Jews stubbornly deny . . . it was not Jehova. This passage is also reproduced with slight alterations in the sermon mentioned above (*LXXX Sermons*, 50. 502): 'This is the name which the Jews falsly, but peremptorily . . . deny ever to have been attributed to the *Messias*, in the Scriptures. This is that name, in the vertue and use whereof, those Calumniators of our Saviours miracles doe say, that he did his miracles, according to a direction, and schedule, for the true and right pronouncing of that name, which *Solomon* in his time had made, and Christ in his time had found, and by which, say they, any other man might have done those miracles. . . . How this name which we call *Iehovah*, is truly to be sounded . . . is a perplext question; . . . our Saviour Christ himselfe, in all those places which he cited out of the Old Testament, never sounded it . . . . Nor the Apostles after him, nor *Origen*, nor *Ierome* . . . they never sounded this name *Iehovah*. For though in S. *Ieromes* Exposition upon the 8. Psalme, we finde that word *Iehovah*, in some Editions which we have now, yet it is a cleare case, that in the old copies it is not so . . . . Neither doth it appeare to me, that ever the name of *Iehovah* was so pronounced, till so late, as in our Fathers time; for I think *Petrus Gallatinus* was the first that ever called it so.'

p. 25, l. 3. A Scedule . . . of Solomon's. The spelling *scedule* is found in the sixteenth and seventeenth centuries, as a variant of the earlier *sedule* and later *schedule*. For the allusion, see Josephus, *Ant.*, VIII. ii. 5.

p. 25, l. 17. Our learnedst Doctor. The marginal reference should be expanded thus, 'Rainolds *de Rom. Eccles. Idol.* lib. ii, c. 3, § 18', according to Jessopp. John Rainolds or Reynolds was President of Corpus Christi College, Oxford, from 1598 to 1607. Bishop Hall described him as 'full of all faculties, of all studies, of all learning'. The reference to him here supports the note in the Dobell MS. of Donne's *Poems*, now in Harvard College Library (Nor. 4506), which supplies the names 'Dr Reinolds and Dr Andrewes' in the margin of *Satire*, IV, 56, to explain 'the two reuerend men of our two Academies' whom Donne named with Beza and 'some Iesuites' as the best linguists. See note in *R.E.S.*, xx. 224.

p. 25, l. 32. But as old age is justly charged. Cf. *Juvenilia*, Paradox vii: 'Yea, that which falls neuer in *young men*, is in them ⟨i.e. old men⟩ most *fantastike* and *naturall*, that is, *Couetousnesse*; euen at their *iourneyes end* to make great prouision.' In both passages Donne was probably drawing on Horace, *Ars Poetica*, 169–71:

> Multa senum circumveniunt incommoda, vel quod
> Quaerit et inventis miser abstinet ac timet uti,
> Vel quod res omnis timide gelideque ministrat.

p. 26, l. 5. An opinion, that by this name of God, Elohim, because it is plurally pronounced in this place. Donne did well to call this attempt to prove the doctrine of the Trinity from the use of a singular verb with a plural form 'this extortion, and beggarly wresting of Scriptures'. Cf. *LXXX Sermons*, 42. 417: 'And therefore, those men in the Church, who have cryed downe that way of proceeding, to goe about to prove the Trinity, out of the first words of *Genesis, Creavit Dii*, that because God in the plurall is there joyned to a Verb in the singular, therefore there is a Trinity in Unity . . . those men . . . who have cryed downe such manner of arguments, have reason on their side, when these arguments are imployed against the Jews . . . .'

p. 26, l. 30. Idiotisme. Idiom.

p. 26, l. 34. Faciamus hominem. Genesis i. 26. In April 1629 Donne preached two sermons before the King on this text (*Fifty Sermons*, nos. 28 and 29).

p. 27, l. 4. Mundum tradidit disputationi eorum. The Vulgate text differs from the Hebrew, which A.V. translates 'also he hath set the world in their heart'. The marginal reference in *1651* 'Sirac. 3. 11' is wrong; the passage is in Ecclesiastes 3. 11. Evidently Donne wrote merely 'Eccl.' which was mistaken for Ecclesiasticus, which is ascribed to Jesus the son of Sirach. See p. 34, where Donne quoting from Ecclesiasticus 43. 27 writes, 'We shall best end in the words of *Sirach's* Son'.

p. 27, l. 11. Anathema, which is consecrated or separated. See *LXXX Sermons*, 40. 401, where Donne distinguishes between two meanings of the word.

p. 27, l. 16. Heresie. Sect (in this passage).

p. 27, l. 21. Cicero speaks. Donne is not quoting directly from Cicero, but from the treatise of Acacius to which a marginal reference was given earlier. Donne quotes from the same treatise in *Biathanatos*, pp. 46, 124, 125.

p. 27, l. 25. Suburbs to Hell. Donne uses this phrase for limbo and purgatory in *Ignatius his Conclave* (1611), p. 5.

p. 28, l. 1. Concurrent. Here used to mean 'a contributory cause', *O.E.D.*

p. 28, l. 8. Opposite and diametrall. Cf. *Juvenilia*, Problem xvii, 'were it never so opposite or diametricall'. For 'diametrall' in the sense of 'diametrical' cf. *LXXX Sermons*, 72. 726: 'There is not so direct and Diametrall a contrariety between the Nature of any Sinne and God, as between him and Pride.'

p. 28, l. 8 n. Aug. contr. advers. leg. Lib. i, cap. xxiii, § 48. (J.)

p. 28, l. 11. Evicts. Proves by argument, evinces.

p. 28, l. 21. In æternum et ultra. 'For ever and ever' is the rendering of the Authorized Version, which does not convey the meaning of '*et ultra*'.

p. 28, l. 27. Omitting the quarrelsome contending of Sextus Empiricus. Jessopp refers to *Hypotyposes*, iii. 14, § 112. L. I. Bredvold in his interesting essay 'The Religious Thought of Donne in relation to Medieval and Later Traditions', in *Studies in Shakespeare, Milton, and Donne* (University of Michigan, 1925), emphasizes Donne's debt to Montaigne, or rather to the sceptical philosophy of Sextus Empiricus, of whom Montaigne was a disciple. As far as I know, this is the only passage in which Donne directly alludes to Sextus, and it does not suggest that he had a high opinion or knew very much of that philosopher's works.

p. 28, l. 29. Laertius. Jessopp quotes from Diogenes Laertius, ix, § 61, and points out that Donne was evidently quoting from a Latin translation. The Greek does not quite bear the meaning attributed to it by Donne.

p. 28, l. 33. Non fit quod jam est, &c. Probably Donne was here using the Latin translation of Sextus Empiricus made by Henri Estienne.

p. 28, l. 37. Lucretius. This quotation is from *De Rerum Natura*, ii. 651. Lucretius was not much read by Elizabethan poets, but the commentators, such as Pererius and Paraeus, made some use of him in order to refute Aristotle's belief in the eternity of the world. Pererius described Lucretius as 'a serious and learned poet', and quoted from him a number of passages taken from the fifth and sixth books of *De Rerum Natura*.

p. 29, l. 2. Quo morbo mentem concusse? Horace, *Sat.*, ii. iii. 295. Donne makes use of the same line in *LXXX Sermons*, 39. 386.: '. . . which the Poet (not altogether in an ill sense) calls a disease of the soule, *Quo morbo mentem concusse? timore deorum.*' Horace, Ovid, Martial, and Juvenal were among the Latin poets who influenced Donne most strongly.

p. 29, l. 4. Nil semine . . . spacio. Lucretius, op. cit. i. 160–81.

p. 29, l. 7. Batter effectually. The metaphor is taken from the operation at a siege; so p. 40, 'underminings and batteries of heretics'. (J.)

p. 29, l. 10. Who is also so simple, that it is impossible to imagine any thing before him of which he should be compounded. According to scholastic philosophy, that which is simple, such as God or the soul, cannot be dissolved, and is therefore immortal. Grierson quotes Aquinas, *Summa*, pt. i, qu. lxxv, art. 6, on this point in his note on *The good-morrow*, 19–21 (*Poems*, ii. 11).

p. 29, l. 25. Impossible to your knowledge, and was ever so to Gods. 'This paragraph is derived from Aquinas, whose determinations on these and kindred points are to be found in the *Summa Theol.* part i, q. xiv; see especially art. 9.' (J.)

p. 29, l. 28. These Idæas and eternall impressions. Plato's doctrine of ideas, handed down through Augustine and Aquinas with some modifications, inspired a number of passages in Donne's sermons; *LXXX Sermons*, 66. 667–8; 69. 700; *Fifty Sermons*, 29. 253; 43. 399.

p. 29, l. 34. Scotus . . . thinks them the Essence of this world. See Ramsay, op. cit., p. 158. John Scotus Erigena and Gerbert, followed later by Duns Scotus to whose *Sententiae* Donne here alludes, held that the Ideas had an eternal existence outside the divine intelligence. Donne follows Aquinas in holding that their existence before the creation was within that intelligence, and can be called eternal only in that sense.

p. 30, l. 2. Obscurum loquitur quisque suo periculo. I have been unable to trace the source of this quotation.

p. 30, l. 3. O man, which art said to be the Epilogue, and compendium of all this world. In this eulogy of man Donne is following not only Pico, to whom he has a marginal reference, but also Ovid, *Metamorphoses*, i. 76–88, who makes the point that all other animals are prone, while man has his 'head erected to heaven', as Donne says.

p. 30, l. 5. Picus. 'Mirandula, *Heptaplus ad Lect.* He says the same again in the *Oratio de Dignitate Hominis*, p. 208.' (J.)

p. 30, l. 7. The Gospel, of which onely man is capable, is sent to be preached to all Creatures. Cf. *LXXX Sermons*, 76. 770, for a discussion of the meaning of *preached to all Creatures*.

p. 30, l. 10. Yet only thy heart of all others, points downwards, and onely trembles. Cf. *The Crosse*, 51–52:

> And crosse thy heart: for that in man alone
> Points downewards, and hath palpitation.
> (Grierson, i. 333.)

The idea comes from Aristotle, *De Partibus Animalium*, iii. 6. 669a: 'man is practically the only animal whose heart presents this phenomenon of jumping, inasmuch as he alone is influenced by hope and anticipation of the future.' (H. L. Gardner.)

p. 30, l. 13. Terram dedit filiis hominum. 'The earth hath he given to the children of men.' Ps. cxv. 16.

p. 30, l. 15. The Divell is Prince of the Air. 'The prince of the power of the air.' Ephes. ii. 2.

p. 30, l. 20. Our soul . . . is a veryer upstart then our body. Donne was fond of the paradoxical depreciation of the soul as compared with the body. See *Juvenilia*, Paradox xi, 'That the gifts of the Body are better than those of the Minde'.

p. 30, *l.* 22. *Being but of the first head.* The phrase was originally used of a deer at the age when the antlers are first developed; hence it is used figuratively of a man newly ennobled or raised in rank. (*O.E.D.*)

p. 30, *l.* 24. *How many souls hath this world, which were not nothing a hundred years since?* The question whether souls were propagated from parents or created separately for each individual was one of intense interest to writers of the sixteenth and seventeenth centuries. Sir John Davies in *Nosce Teipsum*, Davies of Hereford in *Microcosmos*, and Milton in *Christian Doctrine*, debated the subject earnestly. Donne has several references to it in the *Sermons*, but his fullest discussion of it is in *Letters* (1651), pp. 16–18: 'Hence it is that whole Christian Churches arest themselves upon propagation from parents; and other whole Christian Churches allow onely infusion from God. In both which opinions there appear such infirmities as it is time to look for a better: for whosoever will adhere to the way of propagation, can never evict necessarily and certainly a naturall immortality in the soul, if the soul result out of matter, nor shall he ever prove that mankind hath any more then one soul . . . . And they which follow the opinion of infusion from God, and of a new creation . . . as they can very hardly defend the doctrin of original sin . . . so shall they never be able to prove that all those whom we see in the shape of men have an immortall and reasonable soul. . . .'

p. 30, *l.* 27. *Such a neighbourhood and alliance with Nothing,* &c. This long passage on 'Nothing' recalls *A Nocturnall upon S. Lucies day* in which Donne plays with the same idea, especially in lines 15–29:

> A quintessence even from nothingnesse,
> From dull privations, and leane emptinesse. . . .
> But I am by her death, (which word wrongs her)
> Of the first nothing, the Elixir grown; . . .

p. 30, *l.* 37. *Even in Hell,* &c. Donne's view of hell here, with the stress laid on torment, is more crude and materialistic than that which he later developed in the *Sermons*. There he writes: 'Privation of the presence of God, is Hell; a diminution of it, is a step toward it. Fruition of his presence is Heaven . . .' (*XXVI Sermons,* 24. 325). Again, 'Hell is presented to us by fire, but fire without light: Heaven by light, and light without any ill effect of fire in it' (*LXXX Sermons,* 36. 355). 'When all is done, the hell of hels, the torment of torments is the everlasting absence of God' (ibid., 76. 776).

p. 31, *l.* 6. *Infinity and corrosiveness of officers. Infinity* is here used in the sense of 'an indefinitely great number' (see *O.E.D.*). *Corrosiveness* is used in the figurative sense.

p. 31, *l.* 11. *Plato's years.* 'Plato's year is the "annus magnus", or cycle of the fixed stars, which complete their revolution in 36,000 years according to the older, or 25,920 years according to the later astronomers. Plato supposed that at the end of this period the old world was destroyed, and a new world began . . . . "The hollowness" is the whole expanse or sphere of the fixed stars, which was supposed not to be infinite, but to have a known measurement. The "first mover" is the "primum mobile" of the

Ptolemaic system, the origin and source of all motion . . . . "Clavius his number" refers to a digression which that mathematician makes in his work on the sphere (ch. i. ad fin. p. 217), where he, "at the request of friends" revives an investigation which Archimedes had carried on before him, and shows how no finite quantity of objects can surpass our power of expressing them in numbers. . . .' (J.)

p. 31, *l.* 17. *Some have prayed to have hils fall upon them.* Rev. vi. 16.

p. 31, *l.* 20. *As reposedly, and at home within himself no man is an Atheist.* For a much more eloquent and detailed exposition of this thought see *LXXX Sermons*, 48. 486.

p. 31, *l.* 34 n. *Piccolomin. Defin. Creat. De Rerum Def.* p. 134. (J.)

p. 32, *l.* 2. *Reduce.* Bring back, a common use in the sixteenth and early seventeenth centuries.

p. 32, *l.* 11. *Francis George in his Harmony. Harmonia Mundi*, cant. i, ton. vi, c. iii. (J.)

p. 32, *l.* 17. *Temporall propriety.* Earthly property

p. 32, *l.* 20. *Qui velit ingenio cedere, rarus erit.* Martial, *Epig.*, VIII. xviii. 10. Donne has more verbatim quotations from Martial than from any other Latin poet. It is in his *Epigrams* and *Paradoxes* that this indebtedness is most evident, but even in the *Sermons* there are several quotations. See E. M. Simpson, 'Donne's Reading of Martial', in *A Garland for John Donne*, pp. 44–49.

p. 32, *l.* 21. *Such as I, who are but Interlopers.* Donne here indicates that he is still in secular life, and has no authority to expound the Scriptures.

p. 32, *l.* 27. *Disseise.* Dispossess.

p. 32, *l.* 36. *These expositions.* See Pererius, op. cit., c. i, §§ 42–45. Donne has already explained that he is merely summarizing what others have previously said.

p. 33, *l.* 10. *Averroes. Comment. in Met. Arist.* lib. i. 70. (J.)

p. 33, *l.* 25. *His Apologist Dornike sayes. In replicis ad Pet. Burg.* pref. to the Postils. (J.)

p. 33, *l.* 35. *In Cicero's words. De Natura Deorum*, II. vi.

p. 34, *l.* 3 n. *Gilbert de Magn.* The importance of this reference to the *De Magnete* of William Gilbert of Colchester has been stressed by C. M. Coffin in *John Donne and the New Philosophy*, pp. 84–87. He translates the passage from Book VI, c. 3 thus: 'Leaving out the ninth sphere, if the convexity of the *Primum Mobile* be duly estimated in proportion to the rest of the spheres, the vault of the *Primum Mobile* must in one hour run through as much space as is comprised in 3000 great circles of the Earth, for in the vault of the firmament it would complete more than 1800.' Gilbert's work helped to overthrow the old cosmology and to establish the 'new philosophy' of Kepler and Galileo, though *De Magnete* was neither astronomical nor mathematical in its main thesis. It was first published in 1600, and Donne's language in *The first Anniversary* suggests that he was familiar with it when writing that poem, probably in 1610.

p. 34, *l.* 8. *How strong and misgovern'd faith against common sense hath he, that is content to rest in their number.* Another allusion to the same chapter of *De Magnete* which is quoted in the previous note. The Ptolemaic catalogue gave 1022 as the number of the stars. Cf. Donne's argument in *Biathanatos*, p. 146: 'Are not St. *Augustines* Disciples guilty of the same pertinacy which is imputed to *Aristotles* followers, who defending the Heavens to be inalterable, because in so many ages nothing had been observed to have been altered, his Schollers stubbornly maintain his Proposition still, though by many experiences of new Stars, the reason which moved *Aristotle* seems now to be utterly defeated?'

p. 34, *l.* 20. *He repented that he made it, and then that he destroyed it.* Genesis vi. 6: 'And it repented the Lord that he had made man on the earth'; see also Gen. viii. 21.

p. 34, *l.* 28. *When we have spoken . . . his labour.* In these quotations from Ecclesiasticus, Donne is again using the Geneva Bible, which followed the Vulgate. A.V. reads 'We may speak much, and yet come short: wherefore in sum, he is all', and 'When a man hath done, then he beginneth, and when he leaveth off, then he shall be doubtful.'

p. 35, *l.* 6. *Earth and Heaven are but the foot-stool of God.* An adaptation of Isaiah lxvi. 1: 'The heaven is my throne, and the earth is my foot-stool.'

p. 35, *l.* 12. *A Job is not within their reach.* Apparently a reference to Job i. 7–10.

p. 35, *l.* 12. *Malaguzzi.* 'Apud Fabritio Romanci. *Thesoro Politico*, Pt. ii, fol. 62.' (J.)

p. 35, *l.* 20. *Prete-Jan.* A variant of *Prester John*, the fabulous medieval Christian monarch, who was identified, from the fourteenth century onwards, with the Negus or Emperor of Abyssinia. Earlier in the Middle Ages he had been supposed to rule over vast dominions in Asia.

p. 35, *l.* 28. *King of Kings.* For these and other extravagant titles applied to kings and emperors see Selden, *Titles of Honour*, i. iii. Cf. *XXVI Sermons*, 4. 59: 'We finde great Titles attributed to, and assumed by Princes, both Spiritual and Temporal: *Celsitudo vestra, et vestra Majestas*, is daily given, and duly given amongst us: and *Sanctitas vestra, et vestra beatitudo*, is given amongst others . . . . It is not hard to name some, that have taken to themselves the addition of *Divus* . . . .'

p. 35, *l.* 33. *Their Baldus. Their* here means 'belonging to the Roman Church'; cf. 'their great Bishop' of Bishop Tostado, or Tostatus, *LXXX Sermons*, 5. 50.

p. 36, *l.* 3 n. *Martial to Domitian.* Epig. viii. ii. 6: 'Terrarum domino, deoque rerum.'

p. 36 *l.* 3 *The whole Earth, whose hills . . . pock-holes.* For the close resemblance between this passage and lines 286–301 of *The first Anniversary,* see Introduction, pp. xvi–xvii.

p. 36, *l.* 9. *Hel it self, though they afford it three thousand great miles.* The marginal reference is to Sebastian Münster's *Cosmographia Universalis*, to which Donne also alludes in *LXXX Sermons*, 73. 747: 'But the Schoolmen are wild; for as one Author, who is afraid of admitting too great a hollownesse in the Earth, lest then the Earth might not be said to be solid, pronounces that Hell cannot possibly be above three thousand miles in compasse . . .' (marginal note, *Munster*).

p. 36, l. 24. Prandere Olus. Horace, *Epist.*, 1. xvii. 13–14: Si pranderet olus patienter, regibus uti | Nollet Aristippus.

p. 36, l. 29. Proprietary. Owner, one to whom something belongs as property.

p. 36, l. 30. Usufructuarius. One who has the use and profit, but not the ownership.

p. 36, l. 32. Nemo silens placuit, multi brevitate. Ausonius, *Epist.*, xxv. 44.

p. 36, l. 34. O Eternall and Almighty power. See Introduction, pp. xii–xiii, for Gosse's suggestion that this and other prayers in the book must have been written in 1617. Any close study of the prayer will reveal that it summarizes what Donne has been writing about the name of God, about 'in the beginning', and the creation of Heaven and Earth out of a pre-existent Nothing. The change in style is natural, for Donne is passing from a minute examination of every word in the text, to a spiritual application to his own soul. He prays that God, the Creator of Heaven and Earth, will deign to create in his own soul and life those thoughts, words, and deeds which will please Him.

p. 36, l. 36. Being, even to Angels but a passive Mirror and looking-glasse. The highest order of Angels were supposed to spend their existence in the contemplation of the Divine Being.

p. 37, l. 32. Negligent of the offices and duties which thou enjoynest amongst us. Cf. *The Litanie*, 143–4:

> From thinking us all soule, neglecting thus
> Our mutuall duties, Lord deliver us.

Cf. also *Fifty Sermons*, 38. 351: 'Man is not all soule, but a body too; and, as God hath married them together in thee, so hath he commanded them mutuall duties towards one another.' The same emphasis on the necessary duties of this life is found in *Letters* (1651), pp. 48–49.

p. 37, l. 35. Thou hast . . . denyed even to Angells, the ability of arriving from one Extreme to another, without passing the mean way between. Cf. *LXXX Sermons*, 48. 482: 'An Angel it selfe cannot passe from East to West, from extreame to extreame, without touching upon the way betweene . . . .'

p. 38, l. 11. I so esteem opinion, that I despise not others thoughts of me. Cf. *LXXX Sermons*, 67. 679: 'Serve not thy selfe with that triviall, and vulgar saying, As long as my conscience testifies well to me, I care not what men say of me; And so sayes that other Father [Augustine], They that rest in the testimony of their owne consciences, and contemne the opinion of other men, . . . They deale weakly, and improvidently for themselves . . . And they deale cruelly towards others.'

EXODUS

p. 39, l. 2. Their round Temples. Jessopp suggests that there is here an allusion to Exodus xxv. 11, xxx. 3, and 1 Maccabees iv. 57. I cannot see that these have any bearing on the subject. Solomon's Temple, and the buildings which followed it, are generally described as rectangular (see I Kings vi. 2). Donne is perhaps referring to the Jewish synagogues.

p. 39, *l.* 2. *God himselfe is so much a Circle as being every where without any corner.* For Donne's use of this imagery, cf. *Poems* (Grierson), i. 348: 'Thee, who art cornerlesse and infinite', and *LXXX Sermons*, 2. 14: 'God is a circle himselfe, and he will make thee one ; Goe not thou about to square eyther circle, to bring that which is equall in it selfe, to Angles and Corners.'

p. 39, *l.* 8. *As well the Pillar of Cloud, as that of Fire, did the Office of directing.* Exod. xiii. 21: 'And the Lord went before them by day in a pillar of a cloud, to lead them the way, and by night in a pillar of fire, to give them light, to go by day and night.'

p. 39, *l.* 16. *Turcism.* The religion of the Turks, i.e. Mohammedanism.

p. 39, *l.* 17. *Seneca. De Ira*, iii. 30, § 3. (J.)

p. 39, *l.* 20. *Iisdem pugionibus . . . consciverunt.* This seems to be a reminiscence of Suetonius, *Julius Caesar*, 89. Cf. North's Plutarch, *Life of Julius Caesar*: 'Cassius . . . being overcome in battle . . . slew himself with the same sword with the which he struck Caesar' ('sword' should be 'dagger'). Jessopp's reference to Pliny *'Panegyric* 30, § 1' is certainly incorrect, but why did Donne write *'Pliny'* ?

p. 39, *l.* 33. *That is Spiritus Oris.* This is the Vulgate rendering of the Hebrew phrase which the A.V. renders 'the breath of his mouth', Ps. xxxiii. 6. (Vulgate numbering, xxxii. 6.)

p. 40, *l.* 1. *That also is not the literall, which the letter seems to present.* Cf. *LXXX Sermons*, p. 183: 'The literall sense is not alwayes that, which the very Letter and Grammer of the place presents.'

p. 40, *l.* 15. *Devast.* Lay waste.

p. 40, *l.* 16. *Gables.* This was a recognized variant of *cables* in the sixteenth and seventeenth centuries (*O.E.D.*). Jessopp corrects it to *cables*, and it is true that this is the form generally used by Donne.

p. 40, *l.* 23. *Importunum ingenium.* Pliny the Elder, *Nat. Hist.*, xxxvi, c. 6.

p. 40, *l.* 32. *I have read of a General.* Untraced.

p. 41, *l.* 3. *In the Temple was admitted no sound of hammer.* 1 Kings vi. 7.

p. 41, *l.* 10. *My first purpose of taking the beginning of every book.* This shows that Donne had planned a much longer book than he actually achieved. He goes on to argue that the writing of books to the glory of God may be 'more honorable to the Church' than the 'multiplication of vocal prayers'.

p. 41, *l.* 20. *Scriptor manu prædicat.* Jessopp quotes from Johannes Gerson (1363–1429), *De Laude Scriptorum Considerati*: 'Scriptor idoneus et frequens librorum, doctrinae salubris, . . . praedicare dici potest.'

p. 41, *l.* 25. *The Author of that book, the Preacher.* See Ecclesiastes i. 1: 'The words of the Preacher, the son of David, King in Jerusalem.'

p. 41, *l.* 27. *Saint Bernard did almost glory, that Okes and Beeches were his Masters.* Jessopp quotes from St. Bernard of Clairvaux, *Epist.*, cvi, *ad Henricum Murdach*: 'Experto crede; aliquid amplius invenies in silvis quam in libris. Ligna et lapides docebunt te quod a magistris audire non possis.' Gosse makes a bad slip when, in conformity with his theory that the *Essays* were written a few weeks before Donne's ordination, he takes the words, 'I shall be content that Okes and Beeches be my Schollers, and witnesses of my solitary Meditations' to mean that Donne was 'threatened with the absence of worthy auditors in a country parish' (*Life and Letters of Donne*, ii. 321). The whole context with its reference to 'unvocal preaching' makes it clear that Donne was speaking of writing a book.

p. 42, l. 27. 52. Hebdomades. Weeks of the year.

p. 43, l. 12. Intemerate. Inviolate.

p. 43, l. 16. Josephus. Antiq., ii, c. 7, § 4. (J.)

p. 44, l. 3. The Senate, after his death, melted all them, &c. Donne has used the account in Dion Cassius, lib. lx, c. 22. It seems that the name of Claudius must have dropped out before 'his wife *Messalina*', for Donne, after reading Dion Cassius, can hardly have supposed that Messalina was the wife of Caligula, as the text would imply. Where a proper name ends in 's' Donne frequently uses 'his' instead of 's' for the genitive, e.g. '*Moses* his book' (p. 42), '*Lazarus* his name' (p. 44). Messalina's 'beloved Player' was Mnester, the pantomime actor. Dion Cassius states that on the triumph for the campaign in Britain, A.D. 44, the brass money issued in Caligula's reign was called in and melted down, and part of the metal was cast into statues of Mnester.

p. 44, l. 10. Lazarus . . . the wicked rich man. The parable of Dives and Lazarus in Luke xvi. 19–31.

p. 44, l. 16. The civill Ephesian Law. Valerius Maximus, lib. viii, c. 14, § 5. (J.)

p. 44, l. 30. Ethnick. Gentile.

p. 45, l. 4. The History is in the Names. Donne's exposition of the meaning of the names of Jacob's sons (recorded in Genesis xxix–xxx) supports the view that he made no use of the Authorized Version, where a different meaning is recorded in the margin for Levi and Gad. In the *Sermons* he often compares the readings of the Geneva and A.V., as in *LXXX.* 50. 506; 67. 679, 681; 78. 800. The absence of any such comparison here suggests that the *Essays* were written before Donne became acquainted with the A.V.

p. 45, l. 37. Brissonius. De Formulis et solemnibus Populi Rom. Verbis, Lib. vii, fol. 604. (J.)

p. 46, l. 3. Lex Fus. Jessopp has altered *Fus.* to *Fur.*, but this change is unnecessary. *Fusius* is the archaic form of *Furius*, and the Law is mentioned as *Lex Fusia Caninia* in *Cod. Just.*, 7. 3.

p. 46, l. 8. Fr. George. Tom. i. *de Hist. Sacram.* Sect. iii, '*de Patriarchis*', prob. 121. (J.)

p. 46, l. 13. She contributed that five which man wanted before. See Donne's poem *The Primrose* (*Poems*, i. 61):

> And women, whom this flower doth represent,
> With this mysterious number be content;
> Ten is the farthest number; if halfe ten

Belonge unto each woman, then
Each woman may take halfe us men.
Or if this will not serve their turne, Since all
Numbers are odde, or even, and they fall
First into this, five, women may take us all.

Throughout the *Essays*, and especially in the chapters on Exodus, Donne shows his preoccupation with the mystical meaning of numbers. See pp. 10, 46, 53, 59. The present passage is derived ultimately from Mirandola, *De Arte Cabbalistica*, pp. 75–76, edited by Archangelus de Burgensis, (Ramsay, op. cit., p. 63, note 2).

p. 46, l. 20. Not only Expounder of secrets, but Saviour of the world. The first is the translation of the margin of the Geneva and A.V., the second that of the Vulgate. Donne discusses the matter more fully in *LXXX Sermons*, 52. 529: 'For when it is said that *Pharaoh* called *Joseph, Salvatorem mundi*, A Saviour of the world . . . there is a manifest error in that Translation which cals *Joseph* so, for that name which was given to *Joseph* there, in that language in which it was given, doth truly signifie *Revelatorem Secretorum*, and no more, a Revealer, a Discoverer, a Decypherer of secret and mysterious things.'

p. 46, l. 29. Gaudent prænomine molles auriculae. Horace, Sat., II. v. 32–3.

p. 46, l. 31 n. Robortellus de Nominibus. In Gruter's *Thesaurus*, vol. i. p. 1404. (J.)

p. 46, l. 36. Paracelsus Name. Donne had already satirized 'the vain and empty fulness' of this name in *Ignatius his Conclave*, p. 22, where Lucifer trembles on hearing the name 'Philippus Aureolus Theophrastus Paracelsus Bombast of Hohenheim', and imagines that it is a new exorcism.

p. 47, l. 8. Quibus consulibus, &c. Gratiar. Actio, § 32. (J.)

p. 47, l. 20. To change the Name . . . is, by many laws, Dolus, &c. See Digest, Lib. xlviii, tit. x, de lege Cornelia de Falsis l. ix. § 3, and l. xiii, pr. &c. (J.)

p. 47, l. 29 n. Acacius de privil. Juris. lib. i, c. ix, § 34. (J.)

p. 48, l. 21. He which goes further, and asks, Why Gods will was so, inquires for something above God. 'Qui rationem quaerit voluntatis Dei aliquid majus Deo quaerit'. Aug. *De Gen. con. Man.* lib. i, c. 2, § 4. (J.)

p. 48, l. 23. Something that enclines God. Encline is here used in the obsolete sense of 'to cause to bow, to bring down, subject'; see *O.E.D.*

p. 48, l. 26. Offuscate. Obscured.

p. 49, l. 14. Spacious and specious. This is one of those word-plays which are frequent in Donne's *Sermons*, e.g. *LXXX Sermons*, 5. 51: 'As God loves Sympathy, God loves Symphony.'

p. 49, l. 23. Fiet unum Ovile. The Vulgate here misrepresents the sense by translating the Greek word for 'flock' as well as the different word for 'fold' by the one word *ovile*, and the A.V. follows it by translating both as 'fold' (John x. 16). Donne saw the difficulty, as appears from a later sentence—'all his sheep are of one fold, that is, *under one Shepherd, Christ*; yet not of one fold, that is, not *in one place*, nor form'. This is but one instance of several which could be adduced to show that at this period Donne had no knowledge of Greek, but relied exclusively on the Vulgate. About the time of his ordination he seems to have made some attempt at a study of New Testament Greek, for in one or two sermons he introduces a few Greek words, e.g. *LXXX Sermons*, pp. 376, 390, 395, 699. In the list of sixty-one books known to belong to Donne's library (Keynes, *Bibliography of Donne*, 2nd ed., pp. 173–80), there is only one Greek book and that is of a quite elementary character, the *Hellenismos* of Angelus Caninius, published in 1613.

p. 50, l. 3. Sectaries of Thomas and Scotus. The Thomists were the followers of Aquinas, and the Scotists those of Duns Scotus. In opposition to Aquinas, who maintained that reason and revelation were two independent sources of knowledge, Scotus held that there was no true knowledge apart from theology based on revelation. Also in opposition to Aquinas he held that the will of man was independent of the understanding. The primacy of the undetermined will (*voluntas superior intellectu*) was the central contention of the Scotists. They also held that all created things possess both matter and form; thus souls and angels have a matter of their own, though it is widely different from corporeal matter. Many minor disputes arose from these premisses. Cf. *LXXX Sermons*, 11. 111: '... let *Scotus* and his Heard think, That Angels and separate soules have a naturall power to understand thoughts, . . . And let *Aquinas* present his arguments to the contrary, That those spirits have no naturall power to know thoughts.'

p. 50, l. 4. Molinas and his Disciples. The Spanish Jesuit Molina issued his *Concordia liberi arbitrii cum gratiae donis, divina praescientia*, &c. at Lisbon in 1558. His book was attacked by the Spanish Dominicans, and an inquiry into it was made by the Inquisition. The subject was brought before Pope Clement VIII at Rome in 1596, but he died in 1605 without having given a decision. His successor Paul V decided in 1607 that the Molinists and their opponents should both have liberty to retain their opinions, and he forbade either side to condemn the other. Molina had attempted to reconcile the freedom of the human will with the efficacy of divine grace in a way which did not commend itself to the Dominicans. Donne mentions the dispute again in *A Sermon of Valediction* (*XXVI Sermons*, 19. 271): 'consider the other faculty, the will of man, by those bitternesses which have passed between the Jesuits and the Dominicans, . . . whether the same proportion of grace, offered to men alike disposed, must necessarily work alike upon both their wills?'

p. 50, l. 35. Principiant. Primary.

p. 51, l. 1. Sodder'd. A form now obsolete, except in dialect, of *soldered*, in the medical sense of 'closed up, re-united'.

p. 51, l. 11. Ecclesia Malignantium. Psalm xxvi. (Vulgate xxv.) 5: Odivi ecclesiam malignantium. 'I have hated the congregation of evil-doers.' (A.V.)

p. 51, l. 20. But one Church, &c. Cf. *Letters*, 1651, p. 29: 'You know I never fettered nor imprisoned the word Religion; not straightning it Frierly . . . nor immuring it in a *Rome*, or a *Wittemberg*, or a *Geneva*; they are all virtuall beams of one Sun . . . .'

p. 51, *l.* 31. *Churches utterly despoyl'd of Ceremonies*, &c. In this paragraph Donne has shown a tolerance unusual in the seventeenth century by admitting that both Rome and Geneva are to be regarded as parts of one universal Church. He now inserts a parenthesis in which he criticizes the deficiencies of Geneva and the superfluities of Rome in a way which anticipates his defence of the Church of England in *Fifty Sermons*, 33. 300: 'the Church of God is not so *beyond Sea*, as that we must needs seek it *there*, either in a *painted Church*, on one side, or in a *naked Church*, on another; a Church in a *Dropsie*, overflowne with *Ceremonies*, or a Church in a *Consumption*, for want of such Ceremonies, as the primitive Church found usefull, and beneficiall for the advancing of the glory of God, and the devotion of the Congregation'. Cf. also *Holy Sonnets*, xviii. 1–4:

> Show me deare Christ, thy spouse, so bright and clear.
> What! is it She, which on the other shore
> Goes richly painted? or which rob'd and tore
> Laments and mournes in Germany and here?

p. 51, *l.* 35. *He gave me my Pasture in this Park, and my milk from the brests of this Church.* This is Donne's way of affirming that as he was born an Englishman, his natural place as a Christian was within the Church of England. By the law of England at the time of Donne's birth, all Englishmen were required to conform in religion to the Church of England.

p. 52, *l.* 9. *He standeth behind a wall*, &c. Donne makes a similar use of this verse from Canticles in one of his Lincoln's Inn sermons. 'Such another wall . . . the Devil hath built now in the Christian Church, and hath morter'd it in the brains and bloud of men, in the sharp and virulent contentions arisen, and fomented in matters of Religion. But yet, says the Spouse, *My well beloved stands behind the wall*, shewing himself through the grates: he may be seen on both sides. For all this separation, Christ Jesus is amongst us all, and in his time, will break downe this wall too, these differences amongst Christians, and make us all glad of that name, the name of Christians, without affecting in our selves, or inflicting upon others, other names of envy, and subdivision.' *Fifty Sermons*, 21. 183.

p. 52, *l.* 15. *That savour of life unto life.* 2 Cor. ii. 16.

p. 52, *l.* 28. *Pererius. In Gen.* sub. loco, § 37. (J.)

p. 52, *l.* 31. *Saint Ambrose says*, &c. 'St. Ambrose does not meddle with the Hebrew, but simply says . . . Quid est "numeravit?" Hoc est elegit, etc. and then passes on to enlarge upon the interpretation. *De Abrah.* i. c. 3, § 15.' (J.)

p. 52, *l.* 32. *Connaturall.* Natural.

p. 53, *l.* 24. *St. Jerome. Ep.* 53 *de Studio Scripturarum*, § 8. (J.)

p. 53, *l.* 30. *Francis George Probl.* Tom. i, *de Hist. Sacram.* Sect. vi, *de Progressu et Pereg. Israel in deserto*, p. 48, Probl. 376. (J.)

p. 53, *l.* 31. *That number of Angels.* Dan. vii. 10. 'Thousand thousands ministered unto him, and ten thousand times ten thousand stood before him.'

p. 53, *l.* 35. *His Name is a Number.* Rev. xiii. 18. 'His number is six hundred threescore and six.'

p. 54, *l.* 37. *Exinanition.* The action or process of emptying or exhausting (*O.E.D.*). Cf. *Fifty Sermons*, 19. 162: 'In the exinanition, and evacuation of himself'; and *XXVI Sermons*, 4. 46.

p. 55, *l.* 31. *Augustine in Enchirid.* c. xvii, § 5. (J.)

p. 56, *l.* 4. *Delated juridically.* Denounced to a judicial tribunal.

p. 56, *l.* 19. *Althemerus.* 'The work referred to is "Conciliationes Locorum Scripturae qui specie tenus inter se pugnare videntur. Norimb. 1561, Andrea Althemero authore".' (J.)

p. 57, *l.* 1. *Insimulated.* Accused. Cf. *Fifty Sermons*, 25. 210: 'It seems that the *Apostles* had been traduced, and insimulated of teaching this Doctrine.'

p. 57 *l.* 7. *Cribrations.* Siftings. Cf. *Letters* (1651), p. 308: 'I have cribrated, and re-cribrated and post-cribrated the Sermon.'

p. 57, *l.* 20. *Misgoverned.* Misguided, compare p. 33: 'governed by the words', i.e. guided.

p. 57, *l.* 30. *Travelled*, i.e. travailed, in the obsolete sense of 'afflicted, troubled'.

p. 58, *l.* 1. *Saint Hierome. Liber de Hebr. Quaest. in Gen.* in loco. (J.)

p. 58, *l.* 2. *Nephews.* Here used for 'grandsons', a frequent use in the sixteenth and seventeenth centuries.

p. 58, *l.* 7. *Conform.* Conformably, in agreement with.

p. 58, *l.* 9. *Junius. Sacrorum Parallelorum Libri tres*, lib. i, par. 92. (J.)

p. 59, *l.* 5. *Exscriber.* Copyist. Cf. *Letters* (1651), p. 308: 'I have now put into my Lord of Bath and Wells hands the Sermon faithfully exscribed.' (J.)

p. 59, *l.* 6. *Deformly.* Deformedly, with distortion.

p. 59, *l.* 8. *Infirming.* Weakening, making less certain.

p. 59, *l.* 10. *Insolence.* Here used in the obsolete sense of 'strangeness, unaccustomedness'. (*O.E.D.*)

p. 59, *l.* 27. *Too Cabalistick and Pythagorick for a vulgar Christian.* Here again we have Donne's half-critical, half-admiring attitude towards the Cabalists, and his preoccupation with the mystical meaning of numbers. Here he dwells on the use of 70 in Scripture, and explains that it is a multiple of the two greatest numbers, seven and ten, for '*Seven* is ever used to express infinite', and '*Ten* cannot be exceeded, but that to express any further Number you must take a part of it again'. Cf. pp. 10, 111, for a note on the number 5.

p. 59 *l.* 31. *Meta-theology.* This is the only instance of this word recorded by the *O.E.D.*: It is formed on the analogy of *metaphysics* to denote 'a profounder theology than that recognized by divines'. Similarly the *O.E.D.* records such compounds as 'metachemistry', 'metamathematics'.

p. 60, *l.* 13. *Have I conceived . . . misery.* Numbers xi. 12–15.

p. 60, *l.* 28. *The 89th Psalm.* Donne uses the numbering of the Vulgate. It is Psalm 90 in the A.V. and other English versions.

p. 62, *l.* 7. *Though God be absolutely simple.* See note on p. 118.

p. 62, *l.* 31. *The Lord doth not long wait for us*, &c. 2 Maccab. vi. 14–16.

p. 63, *l.* 21. *Vegetius. De Re Militari*, lib. iii, c. 5. (J.)

p. 63, *l.* 29. *His Mercy is infinite in Extent.* This passage on God's mercy should be compared with the far finer passages in the *Sermons,* especially *LXXX Sermons,* 2. 13: '. . . his mercies are ever in their maturity . . . now God comes to thee, not as in the dawning of the day, not as in the bud of the spring, but as the Sun at noon to illustrate all shadowes, as the sheaves in harvest to fill all penuries, all occasions invite his mercies, and all times are his seasons.'

p. 63, *l.* 31. *The Ideating of this world.* Forming the idea of this world. Cf. *Pseudo-Martyr,* p. 4: 'That form of a State which Plato ideated', and p. 248: 'These men have Ideated what a Pope would be.' Also *Biathanatos,* p. 73.

p. 64, *l.* 4. *Non continebit,* &c. Ps. lxxvi. 10 (Vulgate numbering).

p. 64, *l.* 29. *Snort.* Jessopp emends to *snore,* but this is unnecessary, as *snort* was commonly used in the seventeenth century as the equivalent of *snore.* Cf. *The Good-morrow,* 4:

> Or snorted we in the seaven sleepers den?

p. 65, *l.* 11. *Hominem homini deum.* The proverb is found in its Latin form in the *Adagia* of Erasmus (ed. Stephanus, 1558), cols. 59, 60. Jessopp quotes an earlier Greek version from Zenob. *Adag. Cent.,* i. 91. in Leutsch. *Paroemiog.* vol. i. p. 29, and vol. ii. p. 8.

p. 65, *l.* 18. *Homo indigus, misericors est.* So Donne, probably quoting from memory. The Vulgate reads *indigens,* but *indigus* is sound Latin. The Hebrew text of the whole sentence is rendered quite differently in A.V.: 'The desire of a man is his kindness' (Prov. xix. 22).

p. 65, *l.* 23. *Miserere animæ tuæ.* Ecclesiasticus xxx. 23. Cf. *LXXX Sermons,* 75. 765: 'He cryes to every one of you, *Miserere animae tuae,* Have mercy upon thine own soule, and I will commiserate it too.' Also *Fifty Sermons,* 42. 395: 'A poorer thing is not in the world, nor a sicker, then *thine own soule* . . . And therefore show mercy to this soule.'

p. 62, *l.* 66. *And to such a chearfull giver, God gives himself.* 2 Corinthians ix. 7: 'God loveth a cheerful giver.'

p. 66, *l.* 11. *Be mercifull then, as your Father in heaven is mercifull.* Luke vi. 36.

p. 66, *l.* 12. *Homines et jumenta salvabis.* Ps. xxxv. 7 (Vulg.); xxxvi. 6 (A.V.).

p. 66, *l.* 13. *By jumenta are understood men,* &c. This is a quite mistaken interpretation of the Hebrew text. *Jumenta* means 'beasts of burden', and the Psalmist thinks of God's mercy as reaching to the animals as well as men.

p. 66, *l.* 22. *Aelian, Varia Historia,* lib. iii, c. 28.

p. 66, *l.* 26. *Let no smalnesse retard thee.* This passage is one of the most delightful in the *Essays* with its reference to 'a plantane, to ease a childs smart; or a grasse to cure a sick dog'.

p. 66, *l.* 28. *Amber, Bezoar, nor liquid gold, to restore Princes.* These were all supposed to have great medicinal value. The bezoar stone was a calculus or concretion found in the stomach or intestines of certain animals, in particular the wild goat of Persia and various antelopes (*O.E.D.*). Donne

refers to it in *LXXX Sermons*, 16. 160, and *Fifty Sermons*, 24. 203. He refers
to the medicinal properties of gold in *The Bracelet*, 112: 'Gold is restorative
. . .' (*Poems*, i. 100).

p. 66, l. 33. Yea rather, prevent the asking. Prevent is here used to mean
'anticipate'. For the counsel given here, compare *Fifty Sermons*, p. 389:
'In many cases, and with many persons, it is a greater anguish to aske, then
to want; and easier to starve, then to beg; . . . Therefore I must . . . enquire after the distresses of such men; for this is an imitation of Gods
preventing grace . . .'

p. 67, l. 1. Cyminibilis. 'Ciminile is a term applied to a basin for alms.
Du Cange.' (J.)

p. 67, l. 3. Panes Lapidosos. Seneca, *De Beneficiis*, ii. 7: 'Fabius Verrucosus
beneficium ab homine duro aspere datum *panem lapidosum* vocabat . . .'
Lapidosus means 'with grit in it' here.

p. 67, l. 8. Plato's definition of liberality. See Plato, *Definitions*, 412d for
the Greek original. Donne refers to another of the 'Definitions' in the
longer (*B, O'F*) version of Problem xiii of the *Juvenilia*.

p. 67, l. 19. The lean kine, which shall devoure the fat. A reference to
Pharaoh's dream, Gen. xli. 20, 21.

p. 67, l. 22. Saith Saint Ambrose. De Officiis, lib. i, c. 30: 'Dominus non
vult effundi opes sed dispensari.' (J.)

p. 68, l. 26. A diligent and exquisite revenge. Exquisite is here used in the
sense 'carefully chosen'.

p. 68, l. 26. David's choice. 2 Samuel xxiv. 13–15.

p. 68, l. 30. A famine of his word. Amos viii. 11.

p. 68, l. 31. In it one may lawfully steal. 'Donne's authority was probably
Arn. Clapmarius *de Jure Dominationis*, lib. iv, c. xvi.' (J.)

p. 68 l. 35. Divine books have Examples. 2 Kings vi. 28.

*p. 69, l. 34. That which is meerly and utterly Nothing, which is Sin, (for
it is but privation).* It was a saying of the medieval Schoolmen, *Peccatum
nihil*, and Donne makes use of the idea in *The Litanie* (*Poems* i. 348): 'As
sinne is nothing, let it no where be', and in the Sermons: 'You know, I
presume, in what sense we say in the Schoole, *Malum nihil*, and *Peccatum
nihil*, that evill is nothing, sin is nothing; that is, it hath no reality, it is
no created substance, it is but a privation, as a shadow is, as sicknesse is;
so it is nothing' (*LXXX Sermons*, 17. 171). He examines the doctrine more
critically in *Fifty Sermons*, 21. 176, 177: 'We must not think to ease ourselves
in that subtilty of the School, *peccatum nihil*; That sin is nothing, because
sinne had no creation, sin hath no reality . . . This is true; but that will
not ease my soul, no more then it will ease my body, that *sicknesse* is
nothing, and *death* is nothing . . . And therefore as we fear death, and fear
damnation, though in discourse and in disputation, we can make a school-
shift, to call them *nothing*, and but privations, so let us fear sin too, for all
this imaginary nothingnesse, which the heat of the School hath smoak'd
it withall. Sin is so far from being nothing, as that there is nothing else but
sin in us . . . .'

p. 70, l. 16. Azorius. Institutiones Morales, lib. xii, c. 28. (J.)

p. 70, *l.* 28. *In a Calenture . . . in a Scurvie*. Donne is drawing his metaphors from his knowledge of the afflictions of an Elizabethan sea voyage. In his poem *The Calme* (l. 23) he mentions the calenture, which the *O.E.D.* describes as 'a disease incident to sailors within the tropics, characterized by delirium in which the patient, it is said, fancies the sea to be green fields, and desires to leap into it'. The scurvy continued for centuries to afflict sailors on a long sea voyage who had no fresh meat and no green vegetables, till the discovery was made that lemons and lime juice would prevent it.

p. 70, *l.* 30. *I dare not conceive any hard opinion*. Here Donne appears less hostile to monasticism than in most of his writings. In a letter to Goodyear he speaks of 'dull Monastique sadnesse' (*Letters*, 1651, p. 46), and in a verse letter written from Amiens he alludes to 'cloysterall men, who, in pretence of feare | All contributions to this life forbeare' (Grierson, i. 222). Here, however, he admits that there are different callings, and that it may be right for some men to choose a dedicated life of celibacy and seclusion.

p. 71, *l.* 14. *Every thing which hath life*, &c. Gen. ix. 3.

p. 71, *l.* 22. *Ten women shall follow one man*. 'Not ten but seven, Is. iv. 1. I suppose the mistake arose from mixing up Is. iv. 1 and Zech. viii. 23.' (J.)

p. 71, *l.* 25. *the Panegyrick justly extols that Emperour*. A fuller account is given in *Fifty Sermons*, 5. 32: 'And therefore the Panegyrique, that raised his wit as high as he could, to praise the Emperour *Constantine*, and would expresse it, in praising his *continence*, and *chastity . . .* by saying that he *married young . . . formavit animum maritalem . . . Novum jam tum miraculum, Juvenis uxorius.*' The quotation is from *Panegyricus Maximiniano et Constantino*, c. iv, the authorship of which is uncertain.

p. 72 *l.* 7. *215. years*. 'Donne here takes for granted that which from St. Jerome's days (*Comment. in Ep. ad Galat.* c. iii) has always been matter of dispute and controversy. Pererius enters into it in his usual thorough manner, and the reader may find it worth his while to refer to him (*Com. in Exod.* c. xii, disp. xix) where the interpretation adopted by Donne, Gal. iii, vs. 17, is referred to.' (J.)

p. 73, *l.* 26. *Naturals*. Here used for '*natives*', a meaning now obsolete but common in Elizabethan English.

p. 75, *l.* 4. *Acacius de privilegiis. Jur. Civ.* lib. i, c. 1, § 14. (J.)

p. 75, *l.* 7. *Prince of Darkness*. Cp. Shakespeare, *All's Well*, iv. v. 44: 'the prince of darkenesse, alias the diuell'.

p. 75, *l.* 13. *Travell*, i.e. travail, labour.

p. 75, *l.* 20. *O my soul, in this Meditation*. The whole of this passage is a welcome relief in the midst of a rather tedious exposition, and it is a fore-taste of the way in which Donne in his sermons can pass suddenly from dialectic into an impassioned meditation.

p. 75, *l.* 26. *Thou hast delivered me*, &c. This one is of the very few passages of personal reminiscence in the *Essays*. Donne recalls the presumption of his youth, and the disappointment of his early hopes, his marriage, the succeeding years of 'painfull and wearisome idlenesse', relieved by the 'necessities of domestick and familiar cares and duties'.

p. 76, l. 24. The faithful and discreet prayers of them which stay behind.
Jessopp suggests that Donne may have had in his mind the prayer in the
burial service: 'beseeching thee . . . shortly to accomplish the number of
thine elect, and to hasten thy kingdom'. In *LXXX Sermons*, 77. 780–6
Donne examines the question of prayers for the dead, and acknowledges
that these were in use in the early Church, and that St. Augustine prayed
for his dead mother, and St. Ambrose for the dead Emperor. He thinks,
however, that the custom is to be condemned, because it has led to the
doctrine of purgatory, and the use of masses for the dead.

*p. 76, l. 33. Angels and our Souls are not delivered from this dependancy upon
him.* For the doctrine that angels are not immortal by nature, but by
special grace from God, see *LXXX Sermons*, 24. 236: 'Hence is it, that the
Fathers are both so evident, and so concurrent in that assertion, that an
Angel is a spirit . . . that is, Immortall, but Immortall by additional
Grace, and not by Nature . . . Because the Angels were produced of
nothing, they may be reduced to nothing . . . Only God is immortall in
himself, and by nature.' For the corresponding doctrine about the soul of
man see *LXXX Sermons*, 27. 269: 'And for the Immortality of the Soule,
it is safelier said to be immortall, by preservation, then immortall by
nature; That God keepes it from dying, then that it cannot dye.'
Compare also the verse letter *To the Countesse of Bedford* (*Poems*, i. 197):
'Soules but preserv'd, not naturally free.'

p. 77 l. 17. The Sacrament of the Pillar. The pillar of cloud by day and
of fire by night was the outward and visible sign of God's presence with
the Israelites (Exod. xiv. 19, 20), and might therefore by an extension of
meaning be compared with the Sacraments of the Christian Church.
Cf. *The Annunciation and Passion*, 31–32:

> His Spirit, as his fiery Pillar doth
> Leade, and his Church, as cloud; to one end both.

In *LXXX Sermons*, 61. 615 Donne speaks of the Church as the Pillar of
fire and cloud: 'They ⟨the Israelites⟩ did see that Pillar in which God, and
that presence, that Pillar shewed the way. To us, the Church is that
Pillar; in that, God shewes us our way. . . . But yet the Church is neither
an equall Pillar, alwaies fire, but sometimes cloud too; The Church is more
and lesse visible, sometimes in splendor, sometimes in an eclipse.' The
standard medieval interpretation was that the pillar of cloud represented the
obscurity of the Old Testament, and that of fire was the light of the Gospel.

p. 78, l. 29. It is Man. The English form is *Manna*, but the Vulgate in
Exod. xvi. 31–35 uses the form *man*, a transliteration of the Hebrew word.
Wycliffe's version of the Bible employed *man* in this passage of Exodus,
and the *O.E.D.* gives two examples of *man* for *manna* in the seventeenth
century.

p. 79, l. 2. Pepons. This is the rendering of the Geneva Bible, following
Wycliffe's version, where the A.V. and other English versions have
'melons'. The obsolete word *pepon* is derived from French *pepon*, Latin
pepo, peponem, a pumpkin.

p. 79, l. 34. Prateolus. 'Elenchus Haereticorum Omnium . . . Verbo Bezani-tae, p. 93.' (J.)

p. 79, l. 38. Nor Omnipotent in the New Testament. In Rev. xix. 6. the A.V. has *Omnipotent*, and the Vulgate *Omnipotens*. Donne may have over-looked this passage, but it is true that the Greek παντοκράτωρ is equivalent to 'Almighty', and for interpretation of this, see the next note.

p. 79, l. 39. It would rather be interpreted All-sufficient, then Almighty. Compare *Letters* (1651), p. 44: 'No man is less of himself then I, nor any man enough of himself. To be so is all one with omnipotence. And it is well marked, that in the Holy Book, wheresoever they have rendered Almighty, the word is Self-sufficient.'

p. 80, l. 22. An union of two Hypostases, Grace and Nature. Here *hypostasis* means 'essence, essential principle'. Donne generally uses the phrase 'hypo-statical union' for the union of two natures, God and Man, in Christ, as in *XXVI Sermons*, 26. 402: 'did the hypostatical union of both natures, God and man, preserve his flesh from this corruption?'

p. 81, l. 12. Nature is the Common law by which God governs us, and Miracle is his Prerogative. This is one of the numerous legal metaphors which remind us that Donne had been a law-student first at Thavies and then at Lincoln's Inn during the years 1591–4.

p. 81, l. 14. Non obstante. 'A licence from the Crown to do that which could not be lawfully done without it.' (Wharton's *Law Dictionary*.) Cf. *Biathanatos*, p. 48, where also *non obstantes* and *prerogative* are linked together. Cf. also *Loves Exchange*, 'A *non obstante* on natures law' (Grierson, i, 34).

p. 81, l. 16. Creation and such as that, are not Miracles. 'The whole of the matter of this page is to be found at large in Aquinas *Summa Theologiae*, pars i. q. cv, arts. 5 to 8 inclusive.' (J.)

p. 81, l. 26. The Cities Order. Jessopp suggests that there is a misprint here, and that we should read '*kingdom*' for '*Cities*'. There is, however, a mistake in his own text, for he has introduced 'for' before 'the Cities'. The text of *1651* is quite intelligible, and needs no emendation.

p. 81, l. 38. Lactantius. Div. Inst. lib. iv, *de Vera Sapientia*, c. xv. (J.)

p. 82, l. 3. Saint Augustine says truly . . . against Nature. Donne had already quoted this passage from Augustine *Contra Faustam*, XXVI. iii. in *Biathanatos*, p. 37: 'Though he (God) can doe a miracle, he can do nothing against nature; because that is the nature of every thing, which he works in it.'

p. 82, l. 15. Such understanders and workmasters, as the Magi were. The reference is to Exodus vii. 11, 22, and viii. 7, 18–19. Cf. *The first Anniver-sary*, 389–90: '. . . such new wormes, as would have troubled much Th'Ægyptian *Mages* to have made more such.'

p. 83, l. 2. Cyniphs. 'A word taken over from the Vulgate where it is applied to the insects which constituted the third plague of Egypt (Exod. viii. 17); variously supposed to be gnats, lice, fleas' (*O.E.D.*). See the com-mentary of Pererius on Exodus for a full discussion of the questions men-tioned by Donne about the nature of the *cyniphs*.

p. 84, l. 34. It contradicts and destroyes the Nature of Miracle, to be frequent. This and the succeeding passage should be compared with Donne's *Sermon to the Virginia Company* (Keynes, *Ten Sermons,* p. 57).

p. 85, l. 7. Miracula B. Virg. 'Apud Tungros, etc. . . . Duaci . . . 1606, lib. iii, c. 34, p. 218.' (J.)

p. 85, l. 15. Those little boys whom they make Exorcists. 'See Jeremy Taylor's *Diss. from Popery,* Part i, c. ii, sect. x, and Bingham's *Antiq.* b. iii, ch. iv, sects. 4 and 5.' (J.)

p. 85, l. 35. The staying of the Sun, and carrying it back. Joshua x. 12, and 2 Kings xx. 9–11.

p. 86, l. 14. That part which was vocall . . . was so short. Gen. ii. 16, 17.

p. 86, l. 29. For we are all mutuall debtors to one another. Cf. *Biathanatos,* p. 116: 'But betweene men who are mutuall Debtors, and naturally bound to one another, it is otherwise.' The preceding sentence with its reference to God's mercy should also be compared with the context here: 'Ever in his forsakings there are degrees of Mercy.'

p. 87, l. 19. A compassion with Christ. A suffering together with Christ. This, the original meaning of the word, is now obsolete.

p. 88, l. 24. The like tempests hath the inquisition De Modo, rais'd in the article of Descent into Hell, even in our Church. 'The most eminent of the belligerents were Hugh Broughton on the one side, and Bishop Andrewes on the other.' (J.)

p. 89, l. 10. Translated. Removed.

p. 89, l. 30. Aviling. Making vile, degrading.

p. 89, l. 32. Orbity. Barrenness. Cf. *The Annuntiation and Passion,* l. 17 (Grierson, i. 335).

p. 90, l. 23. Disceptation. Disputation, debate.

p. 90, l. 24. Simplicist. One who has a knowledge of medicinal simples, or herbs.

p. 90, l. 25. Peccant quality of every herbe. 'Peccant' is here used to mean 'causing disorder of the system, inducing disease'.

p. 90, l. 31. Complexioned. Having a certain colour or aspect.

p. 91, l. 31. Galatinus. De Arcanis Catholicae Veritatis, lib. xi, c. 3. (J.)

p. 92, l. 2. God himself in that last peice of his, which he commanded Moses to record, that Heavenly Song, &c. The whole of this sentence should be compared with *The first Anniversary,* 461–6:

> Vouchsafe to call to minde that God did make
> A last, and lasting'st peece, a song. He spake
> To *Moses* to deliver unto all,
> That song, because hee knew they would let fall
> The Law, the Prophets, and the History,
> But keepe the song still in their memory.

(Grierson, i. 245)

p. 93, l. 33. Our law which makes Multiplication Felony. 'By a statute made

5 H. iv. c. 4, it is ordained and established, that none from henceforth shall use to multiply gold or silver, nor use the craft of multiplication, and if any the same do, he shall incur the pain of felony; and it was made upon a presumption that some persons skilful in chemistry could multiply or augment those metals.' Cowel's *Law Dictionary*, quoted by Jessopp.

p. 93, *l.* 37. *Felony to feed a Spirit.* 'Statute i. Jac. i. c. 12, is an act against conjuration, witchcraft, and dealing with evil and wicked spirits. "Offenders are divided into two degrees . . . secondly [those] that consult, covenant with, entertain, employ, or reward any evil spirit, to any intents, etc." Cunningham, *Law Dictionary*, article conjuration.' (J.)

p. 94, *l.* 20. *As the frame of our body hath 248 bones, so the body of the law had so many affirmative precepts.* Donne's marginal reference to Francis George's *Problemata* reminds us that it was the excessive ingenuity of this writer which he had satirized in *Catalogus Librorum*, No. 6: 'That the Book of Tobit is canonical; in which, following the Rabbis and the more mystical of the Theologians, the hairs of the tail of his Dog are numbered, and from their various backward twists and intertwinings letters are formed which yield wonderful words, by Francis George, a Venetian' (*The Courtier's Library*, p. 44).

p. 96, *l.* 1. *Prayers.* The flatness of the ending of the essays proper is redeemed by the four prayers which follow. The first of these gives us the key to the second part of the book. Donne's interest in the story of Exodus is threefold. First we have his prosaic and rather wearisome discussion of the details of the history. Secondly, as he has already indicated in pages 74–76, there is the allegorical meaning, which had been fully worked out by the Fathers and the commentators from hints found in the New Testament. They saw the Exodus as a foreshadowing of the deliverance of the Church ('the Israel of God', as St. Paul calls it) from the slavery of the devil, through the Red Sea of Christ's blood, followed by the wilderness of persecution, into the Promised Land. This interpretation has been constantly in Donne's mind throughout the book, as when he speaks of the devil as 'That great *Pharaoh*, whose Egypt all the world is by usurpation', and continues 'And then, camest thou, O Christ, thine own *Moses*, and deliveredst us; not by doing, but suffering; not by killing, but dying.' The third interpretation arises out of the second, but it shifts the scene of the action from history to the individual soul. Here it is not the Church as a whole, but the soul of John Donne which has been in bondage to 'mine own corruption, mine own *Pharaoh*', and which is now in the wilderness of 'a more solitary and desart retiredness'. Here at last we feel a link with the *Holy Sonnets*, where the same spiritual conflict is described. In this first prayer Donne finds in his own heart 'Legions of spirits of Disobedience, and Incredulity, and Murmuring,' and implores God to overpower the wilfulness and stubbornness which he himself is unable to remove. Compare this with *Holy Sonnets* 11 and xiv throughout.

p. 96, *l.* 24. *Both thy Mannaes, thy self in thy Sacrament, and that other, which is true Angells food, contemplation of thee.* Manna is often used as a symbol of the Sacrament, especially in the Eucharistic hymns; see John vi.

31–33, 48–51. For Donne's practice of contemplation see Walton, *Life of Donne* (1670), p. 80: 'He did much contemplate (especially after he entred into his sacred calling) the *mercies* of Almighty God, . . . and would often say, *Blessed be God that he is God, divinely like himself.*' See also *LXXX Sermons*, 27. 274: 'The contemplation of God, and heaven, is a kinde of buriall, and Sepulchre, and rest of the soule; and in this death of rapture, and extasie, in this death of the Contemplation of my interest in my Saviour, I shall finde my self, and all my sins enterred, and entombed in his wounds, . . .'

p. 98, *l.* 7. *We have betrayed thy Temples to prophaneness, our bodies to sensuality.* Cf. *The Litanie*, stanza iii:

> O Holy Ghost, whose temple I
> Am, but of mudde walls, and condensed dust,
> And being sacrilegiously
> Halfe wasted with youths fires, of pride and lust,
> Must with new stormes be weatherbeat; . . .

Also *Holy Sonnets*, II. 5–8:

> I am . . . thine Image, and, till I betray'd
> My selfe, a temple of thy Spirit divine.

p. 98, *l.* 32. *And though our sins be as red as scarlet.* Isa. i. 18: 'Though your sins be as scarlet, they shall be as white as snow.'

p. 99, *l.* 9. *We have found by many lamentable experiences,* &c. Cf. *Holy Sonnets*, XIX, throughout, and *A Hymne to God the Father*, 3–4:

> Wilt thou forgive that sinne through which I runne,
> And do run still: though still I do deplore?

p. 99, *l.* 35. *Suffer not, O Lord, so great a waste.* The thought comes from two lines of the *Dies Irae*:

> Redemisti crucem passus,
> Tantus labor non sit cassus.

Cf. *The Litanie*, stanza xxviii:

> Gaine to thy self, or us allow;
> And let not both us and thy selfe be slaine.

PRINTED IN
GREAT BRITAIN
AT THE
UNIVERSITY PRESS
OXFORD
BY
CHARLES BATEY
PRINTER
TO THE
UNIVERSITY